Little Red Riding Hood

D0951448

"When she climbed up on the bed she was astonished to see how her grandmother looked in her nightgown." (Perrault)

"There lay her grandmother with her cap pulled down over her face giving a strange appearance." (Grimm)

This illustration of the celebrated "bedroom scene" in which the wolf archly attempts to conceal his identity comes from *Little Red Riding Hood* (New York: McLoughlin Brothers, circa 1890s) courtesy of Professor Jack Zipes.

Edited by

ALAN DUNDES

Little Red Riding Hood

A Casebook

The University of Wisconsin Press

The University of Wisconsin Press
114 North Murray Street
Madison, Wisconsin 53715

The University of Wisconsin Press, Ltd.
1 Gower Street
London WC1E 6HA, England

5   4   3   2   1

Printed in the United States of America

Library of Congress Cataloging-in-Publication Data
Little Red Riding Hood.
   Bibliography: pp. 239–247.
   Includes index.
   1. Little Red Riding Hood (Tale).   I. Dundes, Alan.
II. Little Red Riding Hood. English.
GR75.L56L58   1989   398.2'1   88-40431
ISBN 0-299-12030-9
ISBN 0-299-12034-1 (pbk.)

Contents

Contents

Acknowledgments

I am indebted to Simone Klugman of the reference department of Doe Library at the University of California, Berkeley, for carrying out a computer search for recent "Little Red Riding Hood" scholarship. I am grateful to the dedicated interlibrary loan staff at the same library for locating copies of several rare studies of the tale. Special thanks to Professor Jack Zipes of the University of Florida for the two illustrations in this volume, which were selected from his important personal collection of "Little Red Riding Hood" book illustrations. Finally, I thank all the authors and publishers who were kind enough to allow me to print or reprint their essays in this casebook.

Introduction

The story of a little girl who wears a red hood or cape and who carries a basket of food and drink to her grandmother is one of the most beloved and popular fairy tales ever reported. The girl, called "Le petit chaperon rouge" in French, "Rotkäppchen" in German, and "Little Red Riding Hood" in English, invariably encounters a villainous wolf in European versions of the tale. Folklorists classify this folktale as Aarne-Thompson tale type 333, The Glutton (Red Riding Hood). In Stith Thompson's 1961 revision of the tale type index, the plot summary includes two segments:

> 1. Wolf's Feast. (a) By masking as mother or grandmother, the wolf deceives and devours (b) a little girl (Red Riding Hood) whom he meets on his way to her grandmother's.
> 2. Rescue. (a) The wolf is cut open and his victims rescued alive; (b) his belly is sewed full of stones and he drowns; (c) he jumps to his death.

This synopsis tends to rely too heavily upon the well-known versions of the tale by Perrault and especially the Grimm brothers, but insofar as these particular versions give the form of the story known to the general public, the summary might appear to be adequate. What is not so well known is that there are authentic oral versions of the tale which reveal important details not contained in either Perrault's or the Grimms' accounts. Unfortunately, most of the significant scholarship inspired by this folktale has been similarly too narrowly based upon the Perrault and Grimm versions alone.

One of the aims of the present casebook is to demonstrate the nature of the oral folktale from which the Perrault and Grimm versions of the story surely derive. In addition, it is intended to sample the rich and diverse scholarship devoted to elucidating the possible meaning and significance of the tale.

The range of interpretations of Little Red Riding Hood runs

the gamut from solar mythology, myth-ritual, and social-historical to a variety of competing psychoanalytic readings of the tale. The advantage of bringing together under one cover a substantial number of efforts to decipher the meaning of this one tale is that it makes it possible for each individual reader to decide which approach or which combination of approaches to the study of folktales seems to be the most persuasive or illuminating. It may well be that none of the interpretations presented is deemed entirely satisfactory. In that event, the reader may be stimulated to construct a new interpretation of his or her own. Several of the essays were not easily accessible to an English-speaking readership and were translated from French, German, and Hebrew especially for this volume.

Perrault's version of the tale of 1697 is followed by the Grimm brothers' seemingly derivative version of 1812. An oral French version, circa 1885, accompanied by French folklorist Paul Delarue's helpful comparative note, provides an initial entrée to the oral (as opposed to the literary) form of the tale. An extended discussion of possible Chinese versions of the story by sociologist-sinologist Wolfram Eberhard broadens the reader's understanding of the basic plot considerably.

The avowedly interpretive portion of the casebook starts with a classic myth-ritual reading by P. Saintyves. Georg Hüsing then questions whether the tale is an authentic one and whether it can appropriately be studied in the light of so-called mythological theories. A fascinating essay by Hans-Wolf Jäger suggests that the tale contains demonstrable echoes of German attitudes towards the French around the time the tale was recorded by the Grimms. Another socio-historical consideration by Jack Zipes, a leading contemporary authority on "Little Red Riding Hood," appears to have been influenced by feminist theory. Zipes astutely points out the consequences of this girls' fairy tale having been initially reported and edited by men, such as Perrault and the Grimms. An intriguing essay by Zohar Shavit seeks to show how concepts of the child and childhood may be extrapolated from different versions of the tale, e.g., from those of Perrault and the Grimm brothers.

From the concept of childhood, we move to sample psychoanalytic interpretations of the tale. A little-known but stimulating Freudian analysis by Géza Róheim is followed by a different, more extended psychoanalytic reading by Bruno Bettelheim. A final overview by the editor brings the volume to a close. A selected bibliography of other essays and books devoted to the tale invites the reader to continue exploring the scholarship inspired by "Little Red Riding Hood." From the essays included and the annotated list of additional sources, a prospective student of a folktale may recognize the value and indeed the necessity of beginning his or her research where previous scholars have ended theirs.

It is hoped that many will come away from this volume with a new and heightened appreciation of the subtlety and interpretive possibilities of a single folktale. In future studies of this or other folktales, the reader may realize the importance of consulting all available versions of the tale rather than unnecessarily and arbitrarily limiting the scope of investigation to one or two standard literary versions no matter how important the intellectual niche such literary versions may occupy in Western civilization.

Little Red Riding Hood

Little Red Riding Hood

The earliest known European recording of the tale of "Little Red Riding Hood" seems to be the highly stylized literary retelling of Charles Perrault (1628–1703). It is Perrault's version, first published in 1697, which has proved to be not only the probable source of the famous redaction of the brothers Grimm (1812), but which has been the point of departure for most scholarly discussion of Aarne-Thompson tale type 333, The Glutton. For this reason, it is imperative that our comprehensive consideration of "Little Red Riding Hood" begin with Perrault's classic text.

Modern scholarship has established that Perrault did not invent the tale, but rather he adapted one that was already popular in French oral tradition. This means the year 1697 provides a useful *terminus ante quem* for "Little Red Riding Hood." The tale must be older than 1697, although we cannot say for certain how much older. We also know that in purely oral fairy tales (Aarne-Thompson tale types 300–749), the initial victim is rarely if ever killed permanently. If the victim is female, either she saves herself, or she is saved by a male hero. Accordingly, we can reasonably assume that insofar as Perrault's version ends with the death of Little Red Riding Hood, it must be a truncated, fragmentary version of the original oral tale. Moreover, authentic oral tales almost never have a didactic or cloying moral attached. Although Perrault's moral is clearly ironic in tone—almost a parody of a moral: Watch out for gentle wolves!—it does suggest that Perrault was attempting to convert an oral fairy tale into a literary fable.

Reprinted from *Perrault's Complete Fairy Tales*, A. E. Johnson, trans. (Harmondsworth, England: Kestrel Books, 1962), 71–77, by permission of Dodd, Mead & Company, Inc.

3

For a detailed consideration of Perrault's tales, see Marc Soriano, *Les Contes de Perrault* (Paris: Gallimard, 1968). For Soriano's comments on Little Red Riding Hood in particular, see his "Le petit chaperon rouge," *Nouvelle Revue Française* 16 (1968), 429–443, and "From Tales of Warning to Formulettes: The Oral Tradition in French Children's Literature," *Yale French Studies* 43 (1969), 24–43. For a fascinating account of Perrault's transformation of the oral tale, see Jack Zipes, *The Trials and Tribulations of Little Red Riding Hood* (South Hadley, Mass., 1983), 2–13. Those interested in learning more about Perrault's life and work may consult Jacques Barchilon and Peter Flinders, *Charles Perrault* (Boston: Twayne, 1981).

Once upon a time there was a little village girl, the prettiest that had ever been seen. Her mother doted on her. Her grandmother was even fonder, and made her a little red hood, which became her so well that everywhere she went by the name of Little Red Riding Hood.

One day her mother, who had just made and baked some cakes, said to her:

"Go and see how your grandmother is, for I have been told that she is ill. Take her a cake and this little pot of butter."

Little Red Riding Hood set off at once for the house of her grandmother, who lived in another village.

On her way through a wood she met old Father Wolf. He would have very much liked to eat her, but dared not do so on account of some wood-cutters who were in the forest. He asked her where she was going. The poor child, not knowing that it was dangerous to stop and listen to a wolf, said:

"I am going to see my grandmother, and am taking her a cake and a pot of butter which my mother has sent to her."

"Does she live far away?" asked the Wolf.

"Oh, yes," replied Little Red Riding Hood; "it is yonder by the mill which you can see right below there, and it is the first house in the village."

"Well now," said the Wolf, "I think I shall go and see her too. I will go by this path, and you by that path, and we will see who gets there first."

The Wolf set off running with all his might by the shorter road, and the little girl continued on her way by the longer road. As she went she amused herself by gathering nuts, running after the butterflies, and making nosegays of the wild flowers which she found.

The Wolf was not long in reaching the grandmother's house.

He knocked. *Toc Toc.*

"Who is there?"

"It is your granddaughter, Red Riding Hood," said the Wolf, disguising his voice, "and I bring you a cake and a little pot of butter as a present from my mother."

The worthy grandmother was in bed, not being very well, and cried out to him:

"Pull out the peg and the latch will fall."

The Wolf drew out the peg and the door flew open. Then he sprang upon the poor old lady and ate her up in less than no time, for he had been more than three days without food.

After that he shut the door, lay down in the grandmother's bed, and waited for Little Red Riding Hood.

Presently she came and knocked. *Toc Toc.*

"Who is there?"

Now Little Red Riding Hood on hearing the Wolf's gruff voice was at first frightened, but thinking that her grandmother had a bad cold, she replied:

"It is your granddaughter, Red Riding Hood, and I bring you a cake and a little pot of butter from my mother."

Softening his voice, the Wolf called out to her:

"Pull out the peg and the latch will fall."

Little Red Riding Hood drew out the peg and the door flew open.

When he saw her enter, the Wolf hid himself in the bed beneath the counterpane.

"Put the cake and the little pot of butter on the bin," he said, "and come up on the bed with me."

5

Little Red Riding Hood took off her cloak, but when she climbed up on the bed she was astonished to see how her grandmother looked in her nightgown.

"Grandmother dear!" she exclaimed, "what big arms you have!"

"The better to embrace you, my child!"

"Grandmother dear, what big legs you have!"

"The better to run with, my child!"

"Grandmother dear, what big ears you have!"

"The better to hear with, my child!"

"Grandmother dear, what big eyes you have!"

"The better to see with, my child!"

"Grandmother dear, what big teeth you have!"

"The better to eat you with!"

With these words the wicked Wolf leapt upon Little Red Riding Hood and gobbled her up.

Moral

From this story one learns that children,
Especially young lasses,
Pretty, courteous and well-bred,
Do very wrong to listen to strangers,
And it is not an unheard thing
If the Wolf is thereby provided with his dinner.
I say Wolf, for all wolves
Are not of the same sort;
There is one kind with an amenable disposition
Neither noisy, nor hateful, nor angry,
But tame, obliging and gentle,
Following the young maids
In the streets, even into their homes.
Alas! who does not know that these gentle wolves
Are of all such creatures the most dangerous!

Little Red Cap
(Rotkäppchen)

Among the most important founders of the academic discipline of folkloristics, the scientific study of folklore, no two
names are better known than Jacob Grimm (1785–1863) and
Wilhelm Grimm (1786–1859). Imbued with strong feelings
of nationalism and romanticism, the two brothers sought to
document the existence of a body of authentic German traditions which included folktales, legends, myths, and legal
antiquities. It was in 1812 that the first volume of their celebrated *Kinder- und Hausmärchen* appeared, and one of the
tales included in that volume was "Little Red Cap." That
version of "Little Red Riding Hood," along with the earlier
text published by Perrault, have provided the sole basis for
the vast majority of scholarly considerations of the tale.

Unfortunately, despite the avowed claims of the Brothers
Grimm that they were reporting pure oral tradition as it fell
from the lips of uneducated German peasants, source criticism of the hallowed Grimm canon of folktales suggests
that this was not always the case. For one thing, as the
Grimms began to assemble more and more versions of the
same tale type, they could not resist the temptation of combining elements from different versions. As a result, the
composite text they published was not really traditional at
all, even though it was made up of traditional elements. The
tale as reported by the Grimms had in fact never been told in
precisely that form by anyone in oral tradition.

The situation with respect to "Little Red Riding Hood" is

Reprinted from *The Complete Fairy Tales of the Brothers Grimm*, translated by Jack Zipes (New York: Bantam Books, 1987), 101–105. Copyright
© 1987 by Jack Zipes. Reprinted by permission of Bantam Books. All rights
reserved.

even more complicated. The direct source of the tale was Marie Hassenpflug (1788–1856), whose background was partly French Huguenot. She was hardly a peasant. After 1820, she served as a lady-in-waiting for a divorced duchess. The upshot of all this is that the Grimm version of "Little Red Riding Hood" did not stem from a German peasant source but rather from a French middle- or upper-class informant. Thus it is really not so surprising to discover that the ultimate source for the Grimm version is in all likelihood Perrault's 1697 text. However, the Grimm version does differ significantly from Perrault's account. For instance, the fairy tale's required happy ending has been reinstated by the Grimms. In any event, since nearly all interpretations of "Little Red Riding Hood" make explicit reference to the Grimm version, it is essential that those interested in such interpretations be thoroughly familiar with it.

For a sample of the abundant scholarship devoted to the Brothers Grimm, see Ludwig Denecke, *Jacob Grimm und sein Bruder Wilhelm* (Stuttgart: Metzler, 1971). For details of how the Grimms altered and amended what were supposed to be oral texts, see Heinz Rölleke, *Die älteste Märchensammlung der Brüder Grimm* (Cologny-Geneve: Fondation Martin Bodmer, 1975) and John Ellis, *One Fairy Story Too Many* (Chicago: University of Chicago Press, 1983). For biographical details about Marie Hassenpflug, see Heinz Rölleke, "The 'Utterly Hessian' Fairy Tales by 'Old Marie': The End of a Myth," in Ruth B. Bottigheimer, ed., *Fairy Tales and Society: Illusion, Allusion, and Paradigm* (Philadelphia: University of Pennsylvania Press, 1986), 287–300. For specific discussion of Perrault's possible if not probable influence on the Grimm tales, see H. V. Velten, "The Influence of Charles Perrault's Contes de ma Mere l'Oie on German Folklore," *Germanic Review* 5 (1930), 4–18, and Rolf Hagen, "Perraults Märchen und die Brüder Grimm," *Zeitschrift für Deutsche Philologie* 74 (1955), 392–410.

Once upon a time there was a sweet little maiden. Whoever laid eyes upon her could not help but love her. But it was her grandmother who loved her most. She could never give the child enough. One time she made her a present, a small, red velvet cap, and since it was so becoming and the maiden insisted on always wearing it, she was called Little Red Cap.

One day her mother said to her, "Come, Little Red Cap, take this piece of cake and bottle of wine and bring them to your grandmother. She's sick and weak, and this will strengthen her. Get an early start, before it becomes hot, and when you're out in the woods, be nice and good and don't stray from the path, otherwise you'll fall and break the glass, and your grandmother will get nothing. And when you enter her room, don't forget to say good morning, and don't go peeping in all the corners."

"I'll do just as you say," Little Red Cap promised her mother. Well, the grandmother lived out in the forest, half an hour from the village, and as soon as Little Red Cap entered the forest, she encountered the wolf. However, Little Red Cap did not know what a wicked sort of an animal he was and was not afraid of him.

"Good day, Little Red Cap," he said.

"Thank you kindly, wolf."

"Where are you going so early, Little Red Cap?"

"To Grandmother's."

"What are you carrying under your apron?"

"Cake and wine. My grandmother's sick and weak, and yesterday we baked this so it will help her get well."

"Where does your grandmother live, Little Red Cap?"

"Another quarter of an hour from here in the forest. Her house is under the three big oak trees. You can tell it by the hazel bushes," said Little Red Cap.

The wolf thought to himself, This tender young thing is a juicy morsel. She'll taste even better than the old woman. You've got to be real crafty if you want to catch them both. Then he walked next to Little Red Cap, and after a while he said, "Little Red Cap, just look at the beautiful flowers that are growing all around you! Why don't you look around? I believe you haven't even noticed how lovely the birds are singing. You march along as if you were going straight to school, and yet it's so delightful out here in the woods!"

Little Red Cap looked around and saw how the rays of the sun were dancing through the trees back and forth and how the woods were full of beautiful flowers. So she thought to herself, If I bring Grandmother a bunch of fresh flowers, she'd certainly like that. It's still early, and I'll arrive on time.

So she ran off the path and plunged into the woods to look for flowers. And each time she plucked one, she thought she saw another even prettier flower and ran after it, going deeper and deeper into the forest. But the wolf went straight to the grandmother's house and knocked at the door.

"Who's out there?"

"Little Red Cap. I've brought you some cake and wine. Open up."

"Just lift the latch," the grandmother called. "I'm too weak and can't get up."

The wolf lifted the latch, and the door sprang open. Then he went straight to the grandmother's bed without saying a word and gobbled her up. Next he put on her clothes and her nightcap, lay down in her bed, and drew the curtains.

Meanwhile, Little Red Cap had been running around and looking for flowers, and only when she had as many as she could carry did she remember her grandmother and continue on the way to her house again. She was puzzled when she found the door open, and as she entered the room, it seemed so strange inside that she thought, Oh, my God, how frightened I feel today, and usually I like to be at Grandmother's. She called out, "Good morning!" But she received no answer. Next she went to the bed and drew back the curtains. There lay her grandmother with her cap pulled down over her face giving her a strange appearance.

"Oh, Grandmother, what big ears you have!"

"The better to hear you with."

"Oh, Grandmother, what big hands you have!"

"The better to grab you with."

"Oh, Grandmother, what a terribly big mouth you have!"

"The better to eat you with!"

No sooner did the wolf say that than he jumped out of bed and gobbled up poor Little Red Cap. After the wolf had satisfied his desires, he lay down in bed again, fell asleep, and began to snore very loudly. The huntsman happened to be passing by the house and thought to himself, The way the old woman's snoring, you'd better see if anything's wrong. He went into the room, and when he came to the bed, he saw the wolf lying in it.

"So I've found you at last, you old sinner," said the huntsman. "I've been looking for you for a long time."

He took aim with his gun, and then it occurred to him that the wolf could have eaten the grandmother and that she could still be saved. So he did not shoot but took some scissors and started cutting open the sleeping wolf's belly. After he made a couple of cuts, he saw the little red cap shining forth, and after he made a few more cuts, the girl jumped out and exclaimed, "Oh, how frightened I was! It was so dark in the wolf's body."

Soon the grandmother came out. She was alive but could hardly breathe. Little Red Cap quickly fetched some large stones, and they filled the wolf's body with them. When he awoke and tried to run away, the stones were too heavy so he fell down at once and died.

All three were quite delighted. The huntsman skinned the fur from the wolf and went home with it. The grandmother ate the cake and drank the wine that Little Red Cap had brought, and soon she regained her health. Meanwhile, Little Red Cap thought to herself, Never again will you stray from the path by yourself and go into the forest when your mother has forbidden it.

There is also another tale about how Little Red Cap returned to her grandmother one day to bring some baked goods. Another wolf spoke to her and tried to entice her to leave the path, but this time Little Red Cap was on her guard. She went straight ahead and told her grandmother that she had seen the wolf, that he had wished her good day, but that he had had such a mean look in his eyes that "he would have eaten me up if we hadn't been on the open road."

"Come," said the grandmother. "We'll lock the door so he can't get in."

Soon after, the wolf knocked and cried out, "Open up,

Grandmother. It's Little Red Cap, and I've brought you some baked goods."

But they kept quiet and did not open the door. So Grayhead circled the house several times and finally jumped on the roof. He wanted to wait till evening when Little Red Cap would go home. He intended to sneak after her and eat her up in the darkness. But the grandmother realized what he had in mind. In front of the house was a big stone trough, and she said to the child, "Fetch the bucket, Little Red Cap. I cooked sausages yesterday. Get the water they were boiled in and pour it into the trough."

Little Red Cap kept carrying the water until she had filled the big, big trough. Then the smell of sausages reached the nose of the wolf. He sniffed and looked down. Finally, he stretched his neck so far that he could no longer keep his balance on the roof. He began to slip and fell right into the big trough and drowned. Then Little Red Cap went merrily on her way home, and no one harmed her.

The Story of Grandmother

In order to understand just how atypical both the Perrault and the Grimm versions of "Little Red Riding Hood" really are, in comparison with the original folktale from which they surely derive, one needs to have two important sets of data. First, it is critical to have some idea of what the original oral tale was like. Second, one should be aware of the fact that a probable cognate of the tale is widely distributed in China, Japan, and Korea. It is sad to report that most of the scholars who have written at length about "Little Red Riding Hood" were not in possession of these two crucial data sets. For the most part, the vital information was known to only a few specialists in folktale studies.

One of these folktale specialists was Paul Delarue (1889–1956), who wrote at some length about the oral versions of "Little Red Riding Hood" in a multi-part essay in a small French folklore periodical in 1951. See "Les Contes Merveilleux de Perrault et la tradition populaire: I. Le Petit Chaperon Rouge," *Bulletin folklorique d'Ile-de-France* (1951), 221– 228, 251–260, 283–291; (1953), 511–517. Delarue's amassing of thirty-five oral versions of the tale was in fact part of a larger, more ambitious project, namely, the compilation of the first French tale type index. In *Le Conte Populaire Français*, the first volume of which appeared in 1957, the year after Delarue's death, one can find oral French versions of Aarne-Thompson tale types 300–366, which of course includes AT 333. These versions of AT 333 are not only from France, but also from French-speaking areas overseas, such as

Canada and the French-American community in Missouri. In his 1951 essay, Delarue discussed not just French oral versions of the tale, but oral versions from Italy and other countries as well. He also commented upon the striking parallels between "Little Red Riding Hood" and a tale found in Asia. From his unique vantage point, Delarue could ascertain the nature of the oral tradition from which Perrault had presumably taken the tale of "Little Red Riding Hood." Delarue could see which details of the oral tale Perrault had evidently chosen to omit and which details he had apparently added to the oral tale, such as the red-colored cap or hood. The red hood may well be the basis of a number of ingenious interpretations of the tale, but the detail was probably not present in the original oral tale.

Delarue summarized his findings about "Little Red Riding Hood" in the brief commentary he wrote for the 1957 tale type index. Essentially the very same commentary was utilized for his note on the tale which appeared in *The Borzoi Book of French Folk Tales*, an anthology he edited and which was translated into English by American folklorist Austin E. Fife in 1956. It is that version of the tale plus commentary which comprises the present essay in this volume.

Delarue's pioneering research on Little Red Riding Hood has inspired other French-language scholarship, including Élisée Legros, "'L'Enfant dans le sac' et 'Le petit chaperon rouge'" *Enquêtes du Musée de la Vie Wallonne* 7 (1954–1956), 305–328, and Yvonne Verdier, "Le Petit Chaperon Rouge dans la tradition orale," *Le Débat* 3 (1980), 31–61. (An earlier version of the latter essay appeared under the title "Grands-mères, si vous saviez . . . le Petit Chaperon Rouge dans la tradition orale," *Cahiers de Littérature Oracle* 4 [1978], 17–55.) For access to Delarue's synopses of thirty-five French versions, see *Le Conte Populaire Français* 1, Nouvelle edition, (Paris: Éditions G.-P. Maisonneuve et Larose, 1976), 373–383.

There was once a woman who had some bread, and she said to her daughter: "You are going to carry a hot loaf* and a bottle of milk to your grandmother."

The little girl departed. At the crossroads she met the bzou,† who said to her:

"Where are you going?"

"I'm taking a hot loaf and a bottle of milk to my grandmother."

"What road are you taking," said the bzou, "the Needles Road or the Pins Road?"

"The Needles Road," said the little girl.

"Well, I shall take the Pins Road."

The little girl enjoyed herself picking up needles. Meanwhile the bzou arrived at her grandmother's, killed her, put some of her flesh in the pantry and a bottle of her blood on the shelf. The girl arrived and knocked at the door.

"Push the door," said the bzou, "it's closed with a wet straw."

"Hello, Grandmother; I'm bringing you a hot loaf and a bottle of milk."

"Put them in the pantry. You eat the meat that's in it and drink a bottle of wine that is on the shelf."

As she ate there was a little cat that said: "A slut is she who eats the flesh and drinks the blood of her grandmother!"

"Undress, my child," said the bzou, "and come and sleep beside me."

"Where should I put my apron?"

"Throw it in the fire, my child; you don't need it any more."

And she asked where to put all the other garments, the bodice, the dress, the skirt, and the hose, and the wolf replied:

---

*Époigne. Épigne, a small loaf of bread, usually made for children, which has slashes on it made with a knife prior to cooking. From Vulgar Latin, poigneia, pugneia, poignée; from the Latin pugnus.

†I asked the storyteller: "What is a bzou?" He replied: "It's like the brou, or garou (werewolf; the modern French form is loup-garou); but in this story I have never heard anything said except bzou."—A. Millien.

"Throw them in the fire, my child; you will need them no more."*

"Oh, Grandmother, how hairy you are!"

"It's to keep me warmer, my child."

"Oh, Grandmother, those long nails you have!"

"It's to scratch me better, my child!"

"Oh, Grandmother, those big shoulders that you have!"

"All the better to carry kindling from the woods, my child."

"Oh, Grandmother, those big ears that you have!"

"All the better to hear with, my child."

"Oh, Grandmother, that big mouth you have!"

"All the better to eat you with, my child!"

"Oh, Grandmother, I need to go outside to relieve myself."

"Do it in the bed, my child."

"No, Grandmother, I want to go outside."

"All right, but don't stay long."

The *bzou* tied a woolen thread to her foot and let her go out, and when the little girl was outside she tied the end of the string to a big plum tree in the yard. The *bzou* got impatient and said:

"Are you making cables?"

When he became aware that no one answered him, he jumped out of bed and saw that the little girl had escaped. He followed her, but he arrived at her house just at the moment she was safely inside.

The Story of Grandmother (T. 333)

Manuscript in the collection of A. Millien. Told by Louis and François Briffault, at Montigny-aux-Amognes, Nièvre, about 1885. A. Millien has given somewhat arranged extracts of this version in Mélusine 3 (1886–1887), 428–429.

---

*For each item of clothing the teller repeats the question of the girl and the reply of the wolf.

I have devoted to this tale a little monographic study published by the *Bulletin folklorique d'ile-de-France** in the series of works that I have undertaken on *Les Contes merveilleux de Perrault et la tradition populaire* (Perrault's tales of the supernatural and folk tradition). Therein I analyze the content of thirty-five French versions that I have encountered and compare them with known foreign versions. I limit myself to summarizing here certain observations and certain conclusions.

The documents assembled by collectors are of three types: oral versions that owe nothing to printed texts (about twenty); published versions that owe everything to the version of Perrault, which returned to oral tradition following an enormous diffusion by the literature of *colportage* and children's books (only two); mixed versions which contain in variable proportions published elements and independent elements, and a few fragmentary versions.

The independent or mixed versions are all localized in an east-west zone that corresponds approximately to the basin of the Loire, to the northern half of the Alps, to northern Italy, and to the Tyrol.

Outside this zone, in France as in foreign countries, versions are very altered or come from the tale of Perrault, directly or through the intermediary of the version of the Grimm brothers, for the Grimm version comes from that of Perrault, as is revealed by a careful comparison and as certain facts explain: it presents the same details, the same literary adjunctions more agreeably developed, the same lacunæ; the Grimm brothers got their version from a storyteller of French descent who mixed in her memory German and French traditions, and she and her sister furnished them for their first edition three other tales of Perrault and one of Mme d'Aulnoy, which were suppressed from subsequent editions. If "Little Red Riding Hood" was retained, it was no doubt because of the different outcome, which made it pos-

*Years 1951 (pp. 221–228, 251–260, 283–291) and 1953 (pp. 511–517).

sible to presume an independent version; but this outcome is a contamination by the German form of the tale of "The Goat and the Kids." Moreover, although for several generations almost all Germans have known from childhood the loveliest tales of the collection of the Grimm brothers, the tale of "Little Red Riding Hood" is not in German oral tradition (two oral versions only, both of them derived from the Grimm version, have been noted up to this time in all of Germany). One cannot insist too much on this origin of the Grimm brothers' tale for invariably theorists have considered it as more complete and more primitive than that of Perrault, and they have found all sorts of symbolic meanings in the episode of the little girl swallowed by the wolf and coming out alive from its body.

The independent oral versions present a remarkable identity from one extremity of the zone of extension of the tale to the other. They permit one to ascertain that the red headdress of the little girl is an accessory trait peculiar to the Perrault version, not a general trait on which one could base oneself to explain the tale. Moreover, many other tales have also a particular version that is called "Red Bonnet," as other tales have titles which evoke a headdress, a piece of clothing, or colored footwear: "The White Bonnet," "The Green Hat," "The White Coat," "The Green Garter," "The Red Shoes"; and all these titles inspired by a detail of the heroine's clothing in a particular version have a character that is accessory and accidental in the story. And one discerns the error of those who have wished to find a symbolic sense in our tale, taking their departure from the name of the heroine with a red headdress in whom they perceive the dawn, the queen of May with her crown, and so on. Nor in most of the versions is the girl named; they begin simply: "*une petite fille,*" "*une petite,*" "*la piteta,*" etc. . . .

In Perrault's version the wolf, after having got information concerning the place where the little girl is going, tells her that he will go "by this road" and she "by that road"; in the folk versions the conversation is quite different. The wolf asks her: "What road are you taking? The Road of Pins or the

Road of Needles?" The little girl takes one road and the wolf takes the other. There are some variations in the names of the roads; one also finds the Road of the Little Stones and the Road of the Little Thorns in *langue d'oc*, the Road of Roots and that of Stones in the Tyrol. But this question of the wolf on the choice of roads is so general that folk story-tellers of the zone of extension of the tale have introduced it into versions which owe everything else to Perrault. These absurd roads, which have surprised adults and provoked scholars, delight children, who find their existence in fairy-land quite natural.

The cruel and primitive motif of the flesh and blood that are laid aside and that the girl is invited to eat is encountered in all of the folk versions with variations in detail. For example, the teeth of the grandmother, which remain attached to the jaws and provoke the questions of the girl, are presented by the wolf as grains of rice in the Tyrol, as beans in the Abruzzi.

The dramatic dialogue and the tragic ending of the story of Perrault form an ending also for the greatest number of the folk variants.

But it will be noted that the version of this collection possesses a happy outcome: the girl, perceiving that she is with a monster, pretends that she has to take care of one of nature's needs, lets herself be tied to a string, from which she frees herself when she is outside, in order to escape. The same ending is encountered in other versions of Touraine, of the Alps, of Italy, and of the Tyrol. It is encountered in the Far East, in versions of a well-known tale in China, Korea, and Japan, "The Tiger and the Children," which, by the subject and number of motifs, seems to be related to the tales of "Little Red Riding Hood" and of "The Goat and the Kids."

When one examines the content of our French versions and of Italo-Tyrolean versions that owe their whole content to oral tradition, one notes that they have common traits which are absent from Perrault's version. It seems unlikely that elements that are so general should have escaped from the version with which he was familiar at a period when the folk tale was much more lively than it was at the moment of modern collections. But the common elements that are lacking in the literary story are precisely those which would have shocked the society of his period by their cruelness (the flesh and blood of the grandmother tasted by the children), their puerility (Road of Pins, Road of Needles), and their impropriety (question of the girl on the hairy body of the grandmother). And it seems plausible that Perrault eliminated them while he kept in the tale a folk flavor and freshness which make of it an imperishable masterpiece.

The Story of Grandaunt Tiger

Because the Asian tradition of "Little Red Riding Hood" is so little-known in the West, we have elected to include a substantial essay treating Chinese versions of the tale. Its author, Professor Wolfram Eberhard of the University of California, Berkeley, is a sinologist and sociologist in addition to being a folklorist.

The essay is based upon fieldwork carried out in 1967–1968 in the Kuting section of the city of Taipei in Taiwan. Informants came from one hundred families selected at random who were all Min-nan people, that is, Chinese whose ancestors immigrated to Taiwan from the southern part of Fukien province of mainland China. Each family had at least one child between the ages of 13 and 17. Eberhard distinguished four levels of education of the head of the household: (a) college educated, (b) high school graduates, (c) elementary school graduates, and (d) illiterates. Four folktales were specifically solicited, one of which, "Grandaunt Tiger," was by far the most popular. Two hundred forty-one texts of "Grandaunt Tiger" were collected and it is these texts that form the basis of the essay. Eberhard was interested in the length of individual stories as well as other variables of concern to sociologists, such as the class and status of the storytellers. The reader will soon discover that the frequent use of tables and statistics marks the author's sociological approach to the data. On the other hand, one cannot help appreciating the richness of a data base consisting of 241 versions of a tale in contrast to a single version of Perrault.

Reprinted by permission of the author from Wolfram Eberhard, *Studies in Taiwanese Folktales,* Asian Folklore and Social Life Monographs, vol. I (Taipei: The Orient Cultural Service, 1970), 14–17, 27–76, 91–95.

Whether or not one considers "Grandaunt Tiger" to be a cognate of "Little Red Riding Hood" depends in part on the relationship, if any, between Aarne-Thompson tale types 123, The Wolf and the Kids, and 333, The Glutton (Red Riding Hood). The first, an animal tale, is summarized as follows in the tale type index: The wolf comes in the absence of the mother and eats up the kids. The old goat cuts the wolf open and rescues them. Other motifs commonly found in the tale include the villain's disguising his or her voice, or putting flour on his or her paws, thereby gaining access to the children. In the tale type index, there is a specific cross-reference to AT 333, which suggests that folklorist Stith Thompson thought there might be some connection between the two tale types.

The problem is largely a classificatory one. It stems from Antti Aarne's original decision to separate so-called animal tales (AT 1–299) from ordinary märchen (AT 300–1199). In other words, if a folktale had animals as dramatis personae, Aarne classified it as an animal tale; if it had human actors, he classified it as an ordinary folktale or as a joke/anecdote. As a result of this arbitrary division of tales, it sometimes happens that the very same folktale plot may have two separate and distinct tale type numbers, depending upon whether the characters in the tale are animals or humans (cf. AT 9B, In the Division of the Crop, the Fox Takes the Corn, the Bear the More Bulky Chaff, and AT 1030, The Crop Division. Of root crops the ogre chooses the tops; of other crops the roots). I believe it is highly likely that AT 123 and AT 333 are basically the same folktale. In any event, it is up to the reader to judge whether the Chinese versions of "Grandaunt Tiger" belong to the same tale type as "Little Red Riding Hood."

The Story and Its Size

The story of "Grandaunt Tiger,"[1] on the average, was told in 300 Chinese words, which in translation would be repre-

Table 1   Social Class and Number of Words per Story[2]

| | Extent of Education of Head of Household | | | | |
	A College	B High school	C Elementary	D Illiterate	Average
Father	274	221	256	250	247
Mother	292	239	249	225	252
Son	299	457	346	334	354
Daughter	332	327	402	329	349
Average	304	308	323	291	308
Number of cases	53	70	65	48	236

sented by about the same number of English words. The variations were very great, from a very few words to one text with 931 words, told by a boy whose father was a high-school graduate. In general, we can say that the length of the story had little relation to the educational level of the story-teller's family (Table 1), but that fathers tended to give the shortest versions, sons the longest. In order to introduce the story, I am giving now the translation of one of the longest and best texts, from a boy whose father was an elementary-school graduate.

Grandaunt Tiger (843 words in Chinese)

There was a family of four persons. When the father was out boar hunting in the mountains, he was eaten by a tiger, so there were left the mother and her two daughters. One day the mother wanted to go to her mother's house to select a son-in-law. On her way, at the Ten-mile Pavilion, she met an old woman. That old woman asked her to give her the things she had in her baggage to eat. So the mother gave her to eat. When the old woman asked for more, she could not refuse it. Later the old woman said she wanted to eat one of her hands. She (the mother) thought that if the old woman ate one hand, she still could go on. So she let her eat it. The woman then wanted the other hand, and the mother could not but let her eat it. The old woman still was not satisfied and ate her all up. After the old woman had eaten her, she went to her house. Arriving at the door, she called, "Open the door, open the door." When the girls heard her calling, the younger girl was about to go and open the door, saying that mother had come back. The older girl said, "Mother went to (the maternal) grandmother's house and will return only tomorrow." The older girl further said, "Mother's voice is like a bell; but her voice is hoarse. This certainly is not mother." When the Grandaunt Tiger heard this, she went into the mountains, drank spring water, and rinsed her throat. Then she returned to the house and called the names of the two girls, because while she had been eating up Mother she had asked her the names of her two daughters. The older girl said cautiously, "Stick your hand inside." She touched it, and it was very coarse. She said, "Mother's hand is not so coarse." So Grandaunt Tiger returned to the rim of the field, took potato leaves, wound them around the hand, went again to the house, put the hand inside and let the older girl touch it, whereupon both girls opened the door. When she came in, the older girl said to her, "On mother's face there were no moles." Grandaunt Tiger said that on her way she had fallen down. Later the Grandaunt Tiger said, "I am not your mother, I am only your (maternal) grandmother, arriving from very far." In the evening, when they wanted to sleep, Grandaunt Tiger asked both girls to sleep in one bed together with her. They slept until deep in the night, when Grandaunt Tiger got hungry and began eating the younger girl. The older girl heard the maternal grandmother eating something and said, "I, too, want to eat." Grandaunt Tiger said, "Small children cannot eat at sleep time." But when she was bothered, she could not but give her her younger sister's finger to eat. The older sister immediately noticed that it was all wet and then knew that the Grandaunt Tiger must have changed herself into the maternal grandmother and had eaten up her sister. So she said to Grandaunt Tiger, she needed urgently to urinate and wanted to go to the toilet. Grandaunt Tiger asked her to urinate into the bed, but she said, "Grandmother came to visit us, so we cannot subject her to the odor. If you, grandmother, are

afraid I might miss the way, you could tie a rope to my leg."
The grandmother could not immediately find a rope, so she
used the intestines of the younger girl and tied them on.
When (the girl) was outside, she untied the intestines and
tied them to the water bucket. Then she climbed a big tree
which was near their house. After a long time, Grandaunt
Tiger thought, "She is gone such a long time, how come she
is still not back?" She pulled the intestines and it felt as
if they were not loose. After further waiting a while, she
pulled again. Then she got suspicious, pulled again, and the
intestines broke. Grandaunt Tiger searched everywhere, but
could not find (the girl). Shortly before it became morning,
Grandaunt Tiger went to the pond and saw a reflection in
the water and looked up: older daughter had hidden herself
on a tree. Grandaunt Tiger asked her, "What are you doing
on the tree?" Older sister said, "I catch birds to give them to
grandmother for breakfast. Please, grandmother, go into the
house and boil oil, bring it to the tree, so that we can fry the
birds in oil. Then I'll ask grandmother to open her mouth
and close her eyes, and give grandmother the birds to eat."
Then the older girl took the boiling oil and poured it down
into the mouth of the Grandaunt Tiger. Grandaunt Tiger
cried out and died.

The Story and Its Variants

We will now go through all the versions of "Grandaunt Tiger," element by element, motif by motif, in the hope to be
able to show that a study of variants is important, even if
one does not use the Finnish method.

The Situation

In almost all versions, the plot is located in the mountains,
never in the city or town. In some cases the family lives in
the mountains, in other cases in a small village. In South
China "mountains" have the connotation of "forest," and

"forest" for a Chinese has always been threatening, being the domicile of wild animals or ghosts. If the location is not described, the story of the action leaves no doubt that it is taking place in a rural, mountainous area.

The family in the story is unusual for Chinese families: it is headed by a mother who has small children. In very few versions (4 percent) the family is headed by a father who later goes out together with the mother. This variant is told by various tellers, and there is no correlation with the teller's family status (father, mother, son, two stories each; daughter, four stories) or educational class (A five stories, C one story, and D four stories). In a few more versions the father is out or dead, but a description of the death, as in our model text, is extremely rare. The mother, since she has fairly young children—if their ages are given, they are around 8–10 years—must be a widow; at least this is the way a Chinese would understand the situation. It is very unusual for a fairly young woman with children to live alone and not with her in-laws, and equally unusual that she has not remarried, the normal thing to do for a lower-class widow not living with her in-laws. How can a woman alone feed a family? No version indicates her social class, but from the fact that there are no servants and that the house is located in the woods and not in the city, it is clear that she belongs to the lower class. None of these things is explained in any version, as if the listener, upon hearing the famous title of the tale, can be presumed to be so interested in the expected actions that details about the special situation can be left out.

A relatively large number of versions (19 percent) leaves out the mother either entirely or as an acting person. Further analysis reveals a significant point: Those among the storytellers who are fathers and sons tend more often to forget about the mother (31 and 27 percent, respectively) than do those who are mothers, and especially daughters (23 and 3 percent). Evidently, a girl telling a story about girls quite automatically will see the mother in an active role. In the versions without an acting mother (where normally also no father is mentioned, as there is no story in which the father takes over the role of the mother), the story begins only after

Table 2 Number of Children in "Grandaunt" Tale

	Father	Mother	Son	Daughter	Total
Two children	23 (55%)	47 (78%)	46 (74%)	57 (79%)	173 (73%)
Two children of different sex	4 (10%)	1 (2%)	2 (3%)	3 (4%)	10 (4%)
Three or more children	8 (19%)	4 (7%)	5 (8%)	4 (6%)	21 (9%)
One child	2 (5%)	2 (3%)	9 (15%)	5 (8%)	19 (8%)
Number unclear	1 (2%)	1 (2%)	—	—	2 (1%)
Motif absent	4 (10%)	5 (8%)	—	2 (3%)	11 (5%)
Number of cases	42	60	62	72	236

the mother has left the children; or the children live alone even without a mother; or the main part of the story takes an unusual turn; or the story is incompletely told, that is, this detail and others are missing.

Normally the widow has two children (Table 2). Stories told by mothers or daughters are more consistent in this respect than those told by fathers and sons. It is clear that the children in the "standard version" are two girls (94 percent of all cases with two children of the same sex) and not two boys (4 percent; 2 percent gender unspecified): that is, no father, only one daughter and two sons, although four mothers told of two boys. In fact, the story can be told either way. The sex change would not require any changes later on in the story although one might say that the end of the story, including tree-climbing and violence, might be more fitting for boys as heroes than for girls. Because some storytellers regarded the tale as "educational," storytellers who have only sons, or tellers telling the story to a group of boys may well decide to replace the girls in the story by boys.

Some tellers offer versions with two children of different sex. This variant is as rare as the variant of two boys, and it also does not influence the rest of the story.

But there are consequences when the number of children is changed. Twenty-one versions (9 percent) have not two but three, and occasionally even four children (fathers prefer this form more often than others do). This change necessitates that either the tiger must kill two children, instead of one, or two children must escape instead of one. There are a few cases in which the storyteller begins by saying "several children" or "three children," and later specifies or corrects this to the normal two children, apparently suddenly realizing that having more than two children would require more changes. To let the tiger eat more than one child may increase the suspense of the story, but forces the teller to explain why the surviving child did not understand what went on when the first child disappeared. It is of course possible to construct a satisfactory story including this motif. To let two children escape causes other difficulties in explaining how they could escape. It seems difficult to construct a satisfactory story if this last change were to be introduced. We will discuss both points later.

Some tellers (most often sons) have only one child in the story (8 percent). In this case, the whole story has to be reconstructed and major changes must be made. It means that the teller, as soon as he has begun telling about only one child, is forced into another type of story; but he is not completely free, because he was asked to tell the story of "Grandaunt Tiger," a name under which our story is generally known.

The variants are not correlated with the educational-social classes of the storytellers, except that significantly more members of the highest class told a version with only one child (19 percent versus [B] 6 percent, [C] 6 percent, and [D] 2 percent), and more members of the lowest class left out the mother (25 percent versus [A] 19 percent, [B] 17 percent, and [C] 18 percent).

The Mother Leaves the Children

In the following account of the plot, ignoring the fact that not all versions assume the children to be girls, we shall often refer to the "children" as "girls," not only because the standard version is about girls, but also because the description will be simpler, particularly in the last part of the story.

The action in the story begins with the mother leaving her children alone in the house. In the few cases in which the father is alive, both parents go out together, or the father is already absent for unknown reasons.

For a Chinese audience the absence of the mother or of both parents has to be explained. In traditional China, there are very few reasons why a mother should leave the house at all. If the family has servants, she need not go out even to shop. None of our texts mentions servants so that in all versions the family presumably was too poor to keep servants. But the story has it that mother leaves the children alone, and the plot requires that she be away overnight, at least from the late afternoon until the next morning. Indeed, some versions indicate that the mother intended to stay away for several days, though most of them seem to schedule her return for the next morning. While in traditional China and in some ethnic groups, peasant women may go out to work in the fields, in most groups women did not work in the fields, and none of our mothers was presumed to do so. In a single version the mother goes to collect firewood. This explanation is not convincing because in such a case she should be back before darkness. There is really only one good reason for a mother to leave the house overnight: a visit with her own parents and kin, which may be necessary when the parents are sick—in fact mentioned in some cases—or when the parents have a birthday (also mentioned), or when there is some other special occasion. Even this raises the question why she does not take her children with her. Usually the age of the children is not mentioned, but from the context of the story and from the few cases in which the age is mentioned, we can assume that the children are between six and ten years old, that is, well able to make a trip together with their mother. None of our versions states why the mother leaves the children at home. We might conclude then, that it is the same reason which still today forces people to leave at least one person at home when the others go out: the fear of burglars and thieves. However, many versions do not indicate a visit at the mother's parents, but simply state: mother went out (Table 3). Only few texts give

Table 3   Explanation of the Mother's Departure

	Father	Mother	Son	Daughter	Total
To visit her family	36%	30%	42%	53%	39%
To go out	28%	37%	26%	40%	32%
Not mentioned	36%	33%	32%	7%	29%
Number of cases	42	60	62	72	246

further details: she went to town, or she went shopping; one text is so explicit as to say that the mother went to buy tea. We can assume that "going out" is probably understood as "going to town" or "going shopping." In one version the mother goes to the south of Taiwan, in another she goes traveling, and in a third she goes to deliver gifts. These three variants may imply that she goes to visit her family, but it cannot be proved. We gain the impression that going out is a "modernistic" trait, because in Taipei all mothers go out shopping, and the townspeople telling the story may well assume that a woman living in an isolated place far from town particularly needs to go to town to shop. In traditional China, a farm woman would have had very few needs requiring a trip to the town and she could have asked a neighbor to buy a necessity for her. The variant "shopping" is not more typical for the younger generation. The preference for this variant may have to do with socio-educational class: members of the highest class prefer this trait (32 percent, versus lowest class 15 percent), and members of the lowest class prefer the visit to the in-laws (24 percent, versus highest class 14 percent), while the middle classes have no true preference. As a general observation one can certainly say that the people of high socio-educational level are the more urbanized, while the illiterates and offspring of illiterate parents are recent immigrants to the city from the countryside. Thus one can conclude tentatively that the more urbanized have a certain preference for the variant "going shopping."

In some versions the mother meets the tiger on the road to town or to the in-laws (Table 4), a detail which girls seem to

The Story of Grandaunt Tiger

Table 4   The Mother's Encounter with the Tiger

	Father	Mother	Son	Daughter	Total
Mother meets tiger	5%	3%	8%	28%	12%
Mother eaten by tiger	10%	—	15%	17%	10%
Tiger knows details	12%	13%	8%	39%	19%
Before eating mother	5%	—	4%	11%	
Without eating					
mother	2%	—	2%	13%	
By overhearing	5%	13%	2%	15%	

prefer. The tiger then may eat her up, either immediately or after some questioning. Some versions do not mention that she meets and talks with the tiger, but merely state that a tiger eats her up. Here the distinguishing feature is that no mother mentions this variant in her version, while among the others more or less equally many tellers use or omit this motif. Perhaps mothers did not want to frighten their children by telling this detail, an additional violence in a violent story. The meeting between mother and tiger, then, can have several meanings: it may just add more violence to the story, or it may help to explain how, later in the story, the tiger succeeds in entering the house of the children. In about one-fifth of our stories, the tiger knows the details about the family. Before eating the mother, the tiger may ask the mother where she lives, where she is going, and how many children, of what age, and with which names she has. The tiger may just ask the mother about the details without eating her. In such cases, the tiger sometimes appears to the mother in human, not in animal shape. But the whole meeting with the mother is not necessary for the continuation of the story, because the tiger can gain all necessary information by just overhearing the words of the mother before she leaves the children. Most stories anyhow state that the mother warns her children when telling them where she is going. Again, all mothers telling this version of the story prefer this solution: the tiger overhears the conversation and thus gains all necessary information. Fathers and boys seem

31

to have some preference for the more dramatic solution: the tiger first gains all information from the friendly mother and then kills her, nevertheless.

The Tiger Enters the House

The next motif in our story, the tiger's ways to achieve entry into the house, appears in a great many variants, some of particular interest because they have close parallels in European versions.

We remember that some storytellers found this story educational since it demonstrates to children not only the need to obey mother's orders—in this case, not to let a stranger into the house—but also to check carefully any person who comes to the door. Only five versions have the detail that the children think the mother has returned when the tiger comes the first time, and they ask why mother has come back earlier than expected ("early-arrival" variant). In three versions, the tiger explains this to the satisfaction of the children, who then open the door. The rest, as well as many others (19 versions altogether), proceed with a second test concerning the tiger's voice: either it is stated that the tiger has changed its voice so that it sounds like the voice of the mother or grandaunt, or the children regard the tiger's voice as wrong, so that the tiger must go away to do something about its voice. The two variants are almost equally common. Only in two versions the children find the voice of the visitor peculiar, but do not object on that ground.

The third testing of the tiger occurs in numerous variants. One gets the impression that the original form is that the tiger's hands are scrutinized (ten versions). The tiger either has already changed his hands before going to the house or is rejected at the house because of his hands, which the children find too hairy or too black and must get rid of hair or color, usually by putting flour on the hands. I tend to regard this detail as original because when it occurs, it occurs together with the test of the voice (eight out of ten cases). Only one other variant is once linked to the test of the voice, and all other variants occur singly, without the voice test. The "early arrival" is also connected with the hand test, and not with the other tests.

In a number of versions the hand test is replaced by a test of the face (face too dark or peculiar or with beard that must be removed), or of the nails (which must be changed), or of the feet, or of the dress (which must look like the expected person's dress). In one quite deviant story, the tiger has only one eye, which is blind, but is accepted nevertheless. There is a special variant of the face test: The children know that their mother (or grandmother) has a mole on her face, and since they do not feel it on the tiger, the tiger must add a mole to its face, usually by pasting something on the face.

There is an interesting difference between what I regard as the original set of motifs and other variants. In the original set, the tests of voice and hands are connected with the dark. It is clearly assumed that it is dark outside, so that the children in the house cannot see the visitor and have to rely on hearing or touch. In the other variants, where the face is in some way peculiar or where the color of the dress is wrong, the children in the house can see the visitor. Yet even in these versions it is intimated, though not stated, that it is dark or almost dark when the tiger appears at the door. Perhaps the tellers of these versions assume that there is light on the street or in front of the house, though this is never said. Therefore it might not be chance that 29 percent of those who tell the visual variants belong to the upper educational classes which, we can assume, are more urbanized and take street lighting for granted, while 60 percent of those who tell the original variants belong to the lower educational classes.

We mentioned above that the tiger often gets information about the children from the mother. While this information is useful for passing the tests, it is not indispensable, since the tiger can pass the tests also by just overhearing the words of the mother to her children. A few versions link the test to the information given directly to the tiger by the mother. These are two cases in which the tiger knows the names of the girls, one in which the tiger knows secrets of the family, and one in which he can describe the girls. When a Chinese mother talks to her child, she does not use the child's formal name. A stranger, therefore, cannot know personal names by overhearing a conversation. Similarly, the tiger can describe the children only because the mother has described them to the tiger. A hidden tiger cannot have seen the children, who were in the house when the mother talked to them before departing.

Most versions now mention in which shape the tiger succeeds in entering the house of the children (Table 5). The variants can be divided into three groups. First, a few versions are unusual with a trait in which the animal assumes the shape of a male or of a sister of the girls. The second group consists of the cases in which the tiger enters the house in the shape of the mother. This is often, but not necessarily, connected with the motif that the tiger meets the mother, kills her, puts on her dress, and changes into her shape either completely or partially. If the change is not complete, the mother-shaped tiger has to pass one or more of the tests discussed above. In general, this variant relies on some degree of belief in magic. In the third type of variant, the tiger assumes the shape of the grandaunt or grandmother. In some versions the tiger is called "aunt," which I believe is a shortened form of grandaunt. The most common address is "grandaunt," naturally, since the standard title of the story is "Grandaunt Tiger." The grandaunt comes to the children's house after the mother has left and tells them that she comes or has been sent to be a babysitter during the mother's absence. Some storytellers mention specifically that the children say they do not know the grandaunt, which the tiger explains by saying that "she has not visited the family for a long time because she lived too far away." Other storytellers let her pass through the tests. In other versions there is no explanation, taking it for granted that the children have numerous maternal grandaunts and may not remember all of them clearly enough to be puzzled by the tiger-grandaunt. In many of the cases in which the tiger appears in the shape of

Table 5   The Shape of the Tiger Entering the House

	Father	Mother	Son	Daughter
Grandaunt (or aunt)	18	17	14	29
Grandmother	2	4	9	8
Mother	7	14	7	7
Relative (unspecified)	—	1	3	—
Older sister	1	—	—	—
Husband	—	—	—	1
Uncle	—	—	—	1
Servant, nurse, friend of mother	—	—	3	—
Old woman (not related)	2	2	2	1
Babysitter	—	3	2	4
Person bringing food	3	—	—	1
Tiger just enters	1	5	4	1
Tiger had been hidden in house	1	—	—	—
Number of cases	35 (83%)	46 (77%)	44 (71%)	53 (74%)

the grandmother, I have the feeling that this is a slip: the teller actually meant to say grandaunt. In a few cases where clearly the grandmother is meant, the whole version differs very much from the normal story, as will be discussed later. The problem is that in most versions the mother goes out to visit the grandmother. Then how can the grandmother come to babysit? The tiger in the shape of the grandmother, logically, could happen only if the mother went to town or elsewhere. But there is no correlation of this sort. Whenever the tiger appears as the grandaunt or grandmother, as a servant, nurse, or old woman, she pretends to be, or to have been sent as, a babysitter. All these variants, as well as the tiger arriving in the shape of the mother, are based on a belief in magic, since the visitor is a tiger and not a woman. The story is certainly more terrifying when the "mother" turns out to be a tiger, than when a more remotely related person is a cannibal. It is perhaps for this reason that children less often than adults have the tiger take the shape of the mother (Table 6). Adults who regard the story as educational may

35

Table 6   The Tiger Enters as Mother or as Grandaunt (Grandmother) (in
percentage of cases that specifically mention entrance of tiger)

	Father	Mother	Son	Daughter
As mother	20%	31%	16%	13%
As grandaunt	57%	46%	52%	70%
Number of cases	35	46	44	53

like to underline with the dramatic turn that children should
be cautious even if the stranger resembles their mother.

Unusual Behavior of the Tiger in the House

After the tiger succeeded in cheating the children and entered the house, the scene is ready for the main event, but
several storytellers add an interlude before coming to it. In
versions such as this, the variants are the same as those occurring in other versions at the point when the tiger is still
in front of the door: the face of the tiger is peculiar (2), the
voice is different (1), the visitor wears glasses and has a big
mouth (1). In seventeen stories, the identity of the visitor is
questioned or becomes questionable: the tiger may suddenly
state that "she" is not the mother, but a grandaunt, or may
reveal the purpose of the visit, which had not been mentioned before. The typical trait is that the tiger, although in
human shape, still has a tail and is unable to change or hide
it. Therefore, the tiger wants to sit on a jar instead of a chair
(told by four fathers, seven mothers, nine sons, fifteen daughters; 14 percent of all stories). Some tellers elaborate even
further: When the visitor is seated on the jar, there is a noise
coming from the inside, caused by the wagging of the tail.
When the children ask about the noise, the visitor explains
that "she" has diarrhea or gives another absurd explanation.
This motif may often simply serve as an amusing relaxation
before the cruel next scene. In some versions, however, it is
used to introduce the suspicion of one of the children—the
one who later is saved. Logically, this can be the case only

when the tiger shares a bed with only one child, not with both children.

In most versions this interlude, which takes place late in the evening or early at night, is followed by the main event. Only two young storytellers introduce something else. One says that the tiger closes the door and windows, which arouses further suspicion. This is not a very ingenious motif since the house was already locked when the tiger arrived, as any house is during the night. The other one mentions that the tiger washed the children, a motif apparently related to the typical form of the competition motif, which follows soon.

The Night of Horror

Normally, soon after the entering of the tiger, the tiger proposes to go to bed. This is arranged in three different ways (Table 7): the tiger may sleep alone and the children in separate beds in one or two separate rooms, or one child in the same room with the tiger and the other child elsewhere. Judging from information about occupancy rates of rooms, one might say that in any story the motifs "more than one bedroom" and "separate beds for small children" are modern variants, while the motif "one bed for several persons" is a more traditional variant, more likely to be told by persons of the lower classes. Our data are too limited to test this hypothesis. In rural and poor urban families it is still common that young children sleep together in one bed. This custom cannot be used in the analysis of our story, as it does nothing to explain the following events. But it is also common that a grandmother or a mother shares her bed with one or two children. In fact, implicitly also in many of our versions, children seem to enjoy it and may regard it as a treat to sleep together with a visiting grandmother or grandaunt.

The children in the story are described, if at all, as small children, and therefore both could sleep together with mother or visitor. Not many of our young storytellers had both children sleep with the visitor; they told more often

Table 7   The Tiger Goes to Bed

	Father	Mother	Son	Daughter	Average
Number of tellers who mention this trait	22 (53%)	40 (66%)	41 (66%)	58 (81%)	
Sleeps with all children	27%	28%	10%	16%	19%
Sleeps with one	55%	67%	85%	81%	75%
Sleeps alone	18%	5%	5%	3%	6%
Number of cases	22	40	41	58	

than older persons a variant in which only one child sleeps with the tiger. In more detailed accounts, the children, if both of them share the tiger's bed, lie down either one on each side or one at the head, the other at the feet of the tiger, never both children side by side. This arrangement is necessary for the plot.

We cannot say that one child sleeping with the tiger and the other separately in the same or an adjacent room indicates a modernized variant, as if it were a consequence of the ability of modern families to afford a bed for each child or separate second bedrooms. This variant merely allows the storyteller to introduce a special motif as well as to decrease the horror of the plot to some degree.

The special motif is that of a competition (Table 8). The tiger wants to eat the children, but cannot possibly eat both children at once and thus must try to eat one without arousing the suspicion of the other. Therefore the tiger declares that only one child may sleep with "her," the one who wins in a competition. The competition is usually that the girls must wash themselves, or more specifically, wash their feet. The one who is cleaner may sleep with the visitor. Occasionally, this detail is varied: the children must fight with one another or make a bet between themselves, and the winner may sleep with the visitor. It seems to me that the washing of the feet is the typical and perhaps original variant, and that women and girls liked it most. It is not wholly impos-

Table 8 Competition Decides which Child Will Sleep with the Tiger

	Father	Mother	Son	Daughter
Competition mentioned	25%	41%	34%	43%
Number of cases	12	27	35	47

Table 9 Tiger Eats a Child

	Father	Mother	Son	Daughter
Tiger eats one	30	52	52	64
Tiger eats two or more	6	3	4	—
Not mentioned	6	5	6	8
Number of cases	42	60	62	72

sible, but cannot be proved, that this motif goes back to the time when the feet of women and of girls above the age of six were bound, customary until roughly 1920. Bound feet had to be cleaned from time to time, to prevent their smelling. But to untie the bands and wash the feet was a painful manipulation, disliked by women and girls. Therefore, in our tale the girl who does it and does it well deserves a reward.

The bet or the fight as a means to decide to whom to give the reward seems to be more appropriate for boys, but as we have seen, the story is usually about girls, not boys.

Once the children are asleep, the tiger eats one child (Table 9). In a very few versions there are not one or two, but three or more children. In these versions, the teller can allow the tiger to eat more than one child. The only function of this variant seems to be to increase horror.

The second girl, who either sleeps on the other side or at the feet of the tiger in the same bed, or in a separate bed in the same or another room, normally notices the noise caused by the tiger's cracking the bones of the sibling (Table 10). In some cases this trait is replaced by one of the following more direct descriptions: the surviving girl hears a cry, hears the tiger grinding a knife, sees the actual murder of the sibling, or simply finds the sibling missing. In these variants the

Table 10   Surviving Child Becomes Suspicious

	Father	Mother	Son	Daughter	Average
Child hears noise	81%	83%	70%	78%	78%
Other reasons for suspicion	—	7%	14%	7%	7%
Motif missing	19%	10%	16%	14%	14%

motif which otherwise follows is left out, as it does not make sense. In the usual variant, where the girl hears the noise, she assumes at first that the "mother" is eating something and asks what the "mother" is eating. In a few versions, the tiger says that children are not allowed to eat during the night, because they are supposed to sleep, whereupon the girl insists more strongly upon getting something to eat. In one version this is the behavior that arouses the girl's suspicion, because "mother always gave us food when we asked for it." But in the great majority of cases, the "mother" answers the question immediately. The answers can be divided into two kinds: the "mother" pretends to eat either a round or an oblong object (Table 11). The round object is normally a peanut, and the cracking of the peanut is supposed to explain to the girl the reason for the unusual noise. One cannot help suspecting that "peanut" is a relatively new variant, peanuts came to China through contact with the Western world, though they were known in China already before the printing of the earliest text known to me in which this tale is mentioned. "Bean," another variant, probably is only a linguistic variant for peanut, as peanut is often called "earth bean." Melon seeds, which also occur, have been the delight of Chinese, especially when roasted. The noise when they are cracked between the teeth may have some similarity with the cracking of bones. Yet, from the continuation of the story, I believe that the other answer of the tiger is the original one: the tiger pretends to eat an oblong object, either a ginger root, a radish, or a chicken bone. Chewing ginger root does not cause much noise, but radish may do so. My reason for assuming that this kind of

Table 11   Surviving Child Believes It Will Receive Something to Eat

	Father	Mother	Son	Daughter	Average
Peanut	36%	25%	55%	53%	43%
Bean, melon seed	7%	13%	3%	4%	7%
Ginger, radish, chicken bone	19%	12%	5%	6%	9%
Cake, candy	—	—	2%	—	—
Food (unspecified)	3%	2%	—	—	3%
Salt	—	2%	—	—	—
Meat	—	2%	—	—	—
Trait mentioned	65%	56%	65%	63%	62%

Table 12   The Survivor Receives the Fatal Food

	Father	Mother	Son	Daughter	Average
Receives finger, hand, nail (or sees tiger eating it)	48%	63%	45%	57%	54%
Receives bone or sees bone	—	—	16%	6%	6%
Sees blood, receives bloody object	2%	—	6%	1%	3%
Sees tiger in animal shape	—	7%	—	—	2%
Not directly mentioned	24%	13%	5%	17%	14%
Motif missing	26%	17%	29%	18%	22%

answer is older is that it fits much better to the next motif: the child asks for a piece of that food and receives a finger of the sibling, that is an oblong object more similar to a ginger root, a radish, or a chicken bone than to a peanut (Table 12). Very few versions replace the common "finger" by either "hand" or "nail." A nail would seem to correspond in size and form to a peanut, but this variant is exceptional. It may not be by chance that the younger generation preferred the "peanut" answer, because of the present popularity of peanuts in Taiwan, while the older generation more often selected the melon seeds and especially the oblong objects.

Some young storytellers do not mention the finger specifi-

Table 13   Who Is the Survivor?

	Father	Mother	Son	Daughter	Average
Younger child	26%	27%	27%	14%	23%
Older child	60%	52%	55%	71%	59%
Not specified	2%	13%	3%	3%	7%
Story incomplete or not applicable	12%	8%	15%	12%	11%

cally, but speak of a "bone" which the survivor receives or which he or she sees instead of the sibling. Others stress the blood. Here one gains the impression that the teller wanted to avoid mentioning the finger for fear of being too naturalistic. In a fairly large number of versions this motif is not directly mentioned (Table 12), but for reasons of logic it should be present. For instance, it is mentioned that the tiger eats something and even answers that he is eating peanuts, but then the narrative shifts over to the next phase, and the listener is left to assume that the surviving child becomes suspicious of the situation without having received the proof of the murder in the form of the sibling's finger. The reason for this omission may be, again, that the teller wanted to avoid his story becoming too horrid.

The surviving girl is not always the same (Table 13): in most versions it is the older one, probably because an older child is smarter and less easily tricked by the tiger. It is often also the older child who refuses to sleep with the tiger or refuses to compete with the younger one for sharing the bed with the tiger. In some versions the dichotomy of clever older child and stupid younger one occurs already in the early part of the plot, when the younger child opens the door without carefully checking the guest's identity or without giving heed to the warning of the older child. In some versions, the younger child is fatter than the older one and, implicitly, the tiger prefers to start eating the fatter child. However, the older child may be the fatter one, and therefore the one who is eaten first. The motif that the older one survives seems to fit better into Chinese concepts. Older children are supposed to give in to the younger ones; an older child often is the one who is slender because he has strenuous child care obligations and much household work to do, while the smaller child has leisure and is spoiled by the mother. In any case, the distribution of this motif does not show that sex, age, and social class of the storytellers have influenced the selection of one or the other alternative.

How to Escape the Tiger

Most of our storytellers do not explicitly state that the visitor, after entering in the shape of grandaunt, mother, or friend, during the night changes back into a tiger to devour the child. Only four women say so, but it is implied in all other cases, since humans do not eat other humans. But many storytellers seem to assume that after eating the child, the tiger again assumes human shape.

In any case, the majority of complete versions proceed to tell about the trick of the surviving girl. The child, now pretty sure that the visitor is malevolent or even an animal, assumes automatically that she will be the next victim and, therefore, plans to escape. It is normal for a young child waking up during the night to say it must go to the toilet (Table 14). Although Chinese have chamber pots, no version mentions one, and doing so would indeed make impossible the continuation of the standard plot. On the contrary, we must assume from the context that the toilet is in a separate outhouse, not adjacent to the bedroom. In a few versions, the tiger tells the girl to relieve herself in the bed or in the room, but the girl objects, saying that it would smell. The girl normally pretends to need to "go to the toilet," implying the need to urinate. But many tellers have the girl say specifically that she needs to urinate. "Going to the toilet," the more frequent term in our texts, seems to be the more "refined" expression, preferred by the top social class, the lowest class preferring specific expression. The differences of the age and sex of tellers seems to be unimportant, though slightly more males used the specific expression.

43

Table 14   The Trick of the Survivor

	According to Sex				
	Father	Mother	Son	Daughter	Average
Pretends to go to toilet	12 (29%)	22 (37%)	22 (36%)	35 (49%)	91 (39%)
Pretends to go urinate	9 (21%)	14 (23%)	15 (24%)	12 (17%)	50 (21%)
Not mentioned	21 (50%)	24 (40%)	25 (40%)	25 (35%)	95 (40%)
Number of cases	42	60	62	72	

	According to Class			
	A	B	C	D
Pretends to go to toilet, defecate	25 (28%)	23 (25%)	28 (31%)	15 (17%)
Pretends to go urinate	6 (12%)	17 (24%)	14 (28%)	13 (26%)
Number of cases	31	40	42	28

The story now could be continued with the girl escaping by means of this trick, but most storytellers love to embellish the episode with more details. The tiger objects to the girl's request to leave the room, fearing that she might run away and be lost. This problem is solved in one of two ways (Table 15): the tiger, in order to prevent the escape, ties a rope to the girl and holds the end of the rope, or the surviving girl herself proposes to be tied by a rope so she cannot run away. Use of a rope is mentioned in 45 percent of all our texts. The idea of the rope is nothing unusual to a Chinese. Toddlers are often prevented from getting into mischief or danger by having a rope tied to their legs, so that they can walk or crawl around but cannot get too far away. In some versions, the tiger tries to be shrewd by telling the girl that the rope serves to prevent her falling into the toilet or getting lost in the dark.

44

Table 15   The Use of a Rope

	Father	Mother	Son	Daughter	Total
Girl proposes use of rope	3 (23%)	8 (35%)	5 (18%)	2 (5%)	18 (17%)
Tiger initiates use of rope	10 (77%)	15 (65%)	23 (82%)	39 (95%)	87 (83%)
Number of cases	13	23	28	41	105

Interestingly enough, only five youngsters among our storytellers say that the rope was tied to the leg, and six youngsters say the rope was tied to the hand or arm. Normally the rope, if mentioned at all, is tied around the waist. More versions told by parents than by youngsters use the variant that the child proposes to be tied with a rope to the tiger. This variant stresses the intelligence of the girl, who devises this clever way to make the tiger willing to let her leave the room. Children in particular, but also the majority of adult storytellers, prefer the other variant in which the tiger initiates the use of the rope. This variant is in general used more by members of the upper classes ([A] 24 percent and [B] 31 percent, versus 22 and 17 percent, respectively, for the tiger's initiative), while storytellers from the lower classes prefer the variant in which the girl proposes the rope ([C] 33 percent, [D] 28 percent).

The girl may now leave the tiger's room and the main house. Out of 105 versions that mention the tying of the rope, 83 also mention the untying, in several variants. Three stories simply mention that the girl unties the rope and runs away, but most stories elaborate upon this motif (Table 16). Two main forms of elaborations are recognizable. In one, which is used more often by parents, the girl unties the rope in the toilet and ties it to a bucket, a tea kettle, a jar, or a chamber pot in such a way that when the rope is pulled, water begins to drip, imitating the noise of urination. In the other main form, the rope is tied to a solid object such as a tree, a rock, or a doorpost, so that, when the rope is pulled, a resistance is felt. The first form can blend into the second: if

45

Table 16   The Child Unties the Rope (mentioned in 34 percent of all
stories)

	Father	Mother	Son	Daughter	Total
Ties rope to bucket	11 (85%)	10 (53%)	8 (40%)	16 (57%)	45 (56%)
Ties rope to other object	2 (15%)	9 (47%)	12 (60%)	12 (43%)	35 (44%)
Number of cases	13	19	20	28	80

the noise of dripping water is not mentioned and if the rope
is tied to a heavy water jar, the teller possibly thought mainly
of the resistance the jar would cause. Yet I have the feeling
that the association is with noise when the rope is tied to an
object containing a liquid, and with resistance in all other
cases. The preference for each variant may be somewhat
linked with social class. The noise is used by 50 percent of
the members of both lower classes, and the resistance by 48
percent. But we observe that in the two upper classes, the
members of class A prefer the resistance (34 percent versus
16 percent for the noise), while members of class B have
similarly strong preference for the noise (33 percent, versus
17 percent for resistance).

The selection of either variant has a certain importance
for the continuation of the plot. After having waited in vain
for the girl to return, the tiger should pull the rope, since
this was the implied reason for tying the rope to the child.
Only two versions vary here: in one boy's version the rope is
not in the hands of the tiger but is tied to a chair; and in one
girl's version the girl is completely tied up so that she cannot
leave the house, but must first untie the rope before being
able to escape. In all other cases, the listener must assume
that the tiger is holding the rope, but the motif of pulling it
is mentioned in only twenty-nine versions (six adults and
twenty-three youngsters). After the pulling of the rope, very
rarely done more than once, has had no success, the tiger begins to search for the girl. If the rope is tied to an object in
the toilet, the tiger first comes to the toilet where he does

not find her and continues the search. In a number of versions with the other variant, the girl has tied the rope to the tree which she climbs, often without having gone to the toilet. In this case, by following the rope the tiger quickly finds the girl. This solution is less dramatic than the continued search, which creates the occasion for exciting details.

We are now at a turning point of the story. Once the girl has untied the rope or has left the toilet, every decision of the teller determines the end of the plot. The girl simply can run away, for instance to neighbors (twelve versions, nine adults and three youngsters), or she can hide on the roof (two versions), the doorpost (one version), or in the kitchen (one version). All these variants belong to incomplete stories, which are brought to an undramatic end.

The two main variants differ in the performance of the flight (Table 17), which occurs in 73 percent of all stories. In one type of variant, the girl goes into the kitchen, either after leaving the toilet or directly from the tiger's room. This kitchen, we must assume, is again in another building, not in the main building—an arrangement typical of traditional Chinese houses. Here the child either finds hot oil or water or, more often, heats up water or oil and takes the hot stuff in a bucket or other container up the tree in which she hides. This variant has several problems: it is nighttime, when normally there is no fire in the kitchen. Therefore the child would have to kindle the fire and wait until the liquid is boiling, a procedure which takes much longer than the pur-

Table 17   The Preparation for Revenge

	Father	Mother	Son	Daughter	Total
Child goes to kitchen	7	5	16	19	47
Child climbs tree with hot oil or water	11 (41%)	9 (20%)	18 (46%)	23 (39%)	16 (36%)
Child climbs tree without hot oil or water	16 (59%)	37 (80%)	21 (54%)	36 (71%)	110 (74%)

pose for which the child left the tiger. We might expect the child to be in great danger of being surprised by the tiger in the kitchen, a solution selected only by one boy storyteller. As, implicitly, the child's family is poor, it is unlikely that a fire is kept burning after dinner. Perhaps we should not be surprised that this variant is less frequently used by females than by males, since women can be assumed to be more realistic about kitchen work. No storyteller, describing first the preparations in the kitchen and then the climbing of the tree with the hot liquid in hand, seems to have realized the problems involved in climbing a tree at night with a heavy, hot container, especially as trees in China (including by implication the tree of our story) have no lower branches. Perhaps some females were aware of this problem, since they prefer the other variant in which the child climbs the tree without the liquid, but no teller is explicit about this problem. In any case, the variant that includes the preparation of the hot liquid and the climbing of the tree with it offers problems. Yet this solution is preferred by upper-class tellers ([A] 28 percent; [B] 35 percent; [C] 30 percent; [D] 8 percent).

In contrast, climbing the tree without the liquid is simpler and without problems at this point—its problems appear only at a later stage.

After simply having waited a long time, or after pulling the rope and recognizing the ruse, the tiger goes out to search for the girl (directly mentioned in 124 stories, 53 percent of all) and finds her, usually in a tree. Here, some tellers introduce an interesting motif that occurs often in Near Eastern tales, but which I have not encountered in other Chinese stories: the tiger comes to some water (or a pond) and sees the child's reflection in the water (Table 18). This clearly is a variant preferred by parents and not by children, and it occurs more often in versions told by lower-class persons (65 percent). At first I suspected that this trait stemmed from a printed version by a literary writer, but only two tellers said they had read the story in a book, while most people said they had heard the story from a family member (59 percent). This variant cannot logically be expected in versions

Table 18   The Reflection

	Father	Mother	Son	Daughter
Number of stories	4	10	2	1
Percentage of total stories	10%	17%	3%	1%

where the child has tied the rope to the tree. But it is once used to bring the story to an abrupt end: the tiger, seeing the reflection in the water, believes that the child is in the water, jumps in and drowns.

The Killing of the Tiger

We now come to the dramatic end of the tale, the killing of the tiger. The tiger has found the girl on top of the tree and wants to get her and eat her.

Almost all versions assume that the tiger in its human shape cannot climb the tree, and the animal has only a few other possibilities (Table 19). There are two sets of variants: it can try to climb up, shake the tree in the hope the child will fall down, gnaw through the trunk of the tree and thus fell it, cut the tree down with implements, or assume its animal shape and climb up as an animal. This last variant is selected in fewer than one-third of the versions with this motif, and it is used more often by parents than by children. The other set of variants consists of the tiger asking the child to come down, threatening the child, waiting until it comes down, or simply asking, "What are you doing in the tree?" (only two versions).

In many versions, the child in the tree now asks the tiger to send up some boiling oil or water (Table 20). This motif, too, contains some logical problems, as it presupposes that the tiger returns to the house, kindles the fire, and heats up oil or water, a lengthy procedure during which the child could easily climb down and disappear. It presupposes also that the tiger is still in human shape. Furthermore, by now the tiger must know that the child has grave suspicions and, therefore, the child's request is hardly reasonable. Finally,

Table 19   The Tiger under the Tree

	Father	Mother	Son	Daughter	Total
Tiger asks child to come down	9 (59%)	16 (57%)	19 (79%)	24 (77%)	68 (71%)
Tiger threatens tree	4 (31%)	12 (43%)	5 (21%)	7 (23%)	28
Trait mentioned	13 (31%)	28 (47%)	24 (39%)	31 (43%)	96 (41%)

Table 20   Murder Instruments the Child Requests

	Father	Mother	Son	Daughter	Total
Oil or water	12 (29%)	26 (43%)	21 (34%)	24 (33%)	83 (35%)
Pipe	5 (12%)	1 (2%)	4 (7%)	5 (7%)	15 (6%)
Number of cases	17	27	25	29	98

how can the oil be brought up? Only a few versions mention that the rope is used for this purpose.

In a few versions, the child also wants to have a bamboo pipe or pole. This element can appear in both variants, where the girl already has the oil in the tree and where she sits there without anything.

The girl must now explain why she needs these objects; or, if she already has brought the objects up the tree, what she will do next. This explanation seems to be a problem for the tellers. In general, we find one of two kinds of explanations: the girl pretends to need the oil for frying birds on top of the tree which she will then drop for the tiger to eat; or she pretends to wish to fry herself, or to wash up so that the tiger will enjoy eating her (Table 21). The second kind of explanation is that the girl needs the objects for coming down. There are usually no details. Only some versions state that the girl wants to slide down, which she can do either by sliding down the tree after the trunk is oiled, or by sliding down the pipe. But in some versions she promises to come down on her own if allowed, first, to have oil (or water) to drink or to eat or to clean herself after defecating. All these explanations are not too convincing, not even for a stupid tiger, and so most versions do not elaborate the point, but state that

Table 21   The Reason for the Objects in the Tree

	Father	Mother	Son	Daughter	Total
To prepare food for tiger	4 (28%)	4 (17%)	8 (38%)	12 (32%)	28 (29%)
To jump or slide down	10 (72%)	20 (83%)	13 (62%)	25 (68%)	68 (71%)
Percentage of total stories	14 (33%)	24 (40%)	21 (34%)	37 (51%)	96 (41%)

Table 22   The Opening of the Mouth

	Father	Mother	Son	Daughter
Tiger should open its mouth	16 (38%)	27 (45%)	23 (37%)	24 (33%)
Tiger should close its eyes	2 (5%)	4 (7%)	9 (15%)	10 (14%)
Number of cases	18	31	32	34

Table 23   The Killing of the Tiger

	Father	Mother	Son	Daughter	Total
By boiling oil	22 (52%)	29 (49%)	48 (77%)	41 (57%)	140 (59%)
By boiling water	7 (17%)	12 (20%)	2 (3%)	12 (17%)	33 (14%)
By people	5 (12%)	4 (6%)	3 (5%)	6 (8%)	18 (8%)
By other means	4 (10%)	2 (3%)	3 (5%)	2 (3%)	11 (5%)
Tiger escapes	—	4 (6%)	2 (3%)	3 (4%)	9 (4%)
Not mentioned	4 (10%)	9 (15%)	4 (6%)	8 (11%)	25 (11%)
Number of cases	38	51	58	64	236

the girl promises to jump down as soon as she has the re-
quested object. The girl's words create the impression that
she will jump or slide directly into the tiger's mouth, and
many versions have her ask the tiger to open its mouth
(Table 22). Many youngsters add to this motif that the tiger
must close its eyes, so it cannot see what happens.

As soon as the tiger has opened its mouth or is otherwise
in the right position under the tree, the girl proceeds to kill
it (Table 23). By far the most common way is that she pours

the hot oil or water into the open mouth of the animal, in the versions where the tiger has been asked to open it. Sometimes the liquid is poured down into the mouth through the bamboo pipe; in other cases the pipe is used to keep the mouth wide open. If the tiger has not been asked to open its mouth, the hot liquid is sometimes poured on the whole animal. All other ways by which the tiger is killed are variants that lack the oil or water motif or that deviate fairly widely in other ways from the normal form: the tiger may be burned by fire (two boys' versions), the rope on which it wants to be taken up breaks (one boy's version), the tree falls down and kills the tiger (a girl's story), the tiger is killed by rocks (a girl's story), the tiger drowns (a man's story), or no detail about the killing is given. If other people kill the tiger, they are normally neighbors, but in one version the killer is a second surviving child and in another the mother who has come back.

We observe that the oil variant is used more by male tellers, the water variant more by female tellers. The oil motif is particularly remarkable. Oil is expensive and the family in the story is poor. Rarely does a poor family have a kettle full of oil in the kitchen, and even more rarely after dinner during the night. More than men and youngsters, women—who do the cooking—seem to be aware of this unlikeliness, but on the whole most tellers seemed to think that a kettle of boiling water might not be hot enough to kill a tiger. I might add that a few tellers do not speak of boiling oil but let the girl throw oil-fried food down, killing the tiger in this unusual way. Similarly, some tellers do not let the girl pour hot water, but soup. One might think that tellers of lower class, assumed to be poorer than those of the upper class, would mention water more often than oil, but this is not the case ([A] 17 percent; [B] 42 percent, [C] 33 percent; [D] 9 percent).

Why does the surviving child not just run away after all the horror, as she does in a few versions? Why all the elaborate preparations? I think that the surviving child, like any loyal family member, automatically assumes the responsibility to take revenge. Only a few tellers say so directly (10 percent of the fathers, no mothers, 10 percent of the boys, and 7 percent of the girls), sometimes at the end of the story, sometimes when the preparations with the oil begin. Upper- and lower-class tellers mention this element less often than the others. I think that for the average Chinese it is not necessary to mention this element specifically.

Normally, the story ends with the death of the tiger, that is, with a successful revenge. A few tellers have added two more motifs. According to some, the tiger reassumes animal shape when it is killed (three fathers, six mothers, eight boys, five girls; tellers of lower-class less often than others). These tellers, then, imply that the being under the tree was a tiger in human disguise. A few other tellers imply that the tiger had reassumed animal shape already when it pursued the child or, at the latest, when it reached the tree. Otherwise, how could it have tried to gnaw at the tree? Most texts leave the question open, saying nothing about it. The most unusual element, which occurs in six stories (one mother, two boys, three girls) is that the devoured sibling, sometimes even together with the mother, comes out of the stomach of the dead animal, alive. This sounds much like a motif from a European tale, but three of these six stories are otherwise very close to the standard type. One is rather incomplete in its earlier parts, one contains other unusual elements at the end, and one very short tale is unusual in most of its elements. None, however, is close to other elements in the European tale. The motif is not known to me in other Chinese folktales, though it occurs in other types of stories.

Irregular Variants of the Story

The overwhelming majority of texts relate essentially the same story, in more or less detail, introducing either many or only a few modifications. However, all those deviant versions which are profoundly different were produced in response to the request to tell the story "Grandaunt Tiger," and each teller regarded his version as the "true" story.

We remember that in the beginning of the story the mother, who lives with her two children, has to go out and warns the children to be careful lest the bad Grandaunt Tiger might come and do them harm. One of the deviant forms has it that the children go out, not the mother. The mother sends one or two children to visit the grandparents, and on the way the children (child) come(s) to a house that seems to be the house of the grandmother. One teller says that the children got tired on the way and decided to stay overnight in the house of a friendly woman, the disguised tiger. In one story, the tiger pretends that their mother, who had already been devoured, is in the house. In any case, the children believe that the woman in the house is a relative or at least a friendly person. In some variants, they utter some doubts, stating for example that grandmother always wears green or has a mole on her face. But these doubts are overcome, the children remain overnight and sleep with the tiger, and then the story proceeds in the familiar way. Ten texts are of this type (one told by a father, four by mothers, three by sons, two by daughters; three by persons of class A, five by B, two by C, none by D). The tellers assert that they have heard the story from unrelated adults (five) or relatives (four); only one girl believes that she has read this story.

Compared to the normal story, the main characteristic of this deviant story is that the mother's role is diminished and the children's role enlarged. I suspect that this variant is the result of contamination with another tale. This suspicion becomes stronger when we study the second set of deviant stories. In these, just as in the texts mentioned above, the mother sends out a child who arrives at a house that resembles the house of the grandmother, enters, and is eaten up by the tiger. Only one story, told by a girl, mentions the strange face and voice of the supposed grandmother, and the tiger straightens this out. All these texts omit the episode of sleeping in the same bed: the child is simply killed or, in two stories (one by a boy, the other by a girl), the tiger pretends to pick lice from the child's head and kills her during this procedure. The story now continues completely differently: the mother, anxious about the child, goes out and searches, and she meets the tiger, who declares it will come this night and eat her, too. The mother goes home crying. Several peddlers successively come to the house and ask her why she is crying, each offering her one piece of his merchandise. The peddlers in the five stories with this trait offer for sale millstones (four stories), snakes (four), nails or needles (five), excrements (four), a bell or a gong (two), a rope or a hammer (one each). The objects are distributed in the house so that the tiger is upon arrival hit by each of the objects. In two stories the tiger is killed by the objects, in two the mother kills the tiger with the hammer or with a knife she had in the house, and in one story a saint comes and kills the tiger. The storytellers are all children (three boys, two girls), and only one boy said he had heard the story from his mother; the others said they had it from a book, which may very well be so. This end to the story belongs to a well-known tale (W. Eberhard, *Typen* no. 14) which occurs independently in the Far East. But we know of mixed forms already in mainland China (see *Typen* nos. 11 and 14), so that this mixed variant is not a new invention of the Taiwanese storytellers. Two more texts show another kind of contamination between the two stories. In one of them (told by a girl) the tiger eats up the only child, and up to this point the story is conventional. Then the mother returns, does not find the son, searches and finds his clothes. When she cries, a passer-by asks about her crying, hears her story, and promises help. The story abruptly ends by saying that the mother later took revenge for the murder. In the other text (told by a mother) everything is normal up to the moment when the oil is poured on the tiger. Now it continues with the statement that the tiger stops moving. In the morning, a peddler passes by and the surviving girl asks him to look at the tiger. The peddler finds the tiger dead, helps the lonely girl, and later marries her. This may be an original attempt to add a "happy ending" to the gruesome story, but it might as well be that the peddler story (*Typen* no. 14) has influenced the teller. Six of the seven stories in which the peddler story is directly mentioned or alluded to are unusually long (average 533 words). The longest of all texts (931 words) is among them.

I think one may say that the story of the Grandaunt Tiger was contaminated with the peddler story already in mainland China before 1940. The reason for the mixture may be that the peddler story lacks a dramatic introduction, which it gains by combining with "Grandaunt Tiger." The interlocking of the two stories may be complete, as in the last texts discussed above, or one story may have exercised only slight influence on the other, as in the first examples where the child goes out, instead of the mother. One has the strong feeling that all seven contaminated texts were ultimately influenced by printed texts (five of the tellers stated that they knew the story from a book, one from a mother, one from a neighbor). In contrast, the truly oral forms of "Grandaunt Tiger" in Taiwan are those variants which we have discussed earlier.

The Core Story

Let me now try to construct the "core" of the story, that is, the minimal form in which the story still is a story and in which it can be transmitted from one teller to another. In order to construct such a core story, I combined those elements and traits which occur in at least one-third of all the texts I have. This is an arbitrary condition. I could not expect to be able to reconstruct a story text that makes sense if I had to take only traits that occur in the majority of my texts, because so many texts are—as admitted by the tellers—incomplete. On the other side, it is difficult to decide which text is incomplete if the teller does not admit it, and such a decision would probably have been much more arbitrary and unquantifiable than the decision that I preferred to make. The "core" is then no "Urform," but a construct, combining those elements of the story which in a certain community, in this case the Min-nan-speaking community of the Ku-t'ing section of Taipei City, are most commonly represented. Here is this "core" story:

A mother (mentioned in 81 percent of all texts) has two children of the same sex (73 percent). She goes out to see her family (39 percent), leaving the children at home. A tiger in the shape of a grandaunt gains entrance into the house (33 percent). During the night, the tiger eats one child (84 percent). The remaining child hears the noise which the chewing tiger produces (78 percent), believes that it will receive a peanut from the tiger (50 percent), but actually receives a finger of the sibling (54 percent). The surviving child, who is the older of the two (59 percent), now pretends to have to go to the toilet (39 percent). The tiger, fearing that the child might run away, ties the child with a rope (37 percent), but the child unties the rope, ties it to another object (34 percent), runs away and climbs a tree (47 percent). The tiger after a while searches for the child, finds it (53 percent), and asks it to come down (41 percent). The child asks to be given a kettle with boiling liquid (35 percent), asks the tiger to open its mouth (38 percent), and, by pouring the liquid on the tiger, kills the animal (59 percent).

If this core story is compared with the form which I reconstructed in my *Typen* no. 11, it can be seen that the form there represents a "maximal" form, not a core form, and that the "Grandaunt Tiger" text translated above is quite close to the maximal form. Since the maximal form requires more words, it lasts longer to tell it and can be expected only if the teller either knows it well or is interested enough to tell the full story, not only an abbreviated version. In spite of the obvious relation of our Taipei core form to the maximal form presented in *Typen*, we can see that the Taipei core story is close only to those few mainland stories which also have the element of scalding. Most of the mainland stories and all of those from Korea and Japan seem to prefer other endings. The astral myth occurring in the Korean and Japanese versions seems to be unknown in Taipei. We further note that only fourteen of the forty-four variants discussed in *Typen* have the tiger as the acting animal. In spite of the fact that the story is called "Grandaunt Tiger" in Taipei, in one variant the actor was a "shaman," comparable to the "cannibal" mentioned in several texts from South China in *Typen*. The number and sex of the children, which vary in Taiwanese texts, varied even more in the texts analyzed in *Typen*, but at least eight tales from all parts of mainland China specified two girls rather than any other combination of children. In thirteen variants in *Typen* the animal questions the mother of the children and then eats her up, while eight texts omitted this detail. One variant that seems to be fairly common in mainland China, namely that the children flee to the second floor of the house (eight texts in *Typen*), did not occur at all in the Taipei texts. Houses with more than one floor are more often urban than rural; our Taipei texts are collected in the city, but all our storytellers seem to have had in mind a completely rural scene. All the other variants of this section of the story in the mainland—that the children call for help, or that the animal does not find them—have their parallels in Taipei. Even for the supernatural help we have one parallel in Taipei.

Some Taipei versions contained the *Typen* no. 14, in which the animal tells the mother, who searches for her lost children, that it will come back to eat her, whereupon peddlers come and help her. This variant, then, is not original in Taipei, since it occurred already on the mainland. Two other endings, however, have no parallel: two texts from Central China contain *Typen* no. 31 (Snake Husband), and several from different parts of China let the animal change into a bird or mosquito. From such differences we cannot conclude that the Taiwanese form of the story is related to stories from only one part of China, say, Fukien. It may well be that stories with the other endings were accidentally more often collected than stories ending in the Taiwanese way, or—perhaps even more likely—that the publisher of the mainland stories regarded the versions with a less cruel ending as more appropriate for printing than the version most popular in Taiwan.

That so many variants of one tale were found in one ethnic group in one quarter of the city of Taipei certainly shows that the Finnish method is not satisfactory as long as we do not have larger surveys for numerous other areas of the Far East. Conclusions drawn from a comparison of, say, one hundred texts from all parts of China may be spurious, since the collection may be heavily biased. Although I believe that my survey allows us to discuss the form of the story among the Min-nan-speaking sector of the Chinese population of Taipei, one must not automatically presume that the Mandarin- or Hakka-speaking inhabitants, even in the same sector of the city, know the story in the same form. Thus far, there is no way even to speculate about the characteristics of their versions. Almost half of our tellers heard the story from a family member, that is, from another Min-nan speaker. Those who had learned the story from other persons often had it from neighbors or friends, and we may assume that these persons were also Min-nan speakers. But when tellers had the story from a teacher, it is not unlikely that they had it from a Mandarin speaker. If they had it from a book, according to my knowledge of the printed story collections it is more likely that they read versions from Central China than a Min-nan version. The only statement we can make now is that thus far the story has been spread mainly through the family and neighbors, people belonging to the same ethnic and linguistic group.

"Grandaunt Tiger" as a Symbolic Tale

If there is the possibility that the teller expresses his own personality by means of selecting those variants of a widely known story, why then do we not enter into an interpretation of the latent meaning of the story? For many years tales have been used as documents in psychoanalytic studies, often in order to make conclusions concerning the "national character" of the ethnic group to which the teller belonged. The frequent objections to this method are well known. It appears to be necessary to point out that the use of a single version of a folktale for psychoanalytic interpretation not of the teller but his society is particularly dangerous, because every version is a "creation" in which at least four influences are amalgamated: firstly, the personality of the storyteller, expressed in the selection of available variants or in the creation of new variants; secondly, the particular culture in which the teller lives; thirdly, the teller's status in society, that is, his social class; and finally, the "original" storyteller's circumstances, that is, the personality and the cultural and social environments of the hypothetical person who created the story. This person is always unknown and may not have lived in the same society where we now find his tale. I do not think that one can neatly separate these four strands, but one can experiment with them, as did Pertev N. Boratav[3] when he told a story to a storyteller and then recorded the epic which the storyteller created out of this "raw material," or as I did when I compared recently printed texts on which contemporary Taiwanese storytellers based their oral presentation.[4]

There is another objection to an uncritical psychoanalytic interpretation of folktales: granting that unconscious emotions and attitudes may be expressed by symbols, one cannot assume that the meanings of symbols are universal. In other words, when working in a culture not our own, we must be intimately familiar with its symbols and their meaning before interpreting a picture or a narrative, even if we think that our interpretation of symbols is "better" than that of the other society. To illustrate this point with a symbol familiar to all Westerners: unfailingly a snake occurring in a Western text is interpreted psychoanalytically as representing a phallus. But before interpreting a snake in a Chinese text, one must consider the specifics. If the whole snake is concerned, it is, indeed, a male symbol also in China; but if only the head is concerned, it symbolizes the female sex organ. Not knowing this leads to absurd mistakes.

The Grandaunt Tiger story offers itself for symbolic interpretation, not only in psychoanalytic terms but also along the lines of the old-fashioned astral-mythological school. In two Korean and one Japanese version (mentioned in *Typen* no. 11) the children, at the end of the story, climb into the sky and the tiger falls down, coloring the millet with his blood. In the Korean versions the children become sun and moon. Soon after the beginning in one of the Korean versions the tiger eats up the mother piece by piece, and we have a text from Taiwan with the same element. Thus we can hypothesize: the mother, disappearing piece by piece, is the waning moon; the tiger is the bad (solar?) spirit causing the disappearance of the moon. One of the children is the new moon appearing in the sky. The variant that two children remain alive, of whom one becomes the sun, causes some, but not insurmountable, difficulties. Once one accepts this much of the interpretation, one can easily proceed—ignoring that this ascent to heaven is not mentioned elsewhere in Chinese literature as far as I know—to conceive of the "rebirth" of the dead child (or the mother or both) out of the stomach of the tiger as a rebirth of the moon. The moon, then, would have to be regarded as female, which in fact is correct according to Chinese symbolism. The tiger generally represents male power, even the essence of masculinity, and it is always connected with the West, that is, the region of death. Within the framework of Chinese mythological thinking, it makes perfect sense to interpret these Korean and Japanese versions as astral myths, because of the motif of the blood (i.e., life essence) of the (male) tiger falling on the earth (female) and causing fertility (the red millet). I have found no similar version in China but I have Chinese versions in which the tiger is buried and on his tomb cabbage begins to grow, out of which seven girls are born. One might hypothesize similarly that the round cabbage represents the new moon, born out of the tiger that devoured the old moon, and the seven girls would symbolize the new moon, each quarter of the moon lasting seven days. One version from Kui-chou (all in *Typen* no. 11) lets the tiger change into thorns and the girls into cherries. The penis is symbolically not called thorn but "stalk" or "lance,"[5] and cherry (ying-t'ao) carries the meaning of "baby (ying)- peach (t'ao)," where "baby" refers symbolically to woman, while "peach" has numerous symbolic meanings. Most commonly it sym-

61

bolizes simply "long life"[6] and occurs as an attribute of the God of Long Life, an old man with rosy, peach-colored cheeks. It is also a symbol of the east, the region of life, and there it is associated with the rooster,[7] symbol of the male sun. But there is still another symbolic meaning, starting from the shape of the peach, which is compared with the female sex organ,[8] and in some modern texts the vagina is called the "Spring of peach blossoms."[9] Just as the peach is connected with the cheeks, the cherry is connected with the lips:[10] "cherry lips" are highly desirable. The vagina may also be called "red gate"[11] or "cinnabar cave"[12] and is compared with the mouth: a woman's small mouth indicates a small vagina.[13] All these comparisons only serve to show that one could interpret also the Kui-chou version of the Grandaunt tale as an astral tale, the tiger representing the male and the sun, the girls the moon. With this kind of reasoning, the birth out of the peach in the Peach Boy story would not surprise anyone since it would be a birth out of the female organ. The speedy growth of the boy in the Japanese versions could be interpreted as the growth of the moon; the boy would have his full strength in his fifteenth year, like the moon which is strongest on its fifteenth day, and on that day the fight is fought against the powers of darkness.

I think that these interpretations are consistent with the line of thinking which existed in the Far East in the past and still exists today, at least partly. However, I think that today it is not the function of our two stories to explain the origin of sun and moon, or of fertility; besides, I think we cannot prove that the stories ever had this function as their main function. Their function today is educational and recreational—which is not to deny that on a deeper level the figures, objects, and events in the tales may well have symbolic meaning, perceived consciously or unconsciously, always or occasionally, by the storyteller and his audience.

Notes

1. Aarne-Thompson 123. Word counts are done in the usual Chinese way. Each written character counts as one word.
2. [Calculations for the average figures in this table do not all appear to tally, e.g., the average for fathers' texts comes to 250, not 247, and the average for A informants comes to 299, not 304. However, it was decided to leave the original tabulations as they were given in the source essay, for this and all subsequent tables. Ed.]
3. In Pertev N. Boratav, *Halk hikâyeleri ve halk hikâyeciliği* (Ankara, 1946).
4. See my "Notes on Chinese Storytellers," *Fabula*, vol. 11 (1969).
5. R. van Gulik, *Erotic Color Prints* (Tokyo, 1951), 231.
6. J. J. M. DeGroot, *The Religious System of China*, vol. 4 (Leiden, 1901), 305.
7. W. Eberhard, *The Local Cultures of South and East China* (Leiden, 1968), 426.
8. Nagai, vol. 1, 415. The term "remains of the peach" (yü-t'ao) means homosexuality (P'an Kuang-tan, *Hsing-hsin-li Hsüeh*, p. 383. (性心理學)
9. In the novel *Chuang-shang-ti nü-jen*, 103, and others. (牀上的女人)
10. As one example for many, see *Ti-i mei-jen yün-shih*, 52. (第一美人韻史)
11. In the novel *Tsei mei-jen*, 35 and others. (賊美人)
12. In the book *Tung-hsüan tse*. (洞玄子)
13. In the novel *Ti-i mei-jen yün-shih*, 2.

Is "Little Red Riding Hood" a Myth?

The question of genre is invariably of interest to folklorists, who, ever since the Grimms, have tried to make fairly rigorous distinctions between myth, folktale, and legend, among other folk-narrative genres. In brief, a myth is a sacred narrative explaining how the world and humanity came to be in their present form; a folktale is a fictional narrative set in no particular place and time (often signaled by an introductory opening formula: "Once upon a time"); and a legend is a story told as true, set in the post-creation real world. From this perspective, it is obvious that "Little Red Riding Hood" is a folktale. Within the folktale genre, it is classified as a fairy tale, that is, a tale falling within the rubric of Aarne-Thompson tale types 300 to 749.

Why then would anyone consider "Little Red Riding Hood" to be a myth? To answer this question, one needs to know that one of the older nineteenth-century theories of folk narrative (espoused by the Grimms) postulated a devolutionary sequence such that sacred myths over time degenerated into secular folktales. According to such a view, one could not understand folktales without reconstructing their presumed original mythic form. The assumption of a mythic origin of folktales also permitted the application of theories of myth (such as solar or lunar mythology) to folktale texts.

Georg Hüsing (1869–1930), a specialist in epic and myth of Persia, writing in a periodical devoted to comparative my-

Reprinted from *Mitra:* Monatsschrift für vergleichende Mythenforschung 1 (1914), 101–104; 290–291. I am indebted to Patricia Sieber for translating this essay from German into English.

thology research in 1914, takes up the matter of the appropriate genre of "Little Red Riding Hood." Not only does he dismiss the idea that the tale has anything to do with the myth genre, but he questions its very authenticity as a proper oral folktale. After publishing his initial essay, Hüsing came upon a Chinese text which gave him pause. One of the first scholars to recognize a possible Chinese cognate to "Little Red Riding Hood," Hüsing remains, however, skeptical. In an addendum to his earlier remarks, he reiterates his generic views of the tale. For a critique of Hüsing's general lunar mythological interpretations of folk narrative, see Rudolf Much, "Mondmythologie und Wissenschaft," *Archiv für Religionswissenschaft* 37 (1941–1942), 231–261.

I

More mythological origins have been attributed to folktale no. 26 of the Grimms' collection, entitled "Rotkäppchen," than to any other folktale. By the same token, these interpretations usually took care of every single detail. The meaning of the tale seems as clear as one can possibly expect: either dawn (or the sea) devours the sun, or the new moon swallows the full moon, or the sun consumes the dawn, or lightning disappears behind the clouds, etc. One could also elucidate the narrative from the perspective of frightening dreams, even though that approach would not be a mythological one. "Little Red Riding Hood" inhibits no one. The tale pleases and delights everybody and has been immortalized in pictures and even in stone monuments. In short, "Little Red Riding Hood" represents one of the most exquisite pearls of—French literature.[1]

"Little Red Riding Hood" is really not one of mankind's ancient myths, but rather it was evidently conceived in the seventeenth century in France. It represents one of the loveliest French literary tales, perhaps being the most successful fake that we have in the entire genre. At the same time, it offers an instructive example of what should *not* be considered a fairy tale.

I am under the following impression: If a reader's appreciation of fairy tales has not been corrupted by the Grimms' collection, he will see that "Little Red Riding Hood" is not an authentic fairy tale. However, we should not argue on the basis of "seeing" and "impressions." Therefore I must have recourse to other methods of explanation. First of all, I need to remind the reader that only the existence of differing versions of the same tale in distant cultures can substantiate the authenticity of a fairy tale. If the tale is completely preserved, it will usually show a variety of individual features, so-called motifs. Generally, the total number of motifs can only be determined by comparing individual variants: one variant usually completes another since the essential "development" of the fairy tale is based on failure to recall.

None of these criteria holds true for "Little Red Riding Hood." The French original appeared in 1697 (as no. 2 in Perrault) and its diffusion has to have occurred since that date. Consequently, around 1700 it may well have crossed the Rhine and the Alps, and it was certainly well received in all of France and beyond the Pyrenees. The tale had many a long day to infiltrate and become rooted in the fairy tale–bearing stratum of the population. Accordingly, in 1800 when Tieck adapted the "fairy tale" based on Perrault's model, a popular version could already be distinguished from this "literary" form. The fact that the editors [the Grimms] of the collection of 1812 had heard the tale from two different people in Kassel[2] does not prove anything with respect to the authenticity of the tale. Further variants were not known to the editors, since the supposedly related ballad in the third volume of a Swedish collection has nothing whatever to do with "Little Red Riding Hood."[3] Reinhold Köhler does not provide any variants either. Moreover, Bolte's notes to the third volume of the *Anmerkungen zu den Kinder- u. Hausmärchen der Brüder Grimm* (1913) demonstrate very clearly that no other versions exist.

One should not misinterpret this argument. In one version, the girl is supposed to be devoured but escapes. In another, she is devoured. In a third, she is devoured and saved. These twists and turns are merely elaborations of the narrative and are entirely unrelated to the formation of true variants of myth. It is difficult and indeed virtually impossible to reconstruct the evolution of myth. Nevertheless, I will at least suggest what kinds of forms a mythological variant might take: Little Red Riding Hood could out of fear turn into stone or be transformed into a bird. However, being devoured by the wolf or escaping from him without having been swallowed (transformed) can hardly be true mythological variants.

The original form of the fake is, of course, unknown, since it cannot be properly ascribed to Perrault. Thus we do not know whether the story that appears in the Grimms' collection as tale no. 5 under the title "The Wolf and the Seven Kids" served from the very beginning as a model or was later incorporated. Perhaps this fusion first occurred in Hesse and, in fact, this scenario seems most likely. All the other more recent French versions which Bolte has listed are apparently embellishments newly borrowed from genuine fairy tales.

I can only partly verify Bolte's further variants.[4] The Gypsy variant does not belong to no. 26 at all, but is related to no. 5. In the Romanian version a boy has a conversation with a "strange grandfather" who is wearing a huge hat, and who sits on the stove while the boy fetches firewood. At the end, the grandfather eats the boy. The Italian (South Tyrolian) narrative also ends with the Orco [ogre], who replaces the wolf, finally devouring the "cappelin rosso." Incidentally, this Tyrolian tale is related to the Gasconian tale in Bladé (III, 189, no. IX). In both tales the girl is supposed to eat the mortal remains of the grandmother and to drink her blood as wine. Even if we include the Portuguese, the Wendish, and the Carinthian variants Bolte mentions, the area of diffusion is still surprisingly limited. At the same time, the content is so scanty that for this reason alone, one cannot speak of a fairy tale any more.

It does seem to me that "Little Red Riding Hood" is no fragment, no folktale remnant. It is a story something like, for instance, "About the Little Gnat" ["vom kleinen Muck"], put together out of remembrance of fairy tales told one bright sunny day.

I cannot pronounce a definitive judgment since I do not have at my disposal all the material that Bolte compiled. Judging from what I know, however, I have every reason to believe that the few versions I am lacking would, if available to me, not change my overall findings. To elucidate these questions for the general reader, I will on another occasion examine other [fake] fairy tales and demonstrate what other internal evidence speaks against seeing "Little Red Riding Hood" as a fairy tale.

As for the narrative being considered a myth, that is beyond the realm of the possible.

II

Earlier I indicated that the so-called "fairy tale" of "Little Red Riding Hood" started as "a remembrance of fairy tales told one bright sunny day." Now we find a narrative made known to us by its appearance in Richard Wilhelm's 1914 translation of a collection of Chinese folktales.[5] This tale, number nine in the collection, reads as if it were derived from oral tradition, but no source is given. The tale, as Wilhelm himself remarks, is "a composite of motifs which also occur in 'Little Red Riding Hood,' 'The Wolf and Seven Kids,' and 'A Pack of Ragamuffins' [Das Lumpengesindel]."[6] The connection between the first two tales is indeed clear—although it is questionable as to what this might mean. However, so far no one has established a link between "Little Red Riding Hood" and "A Pack of Ragamuffins," the tale about the willful household goods.

Insofar as the tale is from China (but from which region?), it is very valuable for our purposes. Nevertheless, it would appear that the Chinese tale was not put together from different tales, including "Little Red Riding Hood." On the contrary, it seems more likely that the underlying basis of "Little Red Riding Hood" might actually be a remnant of a fairy tale, a tale in which up to now no trace of Little Red Riding Hood could be detected. No real proof has been furnished that Little Red Riding Hood herself forms part of this original fairy tale since mention of Little Red Riding Hood is confined to France and its nearest neighbors.

We cannot be entirely certain about the possible connection between "Little Red Riding Hood" and the Chinese tale. In the Chinese story, the mother plays the part of the "old she-goat," but she also visits the grandmother in place of Little Red Riding Hood. On her way there, a panther stops her, offering to comb her hair. Reluctantly the mother agrees, only to have two pieces of skin torn off her scalp. However, it is quite out of the question to link the resulting bloody wound—which is not even explicitly mentioned— with the red cap, particularly since immediately afterward, the mother is completely torn apart and devoured. Moreover, she is not revived and neither is the son who accompanied her. At home, the two daughters play the part of the young kids when faced with the dissimulating panther. Eventually the girls are given the willful household goods which ultimately kill the panther.

This postscript may show just how far we still are from a definitive judgment—this mostly from a lack of material. At the same time, we can see that the often interpreted "Little Red Riding Hood" of the Grimms' collection really cannot be considered a myth.

Notes

1. See also Reinhold Köhler's comments on the tale of the nightingale and the blind-worm in *Zeitschrift des Vereins für Volkskunde* 1 (1891), 53ff.
2. The two are Jeanette Hassenpflug and the "old Marie" who lived in the chemist Wild's house; she "fed" Dorothea Wild in her child-

hood with stories. The note in the third volume, "From the area of the Main," is therefore a somewhat unjustified generalization even if Wilhelm Grimm may have heard that other people in the neighborhood knew the fairy tale. Only "old Marie" told the tale in its corrupted form, in which the girl is not devoured. But it holds true for both sources that it would be sheer hypothesis if anyone were to claim that they were not derived from Perrault's collection.

3. [Hüsing seems to be correct in asserting that the Swedish ballad adduced by the Grimms themselves as a possible parallel to "Little Red Riding Hood" is totally unrelated. The plot has to do with a werewolf rather than a wolf. Typically in this ballad, found throughout Scandinavia, a girl meets a wolf in the woods. She climbs a tree to escape, but the wolf pulls the tree down and tears her unborn child from her body. Her betrothed arrives on the scene too late to save her, whereupon he kills himself. See Type A 20 Varulven— Girl killed by werewolf, in Bengt R. Jonsson, et al., eds., *The Types of the Scandinavian Medieval Ballad* (Oslo: Universitetsforlaget, 1978), 30. Ed.]

4. Anyone interested in investigating the question further might compare a fairy tale reported in E. Cosquin, *La Chaudiere bouillante et la feinte Maladresse* (Rennes, 1910), 34, where the wolf finally falls through a chimney into a vat of boiling water.

5. [For the tale in question, see Richard Wilhelm, *Chinesische Volksmärchen* (Jena: Eugen Diederichs, 1917), 19–22. Ed.]

6. [For Wilhelm's brief remarks, see his notes to tale 9, Der Panther, p. 387. Ed.]

P. SAINTYVES [E. NOURRY]

Little Red Riding Hood or
The Little May Queen

One of the prominent theories of folk narrative consists of the so-called myth-ritual approach. According to advocates of this theory, folktales and many other forms of folklore derive from original rituals. Typically the ritual origins proposed for any particular folktale involve agricultural fertility, often referring to an alleged battle of seasons in which spring conquers winter.

A major difficulty with myth-ritual theory is that rarely if ever is any origin postulated for the supposed ritual. In other words, myth-ritual theory provides only a limited answer to the inevitable question of origins. Myth or folktale may stem from ritual, but what then is the ultimate origin of the generating ritual? Another common problem with ritual explanations of folk narratives is the failure to adduce solid, empirical evidence of the existence of the alleged ritual. More often than not, the would-be ritual is simply asserted to have existed some time in the distant past. Few modern folklorists take myth-ritual theory seriously, but one occasionally finds adherents in classics or literature, most of whom are blithely unaware of some of the devastating critiques of the theory.

Of those scholars who favored a myth-ritual approach to folklore, none argued more persistently or persuasively than French folklorist Émile Nourry (1870–1935), who published his many books and articles under the pseudonym of P. Saintyves. Saintyves was a prolific writer, but of all his many

Reprinted from P. Saintyves, *Les Contes de Perrault* (Paris: Émile Nourry, 1923), 211–229. I thank Catherine Rouslin for translating the essay from French into English.

71

monographs and essays, probably his best-known work was *Les Contes de Perrault et Les Récits Parallèles: Leurs Origines* (Coutumes Primitives et Liturgies Populaires) published in Paris in 1923. In this book, Saintyves seeks origins for Perrault's eleven folktales. For some, such as "Sleeping Beauty," "Cinderella," and "Little Red Riding Hood," he claims seasonal or seasonal ritual beginnings; for others, such as "Tom Thumb" and "Blue Beard," he finds echoes of initiation ritual origins. The following essay is Saintyves' exegesis of "Little Red Riding Hood."

For more about Saintyves, see Francis Bauman, "P. Saintyves, Savant et Philosophe," *Revue Anthropologique* 45 (1935), 293–307. For a sample of Saintyves' theoretical writings on folklore, see "De la méthode dans l'étude des mythes," *Revue des Idées* 9 (1912), 302–311; "La définition et l'objet du folklore," *Revue Anthropologique* 36 (1926), 147–153; "Folklore," *Revue de Synthese* 1 (1931), 81–93; and "Le Folklore. Sa définition et sa place dans les sciences anthropologiques," in an obituary supplement to *Revue de Folklore Français* 6 (1935), 29–58. For Saintyves' bibliography, see *Revue Anthropologique* 45 (1935), 356–363. For later attempts to find ritual elements in "Little Red Riding Hood," see Anselmo Calvetti, "Tracce di Riti di Iniziazione nelle Fiabe di Cappuccetto Rosso e delle Tre Ochine," *Lares* 46 (1980), 487–496; Yvonne Verdier, "Le Petit Chaperon Rouge dans la tradition orale," *Le debat* 3 (July–August, 1980), 31–61. For critiques of myth-ritual theory, see Joseph Fontenrose, *The Ritual Theory of Myth* (Berkeley and Los Angeles, 1966), and Robert A. Segal, "The Myth-Ritualist Theory of Religion," *Journal for the Scientific Study of Religion* 19 (1980), 173–185.

If we had no versions of "Little Red Riding Hood" other than Perrault's version,[1] we could consider this charming story a fable and suppose that it was invented in order to teach young girls that they should not talk to strangers. This approximates Perrault's own interpretation:

From this story one learns that children,
Especially young lasses,
Pretty, courteous and well-bred,
Do very wrong to listen to strangers,
And it is not an unheard thing
If the Wolf is thereby provided with his dinner.
I say Wolf, for all wolves
Are not of the same sort;
There is one kind with an amenable disposition
Neither noisy, nor hateful, nor angry,
But tame, obliging and gentle,
Following the young maids
In the streets, even into their homes.
Alas! who does not know that these gentle wolves
Are of all such creatures the most dangerous!

For Collin de Plancy, it is also nothing else but an allegory in which seducers are depicted as having the traits of wolves. To prove his point, he adds, "Many stories have the same moral without providing us with such a tragic outcome. In Finistère, the story of a pretty villager is told. She meets a young man at a place in the woods, listens to his sweet talk, and even lets him kiss her. But when she returns home, people screamed with fright when they saw her blackened and withered face: the lover to whom she had listened was a demon whose breath had ruined her face."

Such in interpretation neglects precisely the only complete and by far the most numerous versions in which Little Red Riding Hood escapes from the belly of the wolf while the latter, filled with stones, perishes.

The Red Hood

Each title of Perrault's tales seems to present one of the essential characteristics of the hero, as can be noted in "Cinderella" and "Sleeping Beauty." Therefore we can presume that the headdress [hood] of the little girl who brings a round flat cake and a pot of butter to her grandmother is not without significance. However, it is difficult to agree with Hyacinth Husson that this headdress represents the first glimmer of morning light, or, as suggested by André Lefèvre, the crimson of dawn.[2]

In times past, the hood was not only the padded headdress with a tail which was so widespread in the Middle Ages, but a coif or crown of flowers. In one story, a fairy-frog's power came from its small hood made of ever fresh and blooming bright red roses.[3] In the recent past, the May Queen wore for a crown a flowery hood made of white or red roses. The crown and the flowery hood have always been used in liturgical, magical, or religious ceremonies. Indeed, we cannot imagine Maïa, Chloris, or Flore, the ancient Queens of the May, without their flowery hoods. Could Little Red Riding Hood be such a liturgical personage?

A fifteenth-century chronicle tells us of men-of-arms wearing a May hat with their festival costume en route to Compiègne in order crown people with green boughs. We also know that in the past, in the month of May, young girls of Echenou (near the town of Saint-Jean-de-Losne, Côte d'or) had to bring a *headdress made of violets* to the prior of Saint Vivant en Amour.[4] The May hat, however, was usually reserved for the king or the queen of this spring month. In Hildesheim (Hanover), people go to the woods to meet the Count of May, who awaits them sitting in a cart lavishly decorated with greenery. The major and the town council offer the May crown to the Count, and May trees and flowers are placed on all the towers to celebrate the installation of the new ruler. In Denmark, the Count of May wears two crowns around his shoulders as he enters town. In the marketplace he is then surrounded by beautiful young girls and he chooses from among them a Countess or May Queen by placing on her head a crown of flowers.[5]

In *Guillaume de Dole*, a romance dating back to the very beginning of the thirteenth century, people not only search for the May tree in the woods, decorate walls, and cover the ground with greenery and flowers, but when the lovely Lienor comes forward, they cry out in one voice: "Here is May, Green May!" By this they mean the May Queen.[6]

In Provence, the tradition of the May Queen dates back to the beginning of time. Already in the writings of Nostradamus we find the following remark: "It is a very ancient custom to choose the most beautiful young girls of the neighborhood. They are gorgeously adorned with *crowns of flowers*, garlands, jewels, and silk costumes. They then are seated on high thrones like young goddesses placed in niches commonly called *Mayes*. Passers-by—at least honorable ones—are invited and obliged to contribute a few silver coins in exchange for a kiss."[7] In 1920, in the port of Toulon, I could still see ten or so young May Queens, every one of them veiled and their heads crowned with flowers. Balleydier tells us that on his way to Valence he met a young girl seated on a high throne decorated with garlands. She was crowned with white roses, carried a sceptre of flowers, and was surrounded by her friends who formed the court of this rural queen called *la belle de mai* (the May Beauty).[8] Today, near Grenoble, the May Queens are mostly children crowned with flowers. They sit under hawthorn greenery at a street corner or at the entrance of a village while one of their friends calls upon passers-by to witness her elaborate creation of the queen's costume.[9] In Lons-le-Saulnier and Château-Chalon (Jura), on the first day of May, young girls between the ages of twelve and fifteen choose the most beautiful girl they can find, dress her up in beautiful clothes, *crown her with flowers,* and carry her from door to door as they sing:

> Greet our bride,
> Here is the month, the pretty month of May
> Greet our bride,
> As a New Year's gift,
> Here is the month, the pretty month of May
> We present it to you.

In the Jura, the May Queen exercised her power for all thirty-one days of the month. She chose maids of honor who had to work for her and who diligently obeyed her every command.[10] The *Maïetta* gave each of them the name of a flower.

In many counties of England, in the month of May, people plant in the center of the village a yew-tree wreathed with roses near which the prettiest of the girls in the area stands *crowned with flowers* like the Mayes in Provence, while her friends dance and sing around her and throw her rose petals as if in homage to her beauty and to her supremacy.[11] In Dunkirk, the May rounds are called *Rozenhoed* or dances of the *hat of roses* because they are held beneath a crown and under garlands of flowers strung across the streets.[12]

From a hood of roses, especially one made of bright red ones, to a red hood involves only a slight shift. One can understand then how the folk mind which changed the Queen of Ash Wednesday into Cinderella could transform the May Queen, the queen of the bright red rose hood, into Little Red Riding Hood.

The choice of the color red instead of white has a magical explanation. On the Island of Lesbos, on the evening before May first, young girls go pick flowers in the countryside. Upon their return, they weave them into wreaths which they hang at night on windows and doors. They also crown themselves with these flowers. Red flowers are mixed with ears of corn or wheat, stinging nettle and garlic: garlic wards off the evil eye, the nettle stings the enemy attempting to enter one's home, the ear of corn or wheat attracts wealth, and the color red brings about gaiety.[13] In Bohemia and in the High Palatinate, it is said that red is frightening to witches and to beings which resemble them.[14]

Prohibitions and the Gifts of May

Having explained the tale's title, we must now seek to illuminate the actual text of the story. If one accepts the idea that the tale originated as nothing more than a commentary upon a ritual of May, how did it become attached to this folk liturgy?

Before her departure for her grandmother's house, Little Red Riding Hood's mother—at least in the German version—advises her to go gently on her way without straying to the right or to the left. Unfortunately, she arrives in the woods where she encounters the wolf who gives her bad advice.

"Little Red Riding Hood, see all those beautiful flowers; why don't you look around? Can't you hear how sweetly the birds are singing? (Yes, indeed, May is upon us!) You are walking straight ahead as if you were going to school whereas it is so much fun to play in the woods."

Little Red Riding Hood looked up and when she saw that everything was in bloom and that the rays of the sun were dancing here and there through the branches, she thought: If I were to bring grandmother a freshly cut bunch of flowers, she would be so happy. It is still early enough so that I will no doubt arrive on time.

She left the path to enter a thicket and started looking for flowers. Upon picking a first one, it appeared to her that further away a more beautiful one grew. She ran to it and in so doing plunged deeper into the woods. Meanwhile the wolf went straight to the grandmother's house.

The little girl had, alas, violated an interdiction. At that time of the year, boys, often in groups, used to invade the woods to pick the greenery and the branches with which they were obliged to decorate the houses of young girls. They also went to cut trees that they planted in the town square or in front of some local dignitary's home. Admittedly, these boys would very much have liked to lure girls into the woods, but this was taboo.[15]

During the first days of May, the woods are haunted by evil spirits and fearsome animals. It is at that time that goblins like to play unpleasant tricks on travelers, and especially on *traveling women*. Most important, though, is for people to avoid entering thickets so as not to disturb the amorous frolicking of men and women in the woods.[16] If we are to believe a Latin saying reported by Bede, there is no point in escaping the voraciousness of the wolf only to be exposed shortly thereafter to the sting of serpents.

Tertius in Maja lupus est,
et septimus anguis

We can trace these beliefs back to Nordic mythology. Bede's saying probably refers to Fenrir the wolf and Midgard the serpent, themselves the sons of sorcerers. Indeed, during the twelve nights following the Walpurgis (May 1st), sorcerers become more daring. These are the last days of their winter reign.

During part of the May celebrations, girls and boys were obliged to stay away from each other. During the Roman feast of *Maïa*, men and all that belonged to the male realm were strictly excluded from places where women celebrated this goddess. Men, for their part, honored *Faunus*. Interestingly enough, still today, little girls turn away little boys who try to take part in their games on the first of May, as the boys hope to participate in the distribution of candies at its close. In terse tones, girls declare that theirs is *not a game for men.*[17]

The child takes to her grandmother—at least in the French version of the tale—a pot of butter and a round flat cake (*galette*). One cannot help but think of butter and the May cake.[18] It was then customary to bake oatmeal cakes (*galettes d'avoine*), which were rolled along on Easter day just as one rolled eggs on that day.[19] Butter prepared on the first of May or during the month of May and mixed with salt and holy water was called May butter. In Savoy, it was offered to the pastor by the mothers of families.[20] In the Berry and Auvergne regions, it was said to possess all sorts of medicinal and invigorating powers as useful to humans as it was to cattle.[21] The gifts offered by the French Little Red Riding Hood then are essentially traditional in origin.[22] This is no less true for the German Little Red Riding Hood who brings her grandmother a piece of cake and a bottle of wine. Little known in France, *May wine* is still very widespread in Germany. This wine, called *maitranck*, is perfumed with woodruff. It is drunk during specially organized outings in the countryside and is prepared on the spot with white wine and bunches of fragrant flowers freshly picked in the woods.[23] In Moldavia, the May wine or May of love, well known under the name of *peline*, is perfumed with absinthe.[24] Here again the tale uses a May custom.

As Little Red Riding Hood carries May gifts through woods filled with flowers and bird songs, she may well represent, don't you think, some little flower queen; but the wolf, what do you make of the wolf?

The Wolf and Solar Theories

Must we agree with Hyacinthe Husson and André Lefèvre that the wolf is the symbol of a voracious sun which devours the dawn? Even if the wolf has had perhaps that allegorical significance in Vedic and Greco-Roman mythology, it does not necessarily follow that it must mean the same thing in our tale. Besides, our solar mythologists are not totally sure of their thesis. "Although we attribute a solar meaning to the wolf in the tale of Little Red Riding Hood," writes Hyacinthe Husson, "We must say, however, that there is a rather frequent contradiction in the history of myth interpretation which stems from different perspectives, according to which contradiction this animal is sometimes thought of as representing darkness or winter. Such is his character in many Teutonic legends, such is Fenris the wolf in the Edda."[25] André Lefèvre tells us, "A rather frequent contradiction in the genesis of myths, justified by the mores of this nocturnal animal, has sometimes likened the wolf to night-time terror and to Maha-Kali, who has a remarkable resemblance to the wolf with her large mouth and long teeth."[26]

Our scholars have dealt successfully with this common contradiction in the history of myth interpretation. Some would suggest that the contradiction has its origin in the inadequacy of their exegeses, which transform all heroes of traditional tales into dawn and make their pursuers into equal numbers of the personification of the sun or of the depths of night.

This criticism cannot be directed at Charles Ploix. According to him,

> Here we find once again the three ordinary characters of the drama: the wolf personifying the night; Little Red Riding Hood as the female representation of light; and the hunter, the man who carries the weapon, identical to the Hellenic hero who delivers the heroine from the mythical monster. As usual, the action takes place in the forest. The young girl, or light, is swallowed by the night. In the morning, the hero cuts open the darkness, causing the light to reappear. Let us recall the young girl's exclamation, "How dark it was inside," and also the term employed by the narrator (Grimm) who reports that upon coming out of the wolf's belly, Little Red Riding Hood is luminous.[27]

For Frédéric Dillaye, on the other hand, the wolf is nothing other than winter or the new year. "At that time of year, the rays of the day-star coming through the mist are tinged with that color tradition chose for the hood. The grandmother could either be the old year or the old dawn. But the autumn sun cannot reach the end of the year without being absorbed by winter. This explains the wolf's action."[28]

The representation of autumn (the waning of the year) or the autumnal sun by a child constitutes an unexpected, perhaps even disquieting symbolic association, but the connection between the wolf and winter seems to be the product of a more fortunate intuition. Let us note that in some variants, the wolf is replaced by a flesh-eating, diabolical ogre. This is the case at least in versions from the Tyrol and the Livournais.[29]

It is very likely that the tale of Little Red Riding Hood has its origins in the north. The German version is in fact much more complete than the French one.[30] In Scandinavia and in Germany, the wolf is essentially a ferocious animal, a personification of evil. This is true for Fenrir the wolf, brother of Hel, death or the infernal giantess, and also for Midgard the serpent, which resides in the deep ocean surrounding the earth, enfolding it completely. These three children of Loki and the witch Angerbode are themselves monstrous sorcerers.[31] European werewolves also bear witness to the affinity of wolves and sorcerers, and everyone knows that the leaders wolves follow at night are themselves strongly suspected of practicing sorcery.

There is no doubt that the wolf of this tale is related to Nordic mythology. Not only is the wolf which devours Little Red Riding Hood a mean, voracious being and a glutton, but how can we fail to recognize the resemblance of this tale to another Nordic fable which takes place precisely during the spring celebrations and which involves Loki, the malicious father of Fenrir, the bad wolf:

> Toser, the prince of the winter giants, has captured Thor's, or Donar's, hammer, the god of thunder, and has hidden it eight leagues beneath the ground. He will return it only if he is given Freya (or Frouwa), the Scandinavian Venus, for his wife. Thor dresses up as a bride, and Loki, the slyest of all the gods, himself dresses up as a servant girl, accompanies him as they set out for the giants' country. During the wedding feast, this strange fiancée eats unaided an entire ox, eight salmon, and all the delicacies intended for the women. She drinks more than three barrels of mead.
>
> "Never have I seen a fiancée eat and drink so much," says Toser.
>
> "It is because she has fasted for eight days, so great was her desire to see you," Loki answers.
>
> With these words, Toser lifts the veil of his betrothed, as he is eager to kiss her. But upon seeing her eyes, he jumps back to the opposite end of the hall and exclaims:
>
> "How terrible are Freya's eyes!"
>
> "It is because she has not slept for eight nights, so great was her desire to see you," Loki answers.
>
> Toser then sends for the hammer to place it on his fiancée's lap, as dictated by custom. Thor seizes it and slays the prince of the giants.[32]

If this is not the first seed of the dialogue between the wolf and Little Red Riding Hood, the analogy at least points to their shared place of origin.

The story of Thor's slaughter of Toser and his friends, the winter giants, refers to a spring celebration[33] and offers indisputable analogies to the activities of the wolf who eats in turn the old grandmother—the former May Queen—and her granddaughter, the last May Queen. In the German version, however, both escape from their temporary prison. But I am getting ahead of myself.

The Rescue of Little Red Riding Hood

It is perfectly clear that if Little Red Riding Hood represents the new year, she cannot remain in the belly of the wolf. It is evident that the versions which abandon her in this living casket are incomplete. Furthermore, a version from the Nivernais exhibits a revealing and significant deformation. Little Red Riding Hood is lying down next to the wolf, but as she realizes that it is not her grandmother, she asks to leave in order to relieve herself. The wolf ties a string to her foot, but the child ties it to a plum tree and runs away, thus deceiving the wolf. One could say that Little Red Riding Hood pulls herself out of the wolf's mouth.[34]

The gobbling up of May queens by the wolf must in fact correspond to a lost ritual which we can reconstruct. In times past, in Alsace, May day was the occasion for a performance of the fight between two characters representing winter and summer. Of course, winter succumbed and was subsequently buried.[35] In Sweden, especially in Gothland, and in Norway, the May game was more complicated.

> Two groups of young and strong men set off on their horses. One group represents winter. These men *wear fur-lined clothes*, hold the winter spear, and attack their adversaries by throwing snowballs and icicles at them. The other group, led by the Count of May, has no weapons; they *are decorated with flowers, leaves and green branches*. The summer and winter riders enter the town ceremonially. They will confront each other in a lively tournament. The winter men throw

ashes and sparks; the defenders of summer throw birch
branches and budding lime boughs. The people soon proclaim
these latter the winners.[36]

This ceremony probably varied from one village to the next
while keeping the same essential character. Now we can
speculate about our tale: A group of young girls, led by their
queen and crowned with flowers, together would visit the
oldest local May Queen in order to offer the butter and May
cakes—everyone knew their magical properties. But a giant
led by a lively troop (an ogre or a wolf they met in the woods)
would pursue them and would be able by force or by cunning
to seize the queen. The Count of May would then intervene
with his troop, overpower the voracious being, and pull from
its bowels the young May Queen, to the great delight of
Little Red Riding Hood and of Spring.

By the way, do you know the ending of the German tale?
Perrault's story is a drama which ends badly. In Germany,
after the dramatic consumption of grandmother and granddaughter, the story continues:

> After the wolf had satiated his voracious appetite, he went
> back to bed, fell asleep, and started snoring loudly. The hunter
> was walking by. He thought, "How loudly the old woman
> snores. Let us see if she needs anything."
>
> He entered the bedroom, and coming near the bed, he saw
> the wolf lying there. "Here you are, at last, old villain!" he
> said. "I have been looking for you for a long time."
>
> He was about to aim his rifle when he thought that the wolf
> might have eaten the grandmother and that perhaps there was
> still time to save her.
>
> Instead of shooting, he took a pair of scissors and started
> cutting open the belly of the sleeping wolf. After two cuts, he
> saw Little Red Riding Hood shining; after two more, the little
> girl cried as she jumped out:
>
> "Ah! What a fright I had! It is so dark inside the wolf!"
>
> Next came the old grandmother, still alive, but having diffi-
> culty breathing.
>
> Little Red Riding Hood hurriedly picked up stones and to-

gether they stuffed them into the wolf's belly. When our villain awoke, he tried getting up, but the stones were so heavy that he fell back; he was dead.

All three were very happy. The hunter left with the wolf skin; the grandmother ate the cake and drank the wine Little Red Riding Hood had brought her and as a result regained her strength, but Little Red Riding Hood told herself: "Never again will you wander away from your path to run into the woods when your mother forbids it."[37]

You may ask, what corresponds to this death of Little Red Riding Hood or the queen of the May? One can assume that the beginning of the Scandinavian or Germanic year was characterized by a period of struggle, trouble, and even eclipse.

Dr. Coremans reminds us that some almost forgotten superstitious ideas were formerly attached to the first twelve nights of May. These superstitions were similar to those that still persist today in connection with the twelve nights of the winter solstice. It is then that the dreadful rear guard of the evil winter spirits often delight in causing as much harm as possible. The tradition of the *damned bird-catcher* is associated with these fearsome nights. This coarse-looking bird-catcher appeared in the most varied aspects, yet his occupation was always the same: he thought only of catching young girls to make them his slaves, and he forced them to spin for him. Many a time in the first nights of May, these unfortunate girls were seen spinning in the cavern where he had locked them up. Fortunately, a hunter killed the bird-catcher with his *crapaudine* (a stone that was thought to come from the head of a toad) and ended these poor girls' captivity.[38]

It is very clear that this damned bird-catcher—whose home is reported in twenty different locations and whose appearance was just as varied, even taking that of the wolf— is another personification of the winter spirit. Called the devil's hole by the people of Thuringer, his cavern recalls the wolf's belly.

The time spent in the belly of the wolf and the work carried out in the dark cavern are symbolic of the preparatory days during which the queen or the new year's queens had to undergo a sort of imprisonment. During that time, they awaited the outcome of the battle fought between the spring knights or the green hunter, and the fearsome winter appearing as the wolf, the ogre, or the damned bird-catcher.

The shortening of our French version can be explained by the transformation of the May ritual under our milder climate and among friendlier people. The wolf was replaced by some daring suitor just as ready to devour girls, but in a different way. We all know the song entitled *Celle qui fait la morte pour son honneur garder* (The girl who plays dead in order to save her virtue).[39] Don't you think it could very well be the last echo of a ritual sleep during which the poor queen, too closely pursued by ardent captains, was buried under a heap of greenery? The following folksong variant sung in the Maine district would allow us to think so:

> In the middle of the meal
> The beautiful one falls dead.
> Where shall we bury her?
> In her father's garden
> *Where there are three May flowers.*[40]

All other versions speak of lilies, but are these not also May flowers? Boisjoli says of the lily: It is the king of flowers and its queen is the rose.

If this were true, we would better understand the unexpected morality in verse which ends Perrault's version a bit preciously.

And what do you say about all this? So many "ifs" and "buts" to tell us that Little Red Riding Hood is a kind of personification of the month of flowers and not of dawn; that the wolf which devours her is a symbol of winter rather than of the sun. But don't you feel that we can deepen our understanding of these charming tales by reconsidering the connections they have to seasons? Don't you agree that by exploring this ritual hypothesis we can truly go back to these tales' magical origins—to a time when the year was divided into two seasons, summer and winter? Don't you think that the long-ago times when these graceful myths spoke of immensely popular scenarios were not so uncivilized as some would like us to believe? People lived the poetry of seasons through wonderfully expressive ceremonies; they celebrated mysteries through delightfully childish stories. All took part in this magic jubilation which came down from the sky to earth with the rays of the new sun and returned from the earth to the stars, chaining them to a chariot through their songs, their rounds, and their cries of joy.[41]

Notes

1. We have not found many variants. Apart from Perrault's story, we can cite: *Rothkappchen* (Little Red Cap) in the Grimms' *Kinder- und Hausmärchen*, no. 26; *Rothkappchen* in L. Bechstein's *Deutsches Märchenbuch* (Leipzig, 1868), 51; *El Cappelin Rosso*, no. 6 in Ch. Schneller's *Marchen und Sagen aus Walchtirol* (Innsbruck, 1867), 9–10; *Le rat et la ratine* in P. Sébillot's *Littérature orale de la Haute-Bretagne* (Paris, 1881), 232–235; *Le Petit Chaperon Rouge*, published in Provençal by G. de M. in *Armena Prouvençau* for the year 1883 and translated into French by E. Rolland in *Mélusine* 3 (1886–1887), 362–364 and 428–429; a portion of a Forezian version given by J. J. des Martels in *Mélusine* 3 (1886–1887), 354; a second Breton version given by P. Sébillot in *Mélusine* 3(1886–1887), 397–398; Stanislas Prato's *La Frittana* (the little omelette), a tale from the Livournais in *La Tradition* 7 (1893), 134–135; and Th. Pirez's *A Serêna d'Almàres* in *Tradiçoes populares alemtejanas*, vol. 2, 61–62. See also other versions in J. Bolte and G. Polivka's *Anmerkungen zu den Kinder- und Hausmaerchen der Brüder Grimm* (1913), no. 26.
2. Hyacinthe Husson, *La Chaîne traditionnelle* (Paris, A. Franck, 1874), 7, and André Lefèvre, *Les contes de Charles Perrault* (Paris, Marpon et E. Flammarion, s.d.), lxv.
3. *La Grenouille bienfaisante* (Troyes, Garnier, s.d. [eighteenth century]), pp. 13, 22.
4. Eugène Cortet, *Essai sur les fêtes religieuses* (Paris, 1867), 161.
5. Dr. Victor Coremans, *La Belgique et la Bohême*, vol. 1 (Bruxelles, 1862), 64.

6. E. Faral, *Le Moyen Age*, eds. Joseph Bédier and Paul Hazard, *Histoire de la littérature française illustrée*, vol. 1 (Paris, 1923), 43.

7. L. -J.-B. Bérenger-Féraud, *Réminiscences populaires de la Provence* (Paris, 1885), 17. See Alfred de Nore, *Coutumes, mythes et traditions des Provinces de France* (Paris, 1846), 17, and Frédéric Mistral, *Lou Tresor dou Félibrige, ou Dictionnaire Provençalfrançias* (Aix, s.d. [1886]) on the term *Bello de Mai*.

8. Cortet, *Essai*, 161.

9. J.-J.-A. Pilot de Thorey, *Usages, fêtes, et coutumes existant ou ayant existé en Dauphiné*, vol. 1 (Grenoble, s.d. [circa 1880]), 40–41.

10. Charles Beauquier, *Traditions populaires. Les mois en Franche-Comté* (Paris, 1900), 66–67.

11. Bérenger-Féraud, *Réminiscences populaires de la Provence*, 18–19. Cf. W. S. Lach-Szyrma, "Le mois de mai en Angleterre," *Revue des Traditions Populaires II* (1887), 264, and John Brand, *Observations on Popular Antiquities*, ed. Henry Ellis (London, 1900), 128–129.

12. Alexandre J. Desrousseaux, *Moeurs populaires de la Flandre française*, vol. 2 (Lille, 1889), 46.

13. G. Georgeakis and Léon Pineau, *Le Folk-Lore de Lesbos* (Paris, 1894), 301–302.

14. Coremans, *La Belgique et la Bohême*, vol. 1, 65.

15. This practice is customary in Swabia, however. Jacob Grimm, *Teutonic Mythology*, trans. James S. Stallybras, vol. 2 (London, 1900), 777.

16. Dr. Victor Coremans, *L'année de l'ancienne Belgique* (Bruxelles, 1844), 22.

17. Bérenger-Féraud, *Réminiscences populaires de la Provence*, 9.

18. A Breton version mentions a *tourterin-tourterette*, obviously a holiday cake; P. Sébillot, *Le Rat et la Ratine*, in *Littérature orale de la Haute-Bretagne*, 233–234. In the Nièvre, it is called *époigne* (*Mélusine* 3 [1886–1887], 352), that is, a small bread in which *beurecaudes* are inserted. This is only done for some celebrations.

19. Coremans, *La Belgique et la Bohême*, vol. 1, 60.

20. Maurice-Marie Dantand, *Gardo soit Recueil d'histoires et légendes du pays de Thonon* (Thon-les-Bains, 1891), 98–100 n.

21. C. Laisnel de la Salle, *Croyances et légendes du centre de la France*, vol. 2 (Paris, 1875), 223.

22. Many different French versions are found in *Mélusine* 3 (1886–1887), 271–272; 352–354; 397–398; 428–429. The *galette* and the pot of butter are found in Provence and in Forez. In the Nièvre, it is

replaced by a bread roll or a cake, and the pot of butter becomes a bottle of milk.

23. Hedwige Heinecke, "Le vin de mai," *Revue des Traditions Populaires* 9 (1894), 245.

24. Princesse Bibesco, *Isvor, le pays des Saules*, vol. 1 (Paris, 1923), 254.

25. H. Husson, *La Chaîne traditionnelle*, 9.

26. A. Lefèvre, *Les contes de Perrault*, lxv.

27. Charles Ploix, *Le surnaturel dans les contes populaires* (Paris, 1891), 203.

28. Frédéric Dillaye, *Contes de Ch. Perrault avec notice, notes, etc.* (Paris, 1885), 217.

29. Stanislas Prato, in *La Tradition*, vol. 7 (1893), 134, 275.

30. The version from Agen, *Le loup et l' enfant*, collected by J. F. Bladé, *Contes populaires de Gascogne*, vol. 3, 189–191, is itself as incomplete as Perrault's version. It even appears to be a distortion of the latter.

31. R. B. Anderson, *Mythologie scandinave* (Paris, 1886), 236–237.

32. Colshorn, *Deutsche mythologie*, 130 ff. In Scandinavian mythology, Toser is called Thrym, but the fable is the same. R. B. Anderson, *Mythologie scandinave*, 178–185.

33. Prato, in *La Tradition*, vol. 7, 136.

34. Achille Millien, in *Mélusine* 3 (1886–1887), 428, 429.

35. Abbé Charles Braun, *Légendes du Florival* (Guebwiller, 1866), 80.

36. Coremans, *La Belgique et la Bohême*, vol. 1, 63, 64, and Grimm, *Teutonic Mythology*, trans. Stallybrass, vol. 2, 779.

37. Grimm, *Kinder und Hausmaerchen*, no. 26.

38. Coremans, *La Belgique et la Bohême*, vol. 1, 71.

39. George Doncieux, *Le Romancéro populaire de la France* (Paris, 1904), 269–279.

40. Mrs. Destriché, in *Revue des Traditions Populaires* 27 (1912), 236.

41. We have purposely neglected an episode found in various French versions. The wolf feeds the remains of the grandmother to Little Red Riding Hood and gives her to drink what is left of the old woman's blood. E. Rolland, in *Mélusine* 3 (1886–1887), 272; P. Sébillot, in *Mélusine* 3 (1886–1887), 398, and A. Millien, in *Mélusine* 3 (1886–1887), 428. Must not we see in this the symbol of the young year feeding itself on the substance of the dead year? Must not we see in it the time or the memory of a sort of ritual meal, reminding us of cannibalism and of the revival of human sacrifices?

Is Little Red Riding Hood Wearing a Liberty Cap? On Presumable Connotations in Tieck and in Grimm

In sharp contrast to a myth-ritual approach to folk narrative is the historical approach. According to the latter view of folktales, valuable historical data is contained in such narratives. In addition, this view argues that the historical time-frame in which a given folktale is created or transmitted must be taken into account in analyzing the content of that tale.

One serious difficulty in applying a historical perspective to fairy tales in particular (as a subset of the larger category of folktale) is that the fairy tale genre appears to be based more on fantasy than fact. (Legends are generally conceded to contain more historical reference than fairy tales, which are typically set in no one place or time.) Another obstacle to extrapolating history from fairy tales is that it is often impossible to ascertain with any degree of accuracy precisely when a specific tale first came into existence.

These problems in historical interpretation are somewhat obviated in the following ingenious analysis of two German versions of "Little Red Riding Hood." One version is the adaptation of Perrault's tale into a fairy tale drama by Ludwig Tieck (1773–1853). For a convenient text of "The Life and

Reprinted from *Literatursociologie*, vol. 2, Joachim Bark, ed. (Stuttgart: Verlag W. Kohlhammer, 1974), 159–180 with the permission of Verlag W. Kohlhammer. I am indebted to Patricia Sieber for translating this essay from German into English.

Death of Little Red Riding Hood: A Tragedy," which first appeared in 1800, see Jack Zipes, *The Trials and Tribulations of Little Red Riding Hood* (South Hadley: Bergin & Garvey, 1983), 81–115. The other version is that of the Grimms in 1812. By drawing upon literary and conventional political associations of red caps and wolves, Professor Jäger of the University of Bremen builds a persuasive case for his hypothesis that the versions of Tieck and the Brothers Grimm reflect some of the sociopolitical anxieties of the time period in which they were written. Specifically, according to Jäger, the versions reveal some of the anti-French sentiment caused by the French occupation of German territory during the first decade of the nineteenth century, the very time the Grimms were engaged in collecting folktales.

In the letter granting permission to reprint his essay, Jäger reminded the editor that the paper was an effort of his youth and that it was written partly under the influence of the radical student movement in Germany and elsewhere in Europe which occurred in the late 1960s. One of the student demands at that time was that scholars pay greater attention to the political significance of historical and literary texts, past and present. He very much hoped that his essay would be understood in that context.

Like the interpretation of Saintyves, Jäger's reading of the tale depends greatly upon such details as the red cap worn by the tale's protagonist. But whereas Saintyves was interested in analyzing the tale in general, Jäger is concerned only with the versions of Tieck and the Grimms. His is a political, not a psychological, understanding of the tale. From a psychological perspective, one cannot help but notice that the name of the author contains two important characters in the tale itself: Wolf and Jäger, which means hunter.

At first glance, our title question [Trägt Rotkäppchen eine Jakobiner-Mütze?] seems absurd since it is known not only that "Little Red Riding Hood" appears in folk traditions dating back before 1789, but that already in 1697 Charles Perrault in his *Contes de ma Mère l'Oye* had fashioned the story into its exemplary literary form.

Various interpretations of the Little Red Riding Hood story have been attempted. According to Husson and Lang, the main figure of the fairy tale symbolized the recurring spring or the awakening dawn.[1] F. Linnig held further that this highly stylized tale verged on myth by explaining,

> Little Red Riding Hood is the dawn, bringing man the message that day returns. Little Red Riding Hood's path as a messenger leads where her predecessor had gone before. The tale tells how she catches up with her ancestor, her grandmother. The wolf is not only a symbol of the sun-being, but also that of darkness. Thus the idea of dawn as a light-being is fused with the second idea of the wolf as a symbol of darkness. The first is devoured by the second, but being a daughter of heaven, she cannot die in the body of the wolf. As a hunter armed with bow and arrow, the sun god comes and liberates her, bagging the devourer and cutting his belly open with his hunting knife, releasing the sun beams.[2]

Equally fanciful are the interpretations of Ernst Siecke, who construed the devouring of Little Red Riding Hood by the wolf as a change from "full moon" to "new moon," whereas Saintyves considered Little Red Riding Hood a "liturgical persona," namely the "Queen of the May" who, adorned with a white and red rose-wreath, appeared at Old French, German, and Scandinavian May festivals.[3]

Classifying "Little Red Riding Hood" as a cautionary tale, the Swedish folklorist von Sydow pointed out older stories and popular educational practices that evoked the wolf to discipline children.[4] Even as early as Boner's late-medieval collection of fables, the mother threatens her screaming child: "The wolf is going to get you."[5]

Marianne Rumpf, the author of a comprehensive folkloristic dissertation on "Little Red Riding Hood," sides with the cautionary interpretation of the tale on the basis of its function: "Questioning the function of the fairy tale resulted in one's having to regard the fairy tale of 'Little Red

Riding Hood' as a cautionary tale, a story which is told to children to warn them of the dangers in the forest. The tale talks about wild beasts and uncanny people dwelling there and waylaying children whom they want to seduce and devour."[6]

Explicit psychoanalytic interpretations are not available. In the context of his theory of neurosis, C. G. Jung subordinates the Little Red Riding Hood story to the "Jonas motif," taking the devouring and wounding wolf as the father. In the constellation of images, Jung sees "problems of procreation and birth" as treated by the unconscious.[7]

In 1973 in his amusing "Märchen-Verwirrbuch," Iring Fetscher wittily twisted the story and, playing the part of a psychoanalytically versed socioeconomist, he exposed its "core": the "hidden dream narrative of the authoritarian and neurotic father of Little Red Riding Hood and [her brother] Little Redhead," and human aggression in the "competitive capitalist age" condensed in and justified by the image of the wolf. But this is a jest without analytic pretensions.[8]

Almost all serious interpretations share the reliance upon that which is universally human, whether in terms of content or form. Either they construe the fairy tale as an expression of constant psychic potentials or problems, or as a pictorial reflex of a timeless perception of nature, or else they describe it typologically in accordance with existential categories: warning, promising, frightening, imploring.

In contrast to this, I will make a few remarks about the version of "Little Red Riding Hood" by Ludwig Tieck (1800) and the version by the Grimm brothers (1812). I will give some indication of the contemporary historical background and of the usage of language and imagery between 1790 and 1810. Perhaps this will highlight the tendency inherent in the Grimms' and in Tieck's fairy tales and their probable reception at the time of their redaction. I will point out historical aspects which, according to my hypothesis, enter into the aforementioned versions.[9]

With the Grimms, whom I wish to discuss first, we are

faced with a consciously editing and arranging team.[10] Their *Kinder- und Hausmärchen* appeared in 1812 (first volume), the Grimms having collected and worked on the edition since 1806–1807. Politically, this period is delimited by the dissolution of the German Empire and Napoleon's defeat outside Moscow. In Germany this period leads to the establishment of new kingdoms and, in many parts, of the imposition of French foreign rule. Since 1805, the brothers have been living in Hesse. Since 1808, Jacob has held the post of librarian in Kassel. Hesse is particularly affected by the expansionist drive of the French high-ranking bourgeoisie. The Grand Duchy is dissolved and annexed by the newly formed kingdom of Westphalia under Napoleon's brother Jérôme, Kassel being its capital. "With the most bitter pain I saw Germany fettered, cast into irons, my native country dissolved, even its name deleted," Jacob Grimm writes about that period.[11] The brothers take an interest in the political events. The "Reestablishment of Hesse" and "at long last the unexpected return of the old Elector towards the end of the year 1813"—after Napoleon's retreat from Germany— imbue them with "indescribable jubilation" and "purest joy."[12] Thus their political partisanship against French rule is evident. However, they do not remain passive, but want to become active in the collection and dissemination of German folk and literary traditions. The zeal with which they conducted their Old German studies should help "to overcome the oppression of those times," Wilhelm writes in his memoirs, and he becomes even more explicit in his explanation that contemporary events drove them towards that "long forgotten literature" which they hoped "could contribute something to the return of another age."[13] To the Grimms, the German language, literature, and folk tradition guarantee the unity and thereby a unified and free future for a Germany reaching beyond the borders of absolutist territories. For the time being, this future has to be asserted against Napoleonic rule.

For instance, since Hartmann von Aue's "Armer Heinrich"

focused on the dedication to one's traditional master, the Grimms put their edition of his work in the service of the struggle for liberation from French foreign rule, striving to serve this patriotic aim in an explicitly financial fashion. "In the fortunate age," the brothers write, "when everybody makes sacrifices for the sake of the fatherland, we want to reissue the simple, profound and heartfelt Old German book of "Armer Heinrich" in which it is shown how people with childlike faith and love devote both blood and life to their masters and are thereby magnificently rewarded by God. Their Royal Excellencies, the Elector and the Electress, have permitted the book to be dedicated to them and the proceeds are destined for equipping the volunteers. A copy costs one *rheintaler* and a copy on vellum paper costs two. . . ." It is expected that "all clergymen of the country" will see to the publicity for such a noble cause and that they will contribute to "the brave Hessians and all Germans willingly accepting our intention and supporting it."[14]

The "Hartmann" edition was envisioned at about the same time as the *Kinder- und Hausmärchen,* so that the latter work may not be untouched by similar political motives. On the occasion of his edition of Grimm, folktale editor Friedrich Panzer speaks positively of "the 1000-year-old possession of the nation" and of "the heritage from time immemorial," assigning the folktale collection to an irrational, collectivistic, and ahistorical dimension. "Thus a work grew in which the early dawn of our beginnings seems permeated with the development of our midday heights—a work, emerging from a spirit of wholeness, as if the genius of the people itself had written it."[15]

However, a few facts and comments speak against such a mythologizing. "You happily collected and sometimes you quite happily helped it along which you naturally do not tell Jacob"—a letter of Arnim to Wilhelm Grimm informs us, thereby qualifying the notion of "the genius of the people itself."[16] The preface of 1812 promises a translation of the *Pentamerone* of the Neapolitan Basile for the second volume, but besides that "also everything else foreign sources offer." The Grimms are also conscious of the fact that their source for "Bluebeard," "Puss in Boots," and "Little Red Riding Hood" is Charles Perrault, "the Frenchman."

In the introduction in which they present their fairy tales to the public, the brothers are not as politically explicit as in their announcement of the "Armer Heinrich" edition. Perhaps this is because Napoleon's Russian campaign having not yet failed at the time of the writing of the introduction, a German popular uprising in the face of Napoleon's weakening could not be expected.[17] So by asserting that the fairy tales, like "all genuine poetry . . . can never exist without reference to life," the preface remains unspecific, perhaps due to caution. At least the preface does mention that "a good lesson, an application to the present results from them."[18] Dated slightly later, Jacob Grimm's letter to Wigand also emphasizes the didactic aspect of the work from which one should "learn" and "which should be considered an educational book."[19] The latter seems to point more towards the book's functioning as promoting the family's bringing up of children. However, the principles for private education reflect public experiences and norms, a statement that can be all the more legitimately applied to the Grimms' oeuvre since the Grimms themselves later on reveal that their stories have a part in the "epic element which developed with the history of the people." Consequently, they reflect political and social experiences.[20]

In the "Tale of the Clever Peasant Girl" one can detect praise of the lower strata of the population, who defend themselves against absolutist and arbitrary judgments with the dogged application of wit and logic. It is the early capitalist experience of the difference between exchange and utility value which shapes "Lucky Hans." So in "Little Red Riding Hood" anti-French and anti-Enlightenment trends come together in a remarkable combination in the redaction of the tale.

In the fairy tale, the sharp contrast between *forest* and *way*, between *nature* and *school* stands out. The wolf takes advantage of the child's innocence ("Little Red Riding Hood did not know what a wicked sort of animal he was and was not afraid of him"). The wolf appeals to a latent aversion to ordered and regulated normalcy ("You march along as if you were going straight to school in the village"). He seductively points out the colorful and sound-filled wilderness ("Just look at the beautiful flowers that are growing all around you! Why don't you look around? I believe you haven't even noticed how lovely the birds are singing").[21]

The dichotomy of freedom/wilderness/nature on the one hand versus school/straight path/order on the other hand occurs on other occasions in German literature. One recalls Hölderlin's poem "Die Eichbäume" (1798) which compares oaks with Titans and contrasts trees growing "happily and freely" and striving towards the sky (towards the clouds / is oriented your sunny top, serene and grand") with the "tamer world," which opposes the free existence of the trees. The poem declares, "None of you has yet gone to the school of men."[22] Goethe's ballad "Die wandelnde Glocke" (1813) talks about a child who does not want to obey regulated and religiously sanctioned convention ("there was a child who never wanted / to get itself to church"):

> It has already directed its way into the field
> As if it ran out of school.

Here we also find the contrast between open nature and the institution of school, which represents traditional order. The repressive bourgeois educational book *Struwwelpeter* of 1847 gives an account of "Hans-Guck-in-die-Luft," who falls into an alien and hostile element, water.[23] The narrative relies on the contrast between the colorful expanse ("clouds, swallows") and the bourgeois institution perpetuating traditions to explain the cause of this fall:

> When Hans went to school,
> He always gazed at the sky.

The antithesis "Nature and School"[24] was already a major anthropological and historico-philosophical problem in the eighteenth century. One may compare Schiller's poem of the same title of 1795, giving a historico-dialectical explanation. This opposition between Nature and School is like the more widely spread antithetical images of forest and formal garden. In this opposition, the Sturm und Drang, the Göttinger Hain and the liberal literati, until the Vormärz [the historical period in German history between 1815 and March 1848, the month the German revolution started], depict the difference between constitutional or republican forms of government on the one hand, and absolutist regimes on the other. One should not consider "Little Red Riding Hood" exclusively in terms of this narrow set of political images. Since the national idea emerged in reaction to foreign rule, one could contrast loyalty toward the native country with its authoritarian rule to foreign rule, which is attractive and seductive on account of its veneer of liberalism.

Written after the winter of 1805–1806, Ernst Moritz Arndt's "Geist der Zeit" frequently talks about the enemies of the French being "indifferent and feeble," "blind," "bewitched," "weak and indecisive." The French for their part "deceive" the nations to be conquered and those already conquered. With "cunning," the French capitalize on the "folly and lethal sleep of the nations."[25] Recommending against fighting the French army with traditional military strategy but advocating a new guerrilla tactic, Arndt clarifies his suggestion in a parable: "Should the ox fight against the wolf with his mouth because the latter has sharp teeth?"[26] This image of the wolf applied to foreign rule as represented by Napoleon is not an isolated instance in his time. In depicting the prospect of a German fight against Napoleon as the battle of the German Cheruscan prince against Varus, and in Rom's expulsion from German soil, Kleist's "Hermannsschlacht" of 1808 calls the invader the "wolf from the banks of the Tiber" (v. 2483) and compares him to the "wolf of the desert" (v. 202). It admonishes:

> The wolf, O Germany, breaks
> Into your fold. . . . (v. 72–73)

Issuing a vehement exhortation to "take revenge" in his 1809 "Germania an ihre Kinder," Kleist instigates a fight against the French, using the image of the wolf hunt:

> A lustful hunt, as if hunters
> Sat on the spoor of the wolf!
> Beat him dead! The world court
> does not ask you for your reasons.

The bloodthirsty "Kriegslied der Deutschen" in the same year also has recourse to the comparison with the wolf.

> The shaggy bear and the panther beast,
> The arrow has vanquished them;
> Only for money in the wired cage
> The kittens are still shown.
>
> On the wolf's head, as far as I know,
> Is set a price,
> Wherever he ravenously appears
> He is hounded.

I skip a few stanzas to show the parallelism more clearly in the wording of the last stanza:

> Only the Frenchman still shows himself
> In the German Empire;
> Brothers, take the cudgel
> So that he also retreats.[27]

This is aimed—according to Arndt—at the French in their worst personification, Napoleon. The Germans succumb to his seduction; in turn, they are devoured by his "tiger-like cruelty and wolf-like voracity" (Arndt), as was Little Red Riding Hood by the wolf. Other epithets for the French conquerors include "brute," "strangler soul," "great corrupter," "monster" which "plays his tiger-cat game with the world." "I used to command human beings, now I command tigers," Arndt has Bernadotte say to describe the cruelty of the French whose revolution has in the meantime turned "into a gluttonous monster."[28]

The description of the French intruders as *wolves* is based upon earlier linguistic usage. After the outbreak of the French revolution and even more so after the Parisian taking of power of the Montagne, the conservative German press identified not only the French revolutionaries but also their emissaries and the local supporters of the Jacobins with the image of the wolf. I am going to elaborate on this below. This image was applied to the determined democrats of the early revolutionary years who originally came peacefully to enlighten and proselytize, but who were then dehumanized by slavish authoritarian propaganda and who consequently took over the attributes of the military and imperialistic agents of the French financial bourgeoisie. And this characterization is not used exclusively by the conservative side, but also by those who—like the Grimms and Arndt—believe in the promises of the German princes, that after the common struggle against the conqueror, bondage and petty, small-state patriotism will be abolished in Germany.

The hunter who "had been looking for the wolf for a long time" liberated Little Red Riding Hood and took the wolf's hide, reminding us of Kleist's songs calling for the hunting of the French. The hunter also evokes other bards of the liberation wars who launched, so to speak, the guerrilla fight against foreign rule with the hunting horn. I quote here Friederich Förster's "Schlachtlied":

> Let us away to the merry hunt
> Be up and about and awake,
> The horns entice and call
> Us today to the first battle . . .
> Scatter powder onto the pan
> You hunters, cock the trigger!
> And now in the name of God
> We are the first upfront;

and Theodor Körner's famous "Lutzows wilde Jagd":

The hurrahs cheer and the rifles crack
The French henchman fall.
And when you ask the black hunters:
This is Lützow's wild and daring hunt.[29]

One could also adduce Körner's "Jägerlied"—"Let us away, you hunters, free and quick"—which conjures up "the wild hunt and the German hunt / for the hangmen's blood and the tyrants."[30]

Would it be wrong to assume that the politically aware and observant Grimms took into consideration the contemporary images of contemporary political events in their adaptation of a traditional story and further that the innocence of the seduced and devoured Little Red Riding Hood and the voracious and cunning manner of the monster reflect the political fate of the German states under foreign rule? I consider my conjectures regarding likely connotations in the Grimms' "Little Red Riding Hood" all the more justified because it occupies a privileged position among the *Kinder- und Hausmärchen*. The Grimm brothers refer expressly to Perrault and Tieck in addition to their oral source, Jeanette Hassenpflug. "Except for our oral version, we have, surprisingly, not found this fairy tale anywhere except in Perrault (Chaperon Rouge), the basis of Tieck's adaptation," they write in their notes to the text.[31] They are conscious of the fact that, being the daughter of an originally French and literary, educated family, the narrator Jeanette Hassenpflug (a friend of Wilhelm's later wife Dorothea Wild and of Lotte Grimm) was certainly familiar with Perrault's version of the fairy tale.[32] Perrault's story turns out badly; the girl is devoured. The *positive* ending of the story—rescue from the wolf's belly—presumably has a reasonable explanation unless it was a spontaneous invention on the part of the Grimms. Such a change could have been motivated as a means of political encouragement which might inspire hope for freedom in an age of bondage. Similarly, the scene where the innocent child is seduced by the comment about beautiful nature—absent in Perrault—could be appropriately understood in the political context of anti-Napoleonic propaganda.

Moreover, the *hunter* does not play a role in any of the well-known versions of the fairy tale, except for Tieck's. The hunter appears to be Tieck's addition to Perrault's version. Besides Little Red Riding Hood, Tieck used Perrault's Bluebeard and Puss-in-Boots as models for his fairy tale plays. The Grimms also included these two fairy tales in their collection. However, they were already deleted by the second edition.[33] And Tieck's fairy tale, like Perrault's, ends unhappily for the main protagonist: the hunter shoots too late. Consequently, in their version with the inclusion of Tieck's hunter figure and the successful and liberating wolf hunt, "Little Red Riding Hood" seems to the Grimms so important that despite its French origin and tradition, they retained this tale of seduction, rape, and final liberation so "intertwined with the history of the people."[34] However, to support this hypothesis, we have to answer the question as to how far Tieck, to whom the Grimms refer, made use of relevant political events in his rendition of the story.

Up until now little has been made of Tieck's "Little Red Riding Hood" play, and in the scholarship the work has practically not been treated at all. In retrospect, Tieck himself in 1828 calls the play a "poetic jest." He even denigrates the "trifle" and the "foolish fairy tale."[35] Twelve years after the initial publication of the small play, Tieck inserted it into the framework story of the "Phantasus." However, the conversations of the "Phantasus" shed little light on the understanding of the play. Tieck's friend Solger considers it "a very lovely small piece which has already delighted me very much." To be sure, he does not see "anything profound . . . in it."[36] The Berlin "Archiv der Zeit" of 1800 warns that "the play should not be taken too lightly. It has been invested with a serious and poetic sense which is not seen at first glance." Unfortunately, the article does not elaborate further.[37] Scarcely better information can be found in Tieck research. The work of Käthe Brodnitz, "Der junge Tieck und seine Märchenkomödien" (1912)[38] offers little more than a series of synopses. And Emilie Pfeiffer's investigation "Shakespeares und Tiecks Märchendramen" (1933)[39] excludes "Little Red Riding Hood" from her analysis without offering any justification for doing so. This silence may indicate an interpretative embarrassment as well as an undervaluing of the play. In my attempt to explain the development of the contemporary usage of images, I will again take up the ideas about "red," "red cap," "wolf," "dog," and "hunter" as they were frequently used in a recognizably metaphorical sense at the turn of the century.[40]

Journals sympathetic to the French revolution include in their titles the red of the Phrygian cap as a sign of this. Thus already in 1791 in Regensburg, J. M. Armbruster publishes "Das rote Blatt."[41] With more journalistic success but under the same name, Joseph Görres follows his example in Koblenz and edits the "Rothe Blatt" towards the end of the revolutionary decade, 1798. He later renames the journal "Rübezahl." Predominantly red cockades adorned the hats of the Republicans as the red cap graced the liberty tree. These symbols inspire horror and anger in the traditionally minded, the supporters of principality, and the absolutist mercenaries. Whenever they can risk it, they curse the Republicans and rage against them with fanatic hatred. When the French occupying forces plant "the loathsome liberty tree very close to [his] home," the Zweibrückenian court painter Johann Christian von Mannlich complains about the "hellish noise." As he continues, one senses plainly his disgust: "Crowned with the red cap of a galley slave, the symbol of their freedom [the liberty tree] was first carried through the city in a solemn ceremony." In the face of powerful bands of French soldiers, only verbal defense was possible, denunciation filled with criminal allusions. In the previous year following French examples beyond the border, the Palatine population expressed their revolutionary desires. They were still on their own and acting spontaneously. The conservative front could then react more openly: "They marched into Bergzabern; the populace was told off, the tree [liberty tree] was cut down and the red cap was kicked into the dust by our soldiers."[42] It is the year 1791.

The liberty cap was not only shown, worn, and planted on the liberty tree, it was also the subject of song. "Le Bonnet de la Liberté" was one of the most well-known revolutionary songs. Friedrich Lehne, a Mainz librarian and one of the most prolific Jacobin poets, translated it under the colorful title "The Journeys of the Red Cap." [43] He calls the red cap a "radiant sign of deliverance" which bestows "magical power" on this traveling freedom.

> From pole to pole its course leads,
> Everywhere it undoes the chains
> Of the common *sansculottes**

The song says and promises:

> The liberty cap will fly around the world
> In a swift journey.

In 1793 the counterrevolutionary weekly *Der Deutsche Menschenfreund* prints a miserable lampooning poem about the "Tree and the Red Cap" to ridicule the Clubbists and the Jacobins. [44] The *Almanac of the Revolution of 1793, Göttingen, by Johann Christian Dieterich*, a similarly counterrevolutionary organ, familiarizes the reader with "various products of the French revolution." Here the association between the liberty cap and defamatory notions such as "foolish," "stupid," and "ridiculous" is already established. Under the title "The Piquen and the Red Caps," the almanac notes:

> The red caps are not possessed of anything extraordinary besides the good fortune they enjoy among the Jacobin lot. Since the king had to endure being adorned with one of them on June 20th, they seem to have reached the pinnacle of their glory. They are made of wool and are entirely of the shape of ordinary caps. They are probably meant to be a symbol of the *bonnet de la liberté;* however, I believe that with regard both to heads they cover and to the ways they are used, one could compare them more appropriately with certain other caps

*[Republicans of the poorer classes in Paris. Ed.]

which indeed are not counted among the most honorable ornaments.[45]

The fashion of the red cap, of the Republican cockade, and of the liberty tree caught hold in Germany. In 1796, Goethe and Schiller dedicate an epigram to the theme which shows how virulent the sign of the "red cap" is in both propaganda and literary self-presentation. In order to censure what for them was absurdly wrong, although vivid and influential, the two wrote: "We will keep annoying you for a long time and will tell you: Red caps, only a little bell is still missing to round off your finery."[46] This is like a hint of an age when only the Mainz carnival reminds one of the Mainz Republic.

By the turn of the century, the sign has not been forgotten although the enthusiasm for freedom and for the French has considerably cooled. Because of the expansionist conquest policies of the bourgeois leaders and Bonaparte's imperial attitude, the German revolutionary democrats have become increasingly silent and resigned. In the spring of 1800 when Tieck wrote his "poetic jest," the events, endeavors, hopes—and also the fashion—of the previous decade are familiar and the cap fashion is absorbed into the play. In 1793, Tieck himself probably followed the French events with considerable sympathy. Inspired, he told his friend Wackenroder about the supporters of the revolution, "eager democrats" whose "enthusiasm" he came to know in Göttingen. He closely observed the developments of the counterrevolutionary invasion in France. "Now I am not happy if I cannot have a newspaper," and he went into rapture, "Oh, to be in France. It must be a grand feeling to fight under Dumouriez, to put the slaves to flight and to fall, too. What is life without freedom? Delighted I salute the genius of Greece which I see hovering over Gaul. France is my thought, day and night. If France is unhappy, then I despise the whole world and I despair of its strength. Then the dream is too beautiful for our century, then we are degenerate alien creatures and not a single drop of blood will tie us to those who fell at Thermopylae, then Europe is doomed to be a dungeon." The execution of Louis XVI transformed overnight many German friends of the revolution into renegades. Wackenroder, however, remarked very calmly, "The execution of the King of France has caused all of Berlin to shy away from the cause of the French, but definitely not me. I think about their cause as usual."[47] And Tieck did not contradict him either.

Tieck's political attitude around the turn of the century is, however, difficult to determine; almost no explicitly political statements can be found. The "Schildbürger" of 1796 remains noncommittal, even in such chapters as "The Revolution breaks out" (12), "A New Constitution Is Introduced" (13), or "The Burgers' Enthusiasm" (16), which do not betray an unequivocal partisanship for or against either monarchy or democracy/republic. This holds true also for the witty political allusions in Puss-in-Boots.

In a central scene in "Franz Sternbald's Journeys" (1798) a dispute flares up. It concerns the question of whether or not art is "useless playing about" and a "harmful pastime," "invented to weary and gradually mortify the better forces in man," or whether on the contrary, "divinity" is inherent in art, a "divinity" which warrants higher values such as "When in a state everything serves One Cause" and people fight "for the welfare of the citizens, for independence . . . for bourgeois freedom," for the "common good."[48] Even Tieck's environment cannot unequivocally grasp the purpose of the novel, which most of the time does not go beyond the antithesis. His acquaintances are not sure whether or not the sweeping raptures about art over political purpose are not to be taken ironically. Caroline Schlegel confesses that even "the second part . . . has not shed any light" as to "whether in Sternbald the love of art has not been intentionally portrayed as a wrong tendency, meant to go off badly"—thus she writes in her letter to Friedrich Schlegel in October, 1798.[49]

Friedrich Schlegel until 1797 was favorably disposed towards the revolution.[50] He sees "the revolutionary spirit at its most beautiful" at work "in physics and poetry."[51] However, in these years not only resignation or opportunism are

reasons for the detachment from the revolution and its consequences, but since the police authorities rigidly persecute
sympathizers, caution is vital. The fates of Geiger, Stäudlin,
or Hölderlin, the trials of high treason against the Jacobins
Riedel and Hebenstreit (and later against Sinclair) testify to
the official attitude towards the supporters of French ideas
and endeavors. This attitude is most succinctly expressed in
Fichte's letter to Reinhold on May 22, 1799. "To me it is
more certain than the most certain thing," Fichte writes,
"that if the French do not gain the most overwhelming pre-
dominance in Germany . . . in a few years no human being
in Germany who is known to have thought a free thought in
his life will find a resting-place anymore."[52] This political
situation fosters a double perspective of the Jacobin in the
eyes of the *detached* observer. One view shows him—in accordance with the Jacobin's self-image—as a noble-minded
person, dedicated to enlightenment, liberation, and political
progress. The other one pictures him—in accordance with
the view of the government in a larger sense—as a dangerous troublemaker and political dissident who has to be
hounded. According to our hypothesis, both views constitute Tieck's *wolf* image. It was already suggested that the
image of the wolf is multifariously used to describe the Jacobin, the patriot, the republican. Moreover, the notion that the
wolf image in the Napoleonic era connotes the Frenchman
derives from the linguistic and imagistic usage of the previous decade. Gleim and Bouterwek call the French revolutionaries "wolves."[53] Wekhrlin, at first a sympathizer, sees
in the rigorous rule of the Montagne "the mean tooth of
wolves" at work.[54] When the Emperor Leopold reestablishes
the Theresianum, which the enlightened Josef II had abolished, Denis thanks him:

> Youth roamed about, fenceless
> Exposed to the teeth of the malicious wolves[55]

Consequently, the influence of those who disseminate
French ideas and who, in Denis's view, seduce the innocent
youth is under control.

In Tieck's play, the *grandmother* first mentions the *wolf*, wishing that "They hunt him perhaps."[56] A *peasant* characterizes the wolf more precisely, accusing him of the same behavior that the conservative propaganda uses to defame the French revolutionary soldiers. He warns that the wolf will "massacre" Little Red Riding Hood. The *hunter*, the real enemy of the wolf, speaks even more clearly of "Monsieur Wolf" whom he wishes to "grab." Thereby the wolf is marked as a Frenchman or as a supporter of the French cause. In Germany until 1800 this means the revolutionary and republican cause. In his first appearance, the wolf reveals himself to be someone who is "outcast and ostracized" because "he cannot dissemble and flatter" and "does not want to debase himself to be a slave." In short, he is somebody who contravenes the dominant (courtly) order and fights against it. The ensuing dialogue with the *dog*, the central scene of the play, clarifies this self-presentation. Almost none of the numerous variants of the folktale contain the figure of the dog.[57] If Tieck arbitrarily introduces the dog as a new figure in addition to the hunter, this is crucially important for his statement. The dog serves as a foil to the wolf "in the service of" and as an accomplice of the hunter. In *courtly* French language he boasts of his "skills," that he is capable of catching "hares." He brags that he "can vex cats and fetch little sticks from the water."

As an "obedient servant" he expresses himself in pedantic style. The wolf alleges that he is in "alliance with our common tyrant"; he reproaches the dog that "he has no will of his own, that he is not free," and dismisses him with the contemptuous rationalization:

> These are the heads, so stupid and shallow
> Whom every fear and apprehension affects,
> Who know nothing about strength and independence . . .

The wolf, in missing an awareness of autarchy and autonomy in the dog, reveals himself to be one who "hoped for tolerance and was disappointed," who abandoned himself to "ideals" and who believed in progress in the "business of humanity":

In childhood, I thought tearfully of
The days of that innocent age,
How I harbored a fervent yearning,
How I nourished an illusion of work and benefit,
How I was ready for glorious deeds!
Nobody can have ideals
As high-flown
Can picture them as splendidly,
As I wanted to dedicate all talents and all powers
Solely to the business of humanity,
To the glorious progress of the century.

At the same time, he is an atheist, not believing in "immortality" and "punishment after this life" but considering "everything superstition" and he contends: "The joys that exist are certainly only grapes hanging too high for us."

This progressive jargon and particularly the term "business of humanity" clearly reveals the allegorical function of the wolf figure. He is enlightened, idealistic, progressive, and thus—this he also relates—he has fallen into traps and ambushes, has been thrashed, "outcast and ostracized." Because of all this he has become a misanthrope. As a result of bad experiences, the disillusioned philanthrope is driven

To hate men whom I loved like brothers,
Whom I called my friends.

Let us again examine the figure of the *dog*. Approving of the status quo, he is the typical pragmatic politician when he pontificates—and such phrases sound current and familiar:

I also know that speculation,
Even the best, and all theory
Must never be mixed into practical life.

Ever since the Sturm and Drang (as Schubart's fable "Der Wolf und der Hund" of 1774 proves) up to the Vormärz, the contrast between wolf and dog serves as an expression of the antithesis between wildness/freedom and bondage/servility.

Bürger notes that performing military service for a prince betrays "the courage of a dog."[58] In the "Eipeldauerlied" of the Viennese Jacobin Hebenstreit, he refers to princely scribes and court councillors when he demands that "all the dogmen be beaten to death!" A later song about the revolutionary Hecker derides the "dogs of the reaction." These are just a few examples.

The hunter is the servant of the prince par excellence, the henchman of absolutist politics. This meaning already originated in Bürger's and Claudius' time: the peasant field has to be accessible at all times to the ravaging hunt of the prince for hares, deer, and wild boars. The peasant's every attempt at taking matters into his own hands is meticulously punished as "poaching." Therefore, the princely hunt symbolizes princely despotism and the aristocratic hunt-entertainment expands into the "image of administrative restrictions against every liberal endeavor of the subjects."[59] The hunter—as we have already mentioned—has for the first time been introduced as an important figure into the "Little Red Riding Hood" story by Tieck.[60]

Tieck's hunter shoots the wolf, but unlike the Grimms' version, this action does not lead to a happy ending. At first, the hunter complains about wolves: "They are impertinent lads who love to show up in all places." Warning Little Red Riding Hood of the wolf, he boasts to the child about his green jacket. This provokes Little Red Riding Hood to praise the color of her cap as being preferable to the green clover color. "The jacket would fit you even better/if it were beautifully red, like my cap." To the hunter's objection that "the whole world cannot be red like your cap," she replies that "no color surpasses red." Having at the beginning of the play told her grandmother that "but still no color surpasses red," Little Red Riding Hood again takes up this statement, which runs through the play like a leitmotif. Perrault and later on the Grimms casually explain the name of the fairy tale and of its main protagonist by saying that relatives presented the child with red headgear which fits her nicely. The red color was more or less accidental. In a majority of the folk traditions this explanation is entirely absent.[61] In Tieck, however, the child becomes obsessed with wearing her cap and she sticks obstinately to her declaration that its color is superb:

> How blissful is he who succeeds
> In seeing on his head
> A beautiful red cap, like mine.

Her entire surroundings present themselves in terms of the color of her cap:

> The whole forest beams with red blossoms.

The wearing of caps and the raptures about red are not well tolerated in Little Red Riding Hood's environment. "They all say it is necessary / that I put aside the little cap," she confesses to herself, only to continue defiantly, "but still no color surpasses red." The grandmother makes plain where the red cap does not fit in and in which realm it is offensive:

> The *Lord God* cannot stand it
> That one bounds to him as if on a dance floor
> Or sings his word *in church* wearing a red hat.[62]

However, the old woman, representing tradition, cannot justify her belief. When Little Red Riding Hood asks how "God could possibly find fault / with such a beautiful red cap," the grandmother acts in an authoritarian fashion: "Oh, shut up, you wicked child! For the time being / you have no understanding of these things." Reacting in an equally authoritarian way, the peasant rails against contemporary children who become "definitely too cheeky" and are not even afraid of the *wolf* any more.

The child's enthusiasm for red exactly parallels her carelessness vis-à-vis the wolf ("with your wolf, there is no trouble"). She protests against the admonitions and warnings about the beast (to the dog she says "You are not quite in your right mind"); she also insists upon wearing her red

cap, not accepting this as youthful folly: "I boldly believe /
I will always be audacious / reaching my adult years / I
will dress as I like / then I shall also wear a red cap!" Defiant
and innocent at the same time, she poses questions which
none of the representatives of the establishment—the grandmother, the hunter, the peasant—can or want to answer.
Therefore, they react imperiously. "She always shows her
precocity and is proud of her enlightenment."[63] Then the
wolf finally devours the "cheeky," pert, careless child. The
shot of the hunter is too late to save her.

Summarizing the features that Tieck adds to Perrault's
story and to the folk traditions possibly known to him:
the varying play with the red cap and the enthusiasm for
the color red, the know-it-all dallying with the danger of the
wolf, the attribution of political and historico-theoretical
concepts to the character of the wolf (revealed in the dialogue with the politically defined dog—another autono-
mous addition to the story), it is difficult to imagine that
Tieck did not want to articulate something of the political
experiences, insights, and tendencies which were current in
the environment of his day. However, the political message
of the play, and the play itself, are in many ways heavily
loaded with infantilisms, superstitious babble, and comic
scenes. In the final analysis, the function and characterization of the wolf as the hounded and the hounder are not un-
ambiguously described. The amalgamate of traditional fairy
tale contents, dramaturgical extravagances, and political allusions does not allow for a systematic allegorization. Similarly, one cannot detect Tieck's political attitude and judgment in this tragedy nor in most of Tieck's works of this
period. On the one hand, the warning adults come off badly
in the characterization; on the other hand, the know-it-all
cheeky child becomes the wolf's prey. On the one hand, the
servile dog receives his share of satire; on the other hand, in
spite of psychological and political explanations, the wolf remains a villain. Nevertheless, the interlarding of adapted
fairy tale elements with allusions to contemporary politics,
the correlation between the enthusiasm for red and for caps,

and the fate of being finally abducted by the wolf seem to reveal one of the major ideas of the tragedy. One could paraphrase it as follows: Whoever, in a fashionable manner and with youthful carelessness, abandons himself too much to ideas of upheaval will ultimately be seized in turn and destroyed by this very upheaval. Or if a person in a faddish way dallies with progress and revolution, albeit innocently, an event could occur which bitterly belies that person's gullibility and innocence. In Little Red Riding Hood's revolt against parents and authorities, the play takes up this message both as a family disciplinary problem and a general political issue. The message voices the consensus of the period, reminiscent of the saying that the revolution devours its own children. Tieck himself remains detached from the message of his play, without offering a point of view or any value judgment. One can reasonably assume that the Grimms, who specifically mention Tieck's fairy tale play in their annotations[64] to their own version, must have understood the allusions to "red cap" and "wolf" as referring to Jacobins, Frenchmen, and revolutionaries, and further that they were likely to have thought of the above-noted main idea in the context of the fairy tale. Their own cautionary tale does not suppress the associations; it warns of seduction and of youthful, innocent intercourse with the corrupter. The second, more purist edition of the fairy tales also retains the originally French "Little Red Riding Hood" and its associated features.

May we, to illustrate, adduce a modern example? In the last few years in the German Federal Republic, left-wing pupils and students had to put up with a saying which goes approximately as follows: "Today you are sporting Marx and Lenin badges but you would/will be wide-eyed if the Russians/Communists really came/come!"

Whoever considers this comparison of the past few years too involved with current affairs to elucidate the Grimms' and Tieck's statements may think of how the Springer's newspapers flogged the old connotations of the political realm and the fairy tale sphere to death. When at the end of the 1960s students demonstrated against U.S. imperialism and anti-working class emergency laws, the Springer press called them "wolves" and "wolves and radicalinskis."[65] Similarly, the *Frankfurter Allgemeine Zeitung* and the *Bayernkurier* caricatured left-wing parties, Marxism and the "socialization" as wolves.[66] In the spring of 1972 on the occasion of the Baden-Wurttembergian state parliament election, the CDU still used the old ideas, associations, and affecting overtones of Little Red Riding Hood to agitate against the alleged innocence of the population, to defame an active political group, and to conjure up the trauma of a regime of fear. The emotive propaganda terms were employed in "Little Red Riding Hood and the SPD," a widely circulating election advertisement. It "narrated": "Little Red Riding Hood believed that the good grandmother was lying in bed. In fact, it was the wolf. He jumped out of the bed and devoured Little Red Riding Hood. Some citizens are as gullible as Little Red Riding Hood. They believe they are electing the old SPD. In fact they are electing the Young Socialists." And the advertisement continues to warn and to terrify: "The radicals gain the majority. But our populace does not want a leftist course. We distrust socialist fantasies. For the socialist reality looks quite different. In the GDR, at the Wall, in Prague."

The CDU recommends itself as hunter, though not literally. It is amazing how long political connotations remain effective and to what extent the political image remains available for irrational propaganda.

Notes

1. H. Husson, *La Chaîne Traditionelle* (1874), 7ff.; A. Lang, *Perrault's Popular Tales* (1888), lix.

2. F. Linnig, *Deutsche Mythenmärchen* (1883), 184, 185.

3. E. Siecke, *Indogermanische Mythologie* (1921), 66; P. Saintyves, *Les Contes de Perrault et les Récits Parallèles* (1923), 215–229. On these mythological interpretations in greater detail, see

Marianne Rumpf, "Rotkäppchen: Eine vergleichende Märchenuntersuchung" (Ph.D. diss., Göttingen, 1951).

4. C. W. von Sydow, "Kategorien der Prosa-Volksdichtung," in *Volkskundliche Gaben: Festschrift für John Meier* (1930), 265, 266.

5. Quoted in, Rumpf, "Rotkäppchen," 116.

6. Ibid., 121.

7. C. G. Jung, *Gesammelte Werke,* vol. 4 (Olten, 1971), 237; the quote here is from the article of 1913, "Versuch einer Darstellung der psychoanalytischen Theorie." cf. also vol. 17, 145.

8. Iring Fetscher, *Wer hat Dornröschen wachgeküsst? Ein Märchen-Verwirrbuch* (Hamburg/Düsselforf, 1973), 27, 39. Being an ironic and slightly arrogant description of GDR editions of "Little Red Riding Hood," Sabine Brandt's article "Rotkäppchen und der Klassenkampf," *Der Monat* (1960), 65–74, unfortunately does not talk of what the title suggests.

9. My methodology could be considered rudimentarily structuralist—cf. H. Gallas, *Strukturalismus als interpretives Verfahren* (Berlin, 1972). However, I refrain from forming long series of paradigms and I do not postulate "collective psychic processes" so much as more or less specific associations.

10. Cf. E. Freitag, "Die Kinder- und Hausmärchen der Brüder Grimm im ersten Stadium ihrer stilgeschichtlichen Entwicklung" (Ph.D. diss., Frankfort am Main, 1929), and W. Schoof, "Zur Entstehungsgeschichte der Grimmschen Märchen," *Hessische Blätter für Volkskunde* 29 (1930), 5ff.

11. H. Gerstner, ed., *Die Brüder Grimm* (Ebenhausen, 1952), 50.

12. Jacob Grimm in his autobiography: "The final hardly hoped for return of the old elector towards the end of the year 1813 was an indescribable joy." Ibid., 69. Compare also Wilhelm: "We celebrated the reestablishment of Hesse with the purest joy, and I have never seen anything more moving and touching than the solemn entry of the princely family." Ibid.

13. Cf. ibid., 56.

14. Cf. ibid.

15. F. Panzer, ed., *Kinder- und Hausmärchen: Vollständige Ausgabe in der Urfassung* (Wiesbaden, ca. 1948), 5, 50, 51. I quote the fairy tale in this edition.

16. Quoted in R. Steig, *Achim von Arnim und die ihm Nahestehenden,* vol. 3 (1913), 319.

17. After Napoleon's defeat in the battle of Aspern the brothers had already once hoped in vain for a "liberation"; thereafter, they

were more cautious in their hopes. Compare Wilhelm's autobiography in Gerstner, *Die Brüder Grimm*, 52. The above mentioned "suscription [to the "Armer Heinrich"] for the benefit of the Hessian volunteers" dates from spring 1813.

18. Ibid., 61. The preface was finished on October 18, 1812, that is, the same month as the ravage of Moscow took place.

19. Letter on January 1, 1813. Ibid., 63.

20. "Über das Wesen der Märchen" (1819).

21. Panzer, ed., *Kinder- und Hausmärchen,* 126. Compare particularly the end of the fairy tale: "As long as you live you shall not run from the path into the forest if the mother has forbidden you to do so."

22. *Grosse Stuttgarter Ausgabe,* vol. 1, 201.

23. On the water metaphor, cf. H.-W. Jäger, *Politische Metaphorik im Jakobinismus und im Vormärz,* 28, 29. In addition to the examples presented there in the sense of "revolutionary chaos," "subversive disorder," etc., one should also note the verses aimed at the Viennese Jacobin Hebenstreit: "Compassion casts them [the "right-hearted hearts"] down / their feelings are moved / because one of their brothers / fell so low into the water." Quoted in A. Körner, ed., *Die Wiener Jakobiner* (Stuttgart, 1972), 218. Convicted of high treason, Hebenstreit was hanged on January 8, 1795, in Vienna.

24. Against the background of this traditional antithesis one comes to understand the current conservative prophecies of doom which warn of the "subversion" and the "political perversion" of the schools (and the universities). In the face of the quantity of left-wing teachers and professors, these prophecies seem hypocritical and obscure the fact that those so suspected are often more concerned to carry out the constitutional tasks than those who suspect them.

25. Ernst M. Arndt, *Ausgewählte Werke,* 16 vols., ed. H. Meisner and R. Geerds (Leipzig, n.d.). The typical expressions quoted here occur particularly in vol. 10, 119, 150, 37; vol. 9, 170.

26. Arndt, *Ausgewählte Werke,* vol. 9, 223.

27. Heinrich von Kleist, *Sämtliche Werke und Briefe,* ed. H. Sembdner (Munich, 1965), vol. 1, 27, 28. On similar images of the French and of Napoleon, cf. M. Schönmann, *Napoleon in der deutschen Literatur* (Berlin, 1930), particularly 5ff. and Jost Hermand, "Napoleon im Biedermeier," in his *Von Mainz nach Weimar* (Stuttgart, 1969). J. Grand-Carteret, *Napoleon I in der Caricature* (Leipzig, n.d.), compiles the following bestial epithets for the French con-

querer: "Cerberus" (pp. 80, 90), "Corsican tiger tearing the English dogs to pieces" (38), "bloodhound" (51, 62, 80), and "fox to be abandoned to a pack of hounds" (22). Particularly Kleist's first poem seems bloodthirsty, especially since it imitates the stanza, verse, and rhyme schemes of Schiller's "An die Freude" (To Joy), the main idea of which is, after all, "All men are brothers." But Schiller himself had excluded this poem from a later edition of his works, because the democratic and Jacobin literati considered it a Marseillaise of sorts; therefore, the poem, in the court counsellor's own words, "accommodated an erroneous taste of the age" and threatened to become a "popular poem." Cf. F. Beissner, "Schillers dichterische Gestalt," in *Schiller: Reden im Gedenkjahr* (Stuttgart, 1955), 150, 151.

28. E. M. Arndt, *Werke*, vol. 10, p. 69. The preceding quotes: vol. 9, pp. 219, 220, and 222; vol. 10, p. 65; vol. 9, p. 177.

29. Quoted in K. Berger, ed., *Freiheit. Stimmen aus der Zeit deutscher Wiedergeburt vor hundert Jahren* (Leipzig, 1913), 103, 158. On the guerrilla warfare, cf. E. M. Arndt's essay of 1813, "Was bedeutet Landsturm und Landwehr?" On the other image of the hunter as the henchman of the prince and as an enemy of all reform and of all reformers and progressives, see below, p. 111.

30. H. Zimmer, ed., *Theodor Körners Werke* (Leipzig/Wien), vol. 1, p. 188.

31. Panzer, ed., *Kinder- und Hausmärchen*, 299.

32. Cf. Rumpf, "Rotkäppchen," 96f. and 98ff. On the tradition also see J. Bolte and G. Polívka, *Anmerkungen zu den Kinder- und Hausmärchen der Brüder Grimm* (Leipzig, 1913), vol. 1, 234ff.

33. On possible reasons, cf. Panzer's preface, particularly 26, 27, and Rumpf, "Rotkäppchen," 96, 97.

34. Cf. note 20.

35. Ludwig Tieck, *Schriften* (Berlin, 1828), vol. 1, xxxvii. This seems to be Tieck's only comment about the play.

36. L. Tieck and F. von Raumer, eds., *Solger's Nachgelassene Schriften und Briefwechsel* (Leipzig, 1826), vol. 1, 8.

37. *Archiv der Zeit* (Berlin, 1800), 471.

38. Käthe Brodnitz, "Der junge Tieck und seine Märchenkomödien" (Ph.D. diss., Munich, 1912).

39. Emilie Pfeiffer, "Shakespeare und Tiecks Märchendramen" (Ph.D. diss., Bonn, 1933).

40. On the frequency and the function of these and similar images, cf. Jäger, *Politische Metaphorik im Jakobinismus und im Vormärz* (Stuttgart, 1971).

41. Anonymous; Berlin is given as the place of publication. According to T. Weller, *Die falschen und fingierten Druckorte*, reprint of the 1863 edition (Hildesheim, 1960) vol. 1, 148, however, this should be read as "Montag in Regensburg."

42. E. Stollreither, ed., J. Christian von Mannlich, *Ein deutscher Maler und Hofmann: Lebenserinnerungen* (Berlin, 1910), 416, 430.

43. F. Lehne, *Versuche republikanischer Gedichte* (Strasbourg, in the third year of the Franconian Republic), 40; reprinted in *Gedichte und Lieder deutscher Jakobiner*, no. 66 (Stuttgart, 1972).

44. The piece from the Aschaffenburgian paper:

> How do you and I come together?
> The red cap said to the tree,
> Since we belong to such different realms,
> I to the animated fauna
> You to the noble flora,
> We do not resemble each other
> anymore than bulls and pineapples,
> I believe, indeed, that we are a dream!
> Strange! How does the ass get a lectern?
> The tree said to the red cap:
> He becomes a Clubbist
> And this, indeed, is not a dream!
> > Pfeffer.

> The Jacobins scream
> The name is misprinted!
> Right, that's how it should be:
> Correct the mistake
> Make an l out of the r
> Put on the red cap
> So the world will know very fast
> That you are not in your right mind.
> > Idem.

This feeble rhymester quite shabbily tries to plagiarize the renowned fable poet Pfeffel, who, living in the Alsace, is a consequent friend of the revolution and an official poet of the new republic. For this as well as the following reference I am indebted to my friend Michael Peter Werlein, an outstanding expert in Jacobin literature and relevant archival records. Gleim's "Mayence Song of Victory" (1793) calls out: "Away with liberty caps and cockades; away with liberty trees"; it assures the German "friends of order" that "cap and tree are bad treasures for a German country" (R. R. Wuthenow, ed., *Epochen der deutschen Lyrik*, vol. 8 (1970), 91. Characterizing the red cap, a nasty anti-French lampoon of 1793 fuses the persecution of intellectuals with criminal allusions; the piece is called "The old French in Germany, even worse behind the new Franconian mask" (Deutschland bei G. Kellermann); the preface says: "It is the scholars in Vienna and Berlin, in Frankfort and elsewhere who want to put on the galley-slave liberty cap as a sign of revolt." On the further history of the motif of the red cap and the color red in the Vormärz as "a signal of Jacobin and the later Communist conviction," cf. Jäger, *Politische Metaphorik*, 17ff.

45. *Almanac of the Revolution of 1793, Göttingen, by Johann Christian Dieterich*, 203, 204.

46. E. Schmidt and B. Suphan, eds., *Xenien 1796* (Weimar, 1893), following the manuscripts of the Goethe and Schiller Archives.

47. *Werke und Briefe von W. H. Wackenroder* (Heidelberg, 1967), 435. The previously mentioned statements from Tieck's letter of December 28, 1792, are on pp. 399, 405.

48. Ludwig Tieck, *Schriften*, vol. 16, 163ff.

49. Quoted in H. Kasack and A. Mohrhenn, eds., *Ludwig Tieck* (Berlin, 1943), vol. 1, 62. Cf. also Brodnitz, "Der junge Tieck," 5.

50. See W. Weiland, *Der junge Friedrich Schlegel: Die Revolution in der Frühromantik* (Stuttgart, 1968).

51. In June 1800 to Schleiermacher. Quoted in Kasack and Mohrhenn, *Ludwig Tieck*, vol. 1, 72.

52. Quoted in A. Stern, *Der Einfluss der französischen Revolution auf das deutsche Geistesleben* (Stuttgart, 1928), 175. On the biographies of the personalities mentioned, cf. C. J. Geiger, *Reise eines Erdbewohners in den Mars*, facsimile of 1790 edition (Stuttgart, 1967), epilogue by Jost Hermand; Jäger, *Politische Metaphorik*, 86, 87, 110ff; P. B. Bertaux, *Hölderlin und die französische Revolution* (Frankfort am Main, 1969); W. Kirchner, *Der Hochverratsprozess gegen Sinclair* (Frankfort am Main, 1969). On Hebenstreit, see note 23.

53. H. Düntzer and F. W. Herder, ed., *Von und an Herder: Ungedruckte Briefe aus dem Nachlass*, vol. 1 (Leipzig, 1861), 222. Also see F. Bouterwek, "Zur Erläuterung des literärischen Jacobinismus," *Literarische Blätter* 1 (Göttingen, 1800), 7.

54. Quoted in F. Valjavec, *Die Entstehung der politischen Strömungen in Deutschland, 1770–1815* (Munich, 1951), 151. There a similarly phrased statement by Johann Friedrich Kleukers.

55. Cf. Bruno Bauer, *Geschichte der Politik, Cultur und Aufklärung des 18. Jahrhunderts,* vol. 2 (Charlottenburg, 1843–1845), 86.
56. L. Tieck, "Leben und Tod des kleinen Rotkäppchens: Eine Tragödie" (1800) in L. Tieck, *Schriften,* vol. 2. Since the text is relatively short, I do not deem it necessary to indicate the exact location of each quotation.
57. Cf. Rumpf, "Rotkäppchen," 42. In a Breton variant a dog asks the girl for a piece of pie. In "Puss-in-Boots" Hinze comments on the despicable character of the dog: "They are not capable of anything but flattery and biting" (II). Cf. Brodnitz, "Der junge Tieck," 7.
58. Quoted in W. Grab and U. Friesel, *Noch ist Deutschland nicht verloren: Eine historisch-politische Analyse unterdrückter Lyrik von der Französischen Revolution bis zur Reichsgründung* (Munich, 1970), 46. The following quotations op. cit., 46, 250. Cf. Jäger, *Politische Metaphorik,* 44: "In 'Caput XII' of 'Deutschland ein Wintermärchen' ('Germany, a Winter Tale') Heine feels compelled to reaffirm his loyalty to the liberal political movement. Located 'in the forest,' the report happens in front of the 'fellow wolves.' The suspicion that the revolutionary has become a 'renegade,' 'a court councillor,' or 'deserted to the dogs' is refuted with the confession:

> I am not a sheep, I am not a dog,
> Not a court counsellor nor a cod—
> I am still a wolf, my heart and
> My teeth are wolfish.

Perhaps this actively reactionary usage of the wolf image by reactionaries such as Menzel and Meinhold partly originated in Hobbes' speech about 'homo homini lupus'; Hobbes sought to describe anarchy and the societal 'bellum omnium contra omnes' and to justify authoritarian rule and servility as necessary to overcome this belligerent chaos. For the conservatives and reactionaries the liberal and even more the republican state seem to reincarnate this wild and chaotic *ur*-state." In his "Märchen-Verwirrbuch" Fetscher approves of this hypothesis: "If one searches for a date when the ideologically motivated reductionist approach to the fairy tale tradition started, the publication of Thomas Hobbes 'De Cive' (1641) seems a watershed: in this work the metaphor 'homo homini lupus' (One man is another's wolf) is for the first time used to describe

human society" (p. 27 in the section "On the Rehabilitation of the Wolves"). It may be a jest, but perhaps it is also true.
59. Cf. Jäger, *Politische Metaphorik*, 139, 140. Cf. also *Kunst der bürgerlichen Revolution von 1830 bis 1848/49*, Catalogue, Neue Gesellschaft für bildende Kunst (Berlin, 1972), 148, 149.
60. Cf. Rumpf, "Rotkäppchen," 17, 18, 27, 42.
61. Cf. Rumpf, "Rotkäppchen," 36, 37.
62. Italics by the author of the present article.
63. Brodnitz, "Der junge Tieck," 77.
64. Cf. Panzer, ed., *Kinder- und Hausmärchen*, 299.
65. Cf. P. Rühmkopf, *Die Jahre, die Ihr kennt* (Hamburg, 1972), particularly pp. 205, 218.
66. *Frankfurter Allgemeine Zeitung* on May 4, 1973; *Bayernkurier* on May 12, 1973; also *Kölner Express* on August 23, 1973. In the *Bayernkurier* on October 6, 1973, F. J. Strauss insinuates that the German Chancellor Willy Brandt is an unsuspecting victim of his allegedly radically left-wing ministers of culture; Strauss calls Brandt "Red Riding Hood in the forest of German education."

"Little Red Riding Hood" as Male Creation and Projection

Of the many scholars who have sought to interpret the tale of "Little Red Riding Hood," few, if any, have had the expertise of Jack Zipes, Professor of German at the University of Florida. In his book *The Trials and Tribulations of Little Red Riding Hood* (1983), he demonstrates his unique mastery of previous versions and discussions of the tale. After a substantial introduction, he proceeds to present in chronological order some thirty-one versions (including parodies) of the story. This book is required reading for anyone seriously interested in examining some of the many forms that "Little Red Riding Hood" has assumed from 1697 to the twentieth century.

Professor Zipes' introduction was too long to reprint in its entirety, but its final section, in which he offers new, feminist-inspired insights as to the particulars of the tale's early appearances in print, is included here. In this selection, he goes beyond mere political allegorizing to suggest the possible long-term effects of males collecting and *rewriting* female-centered fairy tales.

For further discussion by Zipes of "Little Red Riding Hood," with special attention to the various illustrations which appear in children's book editions, see "A Second Gaze at Little Red Riding Hood's Trials and Tribulations," *The Lion and the Unicorn* 7–8 (1983–1984), 78–109.

Reprinted from Jack Zipes, *The Trials and Tribulations of Little Red Riding Hood* (South Hadley: Bergin & Garvey, 1983), 54–57, by permission of Bergin & Garvey Publishers, Inc., and the author.

By the time Perrault began to revise the oral folk tale of "The Grandmother," it was no longer necessary to believe in witches or werewolves, especially if one were a member of the upper classes, for the witch craze had subsided and was no longer fashionable. It was now necessary to project an image of woman as innocent, helpless, and susceptible to the chaotic, somewhat seductive, forces of nature, capable of making a pact with the devil or yielding to her fancy. Delarue is quite right when he points out that Perrault decided to change the werewolf into a simple wolf because werewolves had lost their significance after the decline of the witch-hunts. Nevertheless, Perrault's audience still identified the wolf with the bloody werewolf, the devil, insatiable lust, and chaotic nature, *if not with a witch.* The wolf as witch may strike readers today as far-fetched, but it was not far from the minds of seventeenth- and eighteenth-century readers. Thus, let us proceed to reinterpret Perrault's tale according to the French ideology of his time.

As we know, numerous modern studies have focused on the red cap in Perrault's tale as a symbol either of the sun or of puberty. Neither viewpoint is correct. Perrault used the word *chaperon,* which was a small stylish cap worn by women of the aristocracy and middle classes in the sixteenth and seventeenth centuries.[1] Since clothing was codified and strictly enforced under Louis XIV, it was customary for middle-class women to wear cloth caps, whereas aristocratic ladies wore velvet. Bright colors were preferred, especially red, and the skull cap was generally ornamental. For a village girl, in Perrault's story, to wear a red *chaperon* signified that she was individualistic and perhaps nonconformist. Perrault probably intended that she bear the sign of the middle class, and by giving her a name he made something special out of her.[2] Again there is something definitely individualistic about Little Red Riding Hood. We already know that she is the prettiest creature around, spoiled by her mother and grandmother. Thus, the image of this young girl suggests that she contains certain potential qualities which could convert her into a witch or heretic. Her *natural* inclinations do in fact lead her into trouble. In the woods, which was a known haunting place of werewolves, witches, outlaws, and other social deviates, Little Red Riding Hood talks naturally to the wolf because she is unaware of any danger. She trusts her instincts. If it were not for the *male* woodcutters (for only men can serve as protectors), the wolf would have indulged his appetite on the spot, in his natural abode. Instead he is forced to make a "pact" with her. Certainly, according to seventeenth-century beliefs, anyone who entered into an agreement with a diabolic figure was contaminated and would have to fight for his or her soul. The motif depicted here was fully and consciously developed in eighteenth-century France by writers of bourgeois morality plays, like Louis Sebastien Mercier and Denis Diderot, who depicted decadent aristocrats seducing young virtuous bourgeois ladies.[3] This dramatic genre, labelled *comédie sérieuse*, became extremely popular and lasted well through the nineteenth century into the twentieth. Interestingly enough, it served as the basis for Boieldieu's 1818 opera *Le petit Chaperon rouge*. In eighteenth-century Germany this type of drama was cultivated by Gotthold Ephraim Lessing in *Miss Sara Sampson* and *Emilia Galotti*, and he was followed by such Sturm und Drang writers as J. M. R. Lenz, Heinrich Leopold Wagner, Friedrich Maximilian Klinger, and even Friedrich Schiller in *Kabale und Liebe*. And, of course, the constellation of diabolic wolf and virtuous bourgeois damsel served as the basis for Part I of Goethe's *Faust*, where the transformed Faust (a type of werewolf) with the aid of Mephistopheles seduces Gretchen, who must pay for *her* sin. It is important to note that Faust is a necromancer doing the devil's work, and it is apparent that Gretchen's bourgeois/village forebear was none other than Little Red Riding Hood. All French and German writers of the eighteenth century knew that Little Red Riding Hood had been punished for her "crime" of speaking to the devil and of laying the grounds for her own seduction and rape.

The eating or swallowing of Little Red Riding Hood is an obvious sexual act, symbolizing the uncontrollable appetite or chaos of nature. Moreover, Little Red Riding Hood becomes at one with the wolf. That is, her "natural" potential to become a witch is realized because she lacks self-discipline. As Honegger has made clear, the flip side of the Maria cult, the supreme virgin, is the witch. All this is summarized in the *moralité* of the fairy tale. The blame for the diabolical rape is placed squarely on the shoulders of naive young girls who are pretty and have correct manners. Ostensibly, the seduction would not have occurred had Little Red Riding Hood not stopped to listen to a stranger. Her "dallying" or her undisciplined ways lead her into the wolf's lair. Perrault obviously extends the definition of wolf to include deceptive male seducers of bourgeois women. Still, the overall notion of the fairy tale concerns the regulation of sex roles and sexuality. Where order and discipline reign—Perrault supported the absolutism of Louis XIV—young girls will be safe from both their own inner sexual drives and outer natural forces. Inner and outer nature must be brought under control, otherwise chaos and destruction will reign.

The cultural code and pattern embedded in "Little Red Riding Hood" make it obvious that this tale in particular was bound to become an immediate favorite in the eighteenth and nineteenth centuries, particularly among members of the aristocracy and bourgeoisie. However, it was not until the Grimms morally improved upon the Perrault version, showing more clemency for Little Red Riding Hood, that the tale became an explicit narrative of law and order. As we know, by the time the Grimms touched up Perrault's tale, a bourgeois Red Riding Hood syndrome had been established throughout Europe and America, and it went under the name of "virtue seduced." Obviously, the middle classes were reflecting in general upon the fact that, if they did not discipline themselves and their children and rationalize their lives, they would be "raped" by the depraved aristocracy or experience a fall due to unruly natural forces. Then they would have to succumb to the uncouth lower classes. Fear of chaos as dangerous for sound and orderly business was overwhelming among members of the third estate, and, even though the French Revolution had brought turmoil with it, this upheaval had been deemed necessary in order to clean out decadent aristocratic squalor and to bring more order, rationality, and just conditions into France. The effect that the French Revolution had on Ludwig Tieck and the Brothers Grimm has already been documented. Now it is more important to note how the Grimms doctored "Little Red Riding Hood" as "Little Red Cap" to make a comment on sexual norms and sex roles.

The Grimms were responsible for making Little Red Riding Hood definitively into a disobedient, helpless little girl. Before she makes a pact with the devil, she makes one with her good mother. Thus, they also prepared the way for clemency. Yet, with this clemency they also introduced more phrases and images suggestive of authority and order, and they elaborated on the woods scene to show that Little Red Riding Hood wants to break from the moral restraints of her society to enjoy her own sensuality (inner nature) and nature's pleasures (outer nature). She is much more fully to blame for her rape by the wolf because she has a nonconformist streak which must be eradicated. But times had changed since Perrault, and the nineteenth-century moralists no longer argued for killing or burning heretics, especially not their own children. First they displayed the power of their authority in the form of the police, in this case the hunter-gamekeeper, and then they set an example of punishment using a misfit or outsider from the lower classes—that is, the wolf. Foucault has thoroughly outlined the panopticum principle of discipline and punishment in the nineteenth century, where a watchful eye is constantly on the alert for social deviates.[4] Thus, in the Grimms' tale, a policeman appears out of nowhere to save Little Red Riding Hood, and, when she is granted the opportunity to punish the wolf by filling his stomach with rocks, she is actually punishing herself. The sterile rocks in his stomach will also prevent her from rising and fulfilling her potential. As she carries out this punishment, she internalizes the restraining norms of sexuality in a political manner. The actual form of the fairy tale narrative partakes in such repressive socialization.

It is impossible to exaggerate the impact and importance of the Little Red Riding Hood syndrome as a dominant cultural pattern in Western societies. In this regard, I want to stress that in her two most popular literary forms, which have fully captured the mass-mediated common imagination in our own day, Little Red Riding Hood is a *male* creation and projection. Not women but men—Perrault and the Brothers Grimm—gave birth to our common image of Little Red Riding Hood. "The point is," as Andrea Dworkin rightly maintains in her book *Woman Hating:*

> We have not formed that ancient world—it has formed us. We ingested it as children whole, had its values and consciousness imprinted on our minds as cultural absolutes long before we were in fact men and women. We have taken the fairy tales of childhood with us into maturity, chewed but still lying in the stomach, as real identity. Between Snow-white and her heroic prince, our two great fictions, we never did have much of a chance. At some point, the Great Divide took place: they (the boys) dreamed of mounting the Great Steed and buying Snow-white from the dwarfs; we (the girls) aspired to become that object of every necrophiliac's lust—the innocent, victimized Sleeping Beauty, beauteous lump of ultimate, sleeping good. Despite ourselves, sometimes unknowing, sometimes knowing, unwilling, unable to do otherwise, we act out the roles we were taught.[5]

Viewed in this light, "Little Red Riding Hood" reflects men's fear of women's sexuality—and of their own as well. The curbing and regulation of sexual drives is fully portrayed in this bourgeois literary fairy tale on the basis of deprived male needs. Red Riding Hood is to blame for her own rape. The wolf is not really a male but symbolizes natural urges and social nonconformity. The real hero of the tale, the hunter-gamekeeper, is male governance. If the tale has enjoyed such a widespread friendly reception in the Perrault and Grimm forms, then this can only be attributed to a general acceptance of the cultural notions of sexuality, sex roles, and domination embedded in it.

All this is not to say that the tale is outmoded and totally negative, that it should be censored by the women's movement and local school boards, or that it should be replaced by nonsexist versions. The problem is not in the literature, nor can it be solved through censorship. Given the conditions in Western society where women have been prey for men, there is a positive feature to the tale: its warning about the possibility of sexual molestation continues to serve a social purpose. At present, where I teach, women are forced to carry whistles (not a red cap) in the library and classroom buildings and on campus because of rape and violence, and this institution of academic learning is not an exception. Until men learn that they need not be wolves or gamekeepers to fulfill their lives, the tale offers a valuable lesson for young girls and women—albeit a lesson based on the perversion of sexuality.

As we have seen, signs of change have already been depicted in the radical "Little Red Riding Hood" adaptations of the twentieth century. However, it took two hundred years of hunting witches and werewolves to give birth to the traditional helpless Red Riding Hood and restrictive notions of sex and nature, then another two hundred years to establish the proper bourgeois image of the obedient Red Riding Hood learning her lessons of discipline; it may take another two hundred years for us to undo all the lessons Red Riding Hood, and the wolf as well, were forced to learn.

Notes

1. Cf. James Robinson Planché, *Encyclopedia of Costume*, vol. 1 (London: Chatto & Windus, 1876), 241–294; Carl Köhler, *A History of Costume* (London: Harrap, 1928), 163–178; Francois Boucher, *20,000 Years of Fashion* (New York: Abrams, 1967), 531–700.

2. Earlier I discussed the significance of the red hat in relation to

Jews, witches, werewolves, and the devil. It is difficult to determine exactly why Perrault used the color red, but we do know that it was associated with witches and the devil in his time. In discussing the initiation ritual of witches, Andrea Dworkin points out:

> Once the neophyte made the decision for the horned god, she went through a formal initiation, often conducted at the sabbat. The ceremony was simple. The initiate declared that she was joining the coven of her own free will and swore devotion to the master of the coven who represented the horned god. She was then marked with some kind of tattoo which was called the witches' mark. The inflicting of the tattoo was painful, and the healing process was long. When healed the scar was red or blue and indelible. One method particularly favored by the witch hunters when hunting was to take a suspected woman, shave her pubic and other bodily hair (including head hair, eyebrows, etc.) and, upon finding any scar, find her guilty of witchcraft. (See *Woman Hating* (New York: Dutton, 1974), 142–43.

Suspected women not possessing such a mark would be given one, such as the scarlet letter "A." Even redheads, natural redheads, were suspected for a long time of being in league with the devil or the offspring of the devil. The famous Austrian playwright Johann Nestroy wrote an entire play about the difficulties encountered by redheads. See *Der Talisman* (1840).

3. See W. W. Pusey, *Louis-Sebastien Mercier in Germany: His Vogue and Influence in the Eighteenth Century* (New York: Columbia University Press, 1939), and Henry Majewski, *The Preromantic Imagination of L.-S. Mercier* (New York: Humanities Press, 1971).

4. See *Discipline and Punish: The Birth of the Prison* (New York: Pantheon, 1978).

5. *Woman Hating*, 33. Cf. Kay Stone, "Things Walt Disney Never Told Us," in *Women and Folklore*, ed. Claire R. Farrer (Austin: University of Texas Press, 1975), 42–50, and Madonna Kolbenschlag, *Kiss Sleeping Beauty Good-Bye* (New York: Doubleday, 1979).

ZOHAR SHAVIT

The Concept of Childhood
and Children's Folktales:
Test Case—"Little Red Riding Hood"

Folklorists are wont to claim that fairy tales belong exclusively to their corner of the academy, but the truth is that fairy tales are equally of interest to educators and students of children's literature. Children's literature, a discipline unto itself, includes both folklore and stories written by known authors.

The perspective of a children's literature scholar may differ from that of a folklorist insofar as the former is very likely to be more concerned with the possible impact of a particular fairy tale upon the psyche of a young child. In the following unusual essay, Zohar Shavit of the department of Poetics and Comparative Literature at Tel Aviv University considers the very definition of "child" and "childhood" in her study of the Perrault and Grimm versions of "Little Red Riding Hood." In this investigation, the particular time-frames of the two classic versions are once again examined, but not so much with respect to political events or to the gender of the collectors-editors.

For other essays written from the perspective of children's literature, see Lee Burns, "Red Riding Hood," *Children's Literature* 1 (1972), 30–36, and Carole Hanks and D. T. Hanks, Jr., "Perrault's 'Little Red Riding Hood': Victim of the Revisers," *Children's Literature* 7 (1978), 68–77. For

Reprinted from *Jerusalem Studies in Jewish Folklore* 4 (1983), 93–124, by permission of the Institute of Jewish Studies, Hebrew University, Jerusalem. I am indebted to folklorist Michael L. Chyet for translating this essay from Hebrew into English.

more of Zohar Shavit's consideration of children's literature, see her *Poetics of Children's Literature* (Athens: University of Georgia Press, 1986).

Children's literature today enjoys centrality in cultural awareness and constitutes such a sizeable proportion of new educational materials that it is hard to imagine publishing activity without it. However, although children's literature is today a "natural" phenomenon taken for granted in any national literature, it is a relatively new development—less than two hundred years old. Books written especially for children were virtually unknown until the eighteenth century, and the children's book industry did not begin to flourish until the second half of the nineteenth century, when adult literature (in the modern sense) had already been established for at least one hundred years.

The reasons contributing to the late development of children's literature are diverse, but undoubtedly among the most important was the total absence of the concepts of "child" and "childhood" as we perceive them today. Before children's literature could be written, "childhood" itself had to come into existence and receive recognition and legitimation as a distinct time period in the life of the individual, or in the words of Townsend: "Before there could be children's books, there had to be children—children, that is, who were accepted as beings with their own particular needs and interests, not only as miniature men and women."[1]

In this article I will analyze along general lines and only in their principal features the creation and crystallization of the prerequisites for the development of Western children's literature—the development of the concept of the "child" in culture—and I will examine the relationships between this concept and texts written for children. In other words, I will ask how the nature of the concept of the child in literature and the meaning that has been given to that nature have to a large extent determined the character and the structure of texts for children, and how the changes that occurred in this concept were largely responsible for the changes that came about in texts for children. In attempting to answer these questions, I will use as a test case different versions of the folktale "Red Riding Hood."

The twentieth century is characterized by the almost obsessive use of the concept of childhood: issues about psychological, physical, and sexual problems of the child do not cease to concern adults. The period of childhood is considered the most important period in one's life, and an adult's behavior is often explained by his childhood experiences. But such a perception of childhood is completely different from the cultural outlook that prevailed two hundred years ago—the concept of childhood as we know it today did not exist then.

In his classic work, Philip Ariès[2] proposes the argument, supported by later research as well,[3] that from the Middle Ages until the seventeenth century a different view of childhood dominated social consciousness, a view which began to develop and to change along lines familiar to us today beginning in the seventeenth century, passing through several transformations as one of the basic concepts of Western civilization.

The Concept of Childhood up to the Seventeenth Century

Up to the seventeenth century the child was not perceived as an entity distinct from the adult, and consequently he was not recognized as having special needs. One of the results of this outlook was the lack of an established educational system for children, and of books written specifically for them.

In the Middle Ages and the ensuing period neither the living conditions nor the prevailing theological standpoint allowed for the concept of childhood. In the conceptual outlook of the day there was no room for the concept of childhood because of the identification between man and nature, as a result of which the life cycle was described as analogous to that of nature, including only the periods of birth, life, and death. In such a system there was no place for the period of childhood, the lack of which in the conceptual framework was no doubt strengthened by the poor chances of survival of children and their high mortality rate, which rendered their continued existence utterly uncertain. In addition, the basic living conditions were a contributing factor: people were wed at a relatively young age, and therefore "left childhood"—in the modern sense of the term—at a very tender age. Upper-class children took an active part in society from an extremely young age (10–13), whereas children of the lower classes were needed in the work force, and began working at a tender age. Consequently, children who successfully survived the first dangerous years of life could not remain children for long, and were quickly forced to enter the adult world and to become part of it.

Relations between the Child's World and the Adult's World: From Unity to Polarization

Up to the seventeenth century children were an integral part of adult society, sharing clothing, lodging, games, and work. Unity prevailed between children and adults in regard to all physical and psychic needs. A process of polarization began to undermine this unity from the seventeenth century on, as can be seen, for instance, from a discussion about the nature of the dress of children and adults of the upper class.[4] Up to the seventeenth century it was customary for children to wear a miniature version of the adults' clothing as soon as they stopped wearing swaddling clothes, which occurred at a relatively late age (3–5 years). With the development of the concept of childhood, the designing of special clothes for children also began. In general it can be said that the child's new wardrobe was characterized by items of attire which formerly belonged to the realm of adult wear and lost their function as such. Children's clothes became systematized through a process of reduction and at times also of simplification, and in the new system they also acquired a new function: they became a symbol of the separation of the world of children from that of the adult. Soon after certain items became children's clothing, they were used exclusively for children, such as breeches, which formerly had been a standard item of adult attire, but later became a trademark of children's dress. Moreover, various items of dress designated different stages of childhood, and permission to wear a certain item marked another stage in a child's maturation, until finally he entered the adult world and began to dress as a full-fledged adult.

The process of the transformation of childhood was expressed in other aspects of daily life, such as children's games, the educational system of the child, and even the fact that there was a special room in the house set aside for children, just as there were special rooms for the parents, for dining, and the like. As Ariès points out, an interesting example of this process of the transformation of elements from the adult's world to the world of the child and their consequent evolution into a trademark of the child's world is the case of the wooden rocking horse. The horse, which had been a primary medium of transportation, lost this function for the adult world at the end of the nineteenth century. It did not disappear from the culture, but rather evolved through a process of reduction and simplification into the wooden horse of the nursery, where it acquired a new function as a toy. Moreover, in addition to this function it became a symbol differentiating the children's room from the adults' room, and a sine qua non in nursery furnishings. (For a similar phenomenon, other dolls and miniature toys can be pointed to which originally had a ritual function for adults and children alike, but which later lost their ritual function, becoming not only part of the child's world, but his exclusive monopoly.)

Hence, in the process of the formation of the concept of

"child," there occurred a polarization between the adult's and the child's world. The system of childhood began to be characterized by a series of elements which migrated from the adult system to the child's system, and took on the function of differentiating between the two systems.

The Spread of the Concept of Childhood into Society: Two Concepts

The polarization between the adult's and the child's world and the spread of the concept of childhood were the result of many processes which occurred in Western society, especially the changes in social and material processes. The Industrial Revolution, the decrease in infant mortality, and the increase in life expectancy undoubtedly all played an important part in the development of the child concept, but changes in man's perception of the world during the Renaissance and the Enlightenment contributed considerably to the fact that the concept of "child" began to rise to consciousness before the physical conditions justified it, that is, before any change occurred in living conditions, and the change in these conditions later aided in the dissemination of the child concept among the middle class as well.

The first signs of the formation of this child concept, and the recognition that the child is a creature distinct from the adult, were already apparent at the end of the sixteenth century in the realm of painting. Here the child served a religious purpose—the infant Jesus, Jesus and the Angels, and the like—being depicted for the first time as sweet, angelic, and innocent, qualities which were also to characterize the image of the child at a later date. In time this iconography acquired a decorative character (viz. the paintings of Putt) beyond its original religious nature, and images of children gradually began to undergo a process of secularization and to hold a dominant position in the realms of painting and iconography. These pictures were the expression of a perception of the child as different from the adult by virtue of the former's innocence, sweetness, and angelic appearance. Gradually depictions of children began to acquire their own legitimacy, and painting children's portraits became more and more common. Thus the depiction of children aided in the spread of the new concept of the child as possessing the qualities portrayed in the paintings, qualities which from the seventeenth century onward made children a source of amusement for adults.

Regarding the child as a source of entertainment began to develop within the family circle. People no longer hesitated to acknowledge the diversion which children provided, and delighting in children, as well as in their sweetness, beauty, and witticisms, became fashionable among the upper classes. Children were invited to the parlor so that adults might be amused by them: the attitude towards children greatly resembled that assumed for cherished pet animals. Fleury described this attitude as follows: "It is as if the poor children had been made only to amuse the adults, like little dogs or little monkeys."[5]

This attitude began to arouse resistance among extra-familial groups, such as moralists and pedagogues, who were opposed to the fashion which prevailed in relation to children. Nevertheless, they accepted the principal concept of considering the innocent child who is closer to God as distinct from the adult. They used this very concept to justify their demand for separating children from the corrupt adult society.

In contrast to the perception that was developing within the extended family circle, which saw the child as a source of amusement, a second perception of the child arose among groups which stood in opposition to the family: the church, the moralists, and the pedagogues, who, because of their awareness of his different nature, felt responsible for the spiritual development of the child. They believed that children need education and discipline, and simultaneous with the new interest in the psychology of the child, they drafted a demand for an educational system that would satisfy these needs. Henceforth the child was perceived as a delicate creature who must be protected, educated, and molded in accordance with the current educational beliefs and goals.

The way to shape children along these lines was first and foremost by means of books, which were considered the primary tool in achieving these "pedagogical" goals. This new "educational" perception of society, unlike the "amusement" perception which preceded it, created for the first time the need for children's books, and became the frame of reference in which the first books were written whose intended audience was specifically children. From then on official children's books were written, based on an understanding of the child as the audience and of his needs, which were different from those of adults. When a change in this understanding came about, texts written for children changed as well.

In order to investigate the relationship between the cultural concept of the child and the norms governing literature for children, I shall analyze as a test-case different versions of "Little Red Riding Hood." The text of "Little Red Riding Hood" has been chosen not only because it is a "classic" of children's literature, but also for reasons of methodological convenience, as there is an extraordinary correspondence between the periods in which the different versions of the text were produced and the parallel developments in the child concept and the changes which occurred in it. Examining this text may therefore shed light on the link between the changes that took place in the child concept in Western civilization at different periods and the changes that occurred in the versions of the text in at least two ways: (1) understanding the child's needs and his comprehension capacity, and (2) seeing the manner in which the child and his world are presented in the texts themselves.

The examination of versions of "Little Red Riding Hood" will deal therefore with these questions and the way in which the "amusement" perception served as a basis for Perrault's version, its transformation into the "educational" version of the Brothers Grimm, and the further transformation of this version to the "protective" version of the twentieth century.

"Little Red Riding Hood":
A Test Case of Attitudes towards Folktales
from the Seventeenth Century on

We have seen how, in the process of the creation of the child concept, elements from the adult world have passed over to the child's world, becoming the exclusive property of the child, after previously being shared by adults and children alike. This process characterized modes of dress, games children played, and folktales, which gradually entered the child's world, until in the twentieth century they were considered an essential component in his development (unlike the first half of the nineteenth century, when they were considered too dangerous for children and were removed from the canon of juvenile literature).

Up until the nineteenth century, folktales were told and read, as were romances, by adults (even among the upper classes). Children, who constituted part of adult society, were acquainted with them in the same way, although the tales were not considered meant for them. However, starting from the second half of the seventeenth century a change occurred in the attitude of the upper class vis-à-vis folktales. This was part of a general change in the prevailing literary fashions. Members of the literary elite, whose tastes were becoming more "sophisticated," regarded folktales as too "simple" and "childish," suitable, in their estimation, only for children and members of the lower classes (who were seen as social equals by the class-conscious of the time).[6] Despite this, it became fashionable to be interested in folktales and to write tales modeled after oral tales, at times pretending to be setting down an oral tale in written form (which was in some cases true). Yet in spite of the fact that folktales were in vogue, the writing and acceptance of them were based on the assumption that they were meant for children and the lower classes. Thus members of high society could enjoy them only vicariously through children, but since the child was perceived in any case as a source of

137

amusement, adults could enjoy elements of the child's world while openly or covertly considering them part of the world of children, part of a culture different from that of the upper classes.

Perrault's Version

Concealing the Author's Identity

This attitude towards children's culture functioned as the background and the motivation as well as the source of legitimation for Perrault's book *Histoires ou Contes du temps passé*. As is known, in 1697 Perrault published a collection of tales, some of which had never before been written down (such as "Little Red Riding Hood"). Perrault's collection was not unusual, but rather belonged to the genre of tales written by upper-class women such as Mme d'Aulnoy, Mlle l'Héritier, and Mme Le Prince de Beaumont which began to flood French literature at the end of the seventeenth and the beginning of the eighteenth centuries. Perrault's collection stirred up a controversy almost immediately after it was published, not only because it was specifically intended for children while being both ironic and very sophisticated, but even more so because it was not signed by Perrault, the distinguished member of the Académie Française, but instead by his seventeen-year-old son Pierre d'Armancour.

The ambiguous nature of the text, which will be discussed below, and its author's mysterious identity raise two questions: (1) Why did the author's identity remain unclear? and (2) For whom was the work intended?

The author's identity became a topic of controversy among researchers, who based their arguments on the following facts. Although the work was by Perrault's son, it was attributed to Perrault himself even in his lifetime. In two volumes of *Le Cabinet des fées* (a vast collection consisting of thirty-seven volumes of tales gathered in that period, evidence for the great interest taken in them), one reads that

Histoires ou Contes du temps passé was written by Perrault, despite its being ascribed to his son.[7]

Soriano, the well-known expert on Perrault, maintains that the text was often attributed to the latter after it became a great success, as if to say that an important name was required. But this claim does not explain why the work was ascribed to Perrault before it attained world renown, or why Perrault never bothered to clarify the issue, as Soriano himself asserts: "The academician knew the truth of this affair, but he did nothing to eliminate the doubt."[8] Moreover, it seems that the opposite can be argued: not only did Perrault fail to clarify unequivocally the issue of the author's identity, he did all he could to leave it ambiguous.

Perrault did not deny the fact that he was a writer. He signed his name to "La Marquise de Salusses ou la Patience de Griselidis," which appeared in *Mercure Galant* together with a comment to the effect that it was given as a lecture in the Académie Française (1691). His name also appeared on the story "Les Souhaits ridicules" which also appeared in *Mercure Galant* (1693). Nevertheless, at the same time Perrault did all he could to conceal the identity of the writer of *Les Contes*. Among the ruses he resorted to was the following: In the second version of "L'Histoire de la Marquise-Marquis de Banneville"—which was written, to all appearances, by Perrault—there is a long digression relating to the author of "La Belle au bois dormant" (February 1696), which contains the following quote: "But I was not at all surprised when I was told the name of the author. It is the son of Master——"[9] Such a comment about a story included in *Les Contes* undoubtedly added to the mystery which surrounded the author's identity.

Guesses as to the identity of the author of the tales were not limited to Perrault's son. Some attributed them to his niece or to other contemporary tale writers because of their resemblance to other literary tales. It must also be borne in mind that similarities between different tales were not necessarily due to familial relations, but rather to the simple fact that all the writers relied on the same literary models and consciously attempted to imitate them, as Soriano rightly points out: "Perrault, his son, Mademoiselle l'Héritier, Perrault's niece, Mademoiselle Bernard, the niece of Fontenelle, the abbot of Choisy, found themselves in the same salons, playing the same society games, intellectually competing with themes which were identical."[10] In addition, it should be noted that Perrault's contemporaries were not particularly impressed by his endeavors to conceal his identity, nor by the similarity between his text and others. They had no doubt about the author's true identity, as is evident from a letter which Dubois wrote to Bayle: "The same publisher also printed the *Contes de ma mere l'Oye* by Monsieur Perrault."[11]

The fact that Perrault deliberately masked his identity as author, preferring officially to attribute the work to his son, can be explained, at least partially, by the fact that as a member of the Académie Française he did not feel comfortable writing texts that it was felt should be written by young people or by upper-class women, whose social status was lower than his. However it seems that there was more than just Perrault's social standing involved in the blurring of the author's identity: otherwise it would have been more logical to identify his son as the sole author of the tales, rather than to play around with two identities. It appears that the main reason for Perrault's behavior is embedded in a social convention current among elite literary circles of the time vis-à-vis folktales. The games around the author's double identity were part of the general pretense regarding folktales. Even though the literary elite knew who the true author was, it preferred to pretend that the work was written by Perrault's son, just as it preferred to pretend that the tales were meant for children. The game surrounding the author's ambiguity paralleled the game around the intended audience's identity. Nevertheless, the manipulation of the text and of the folktale model, and more particularly their satiric and ironic tone, left no doubt as to the true identity of both the audience and the writer.

*Manipulating the Model: The Ambiguity
of "Little Red Riding Hood"*

As stated above, Perrault was the first person to set down
"Little Red Riding Hood" in writing. Scholars are still un-
decided on the question of whether or not Perrault's text is
based on an existing folktale, mainly because of the atypical
tragic ending of his text, a phenomenon unheard of in folktales. At any rate, even those scholars who believe that his
text is based on an original folktale agree that Perrault doctored the text, altering part of its formal structure in order to
make it more sophisticated.

For instance, Perrault changed the formulaic structure of
the dialogue, which is generally characterized by completely
symmetrical repetitions. Perrault violated this semi-sacred
symmetry in the following manner:

> The *better* to embrace you,—
> The *better* to run with,—
> The *better* to hear with,—
> The *better* to see with,—
> To eat *you* with.[12]

Nevertheless, Perrault took pains to create the illusion of
a folktale, mainly by means of stylistic devices, as Soriano
asserts: "An attentive study of vocabulary shows that many
of the turns of phrase utilized by the tale-teller were already
considered old at that time—it is in sum a reconstitution, a
sort of "in the manner of."[13]

The function of the stylizing of the text was not only to
lend it the qualities of "authenticity" and "antiquity," but
also, and perhaps primarily, to emphasize who its official audience was. The desire to stress the intended audience, that
is, the child, would explain why Perrault used in the text
words which were at that time considered to belong exclusively to the language of children, words such as *la bobinette*
and *la chevillette,* which were not part of the accepted written language. The very act of inserting such vocabulary

items into the texts was a striking departure from the norm, thus serving an important stylistic function.

However, together with the attempt to characterize the work as "authentic" and as intended for children through the use of elements whose stylistic identity was clear, Perrault did not hesitate to deviate from the formulas of the folktale even at key points, such as the addition of a tragic ending, or in typical structures, such as the repetitions. In this manner he created a text which cannot be considered unequivocally either a folktale or a literary tale, possessing instead an ambiguous nature.

The Basis for the Ambiguous Nature of the Text

It seems that the ambiguous nature of the text can be explained by its official and unofficial audience. This ambiguity enabled Perrault to address two different audiences at one and the same time. On the one hand, he was able to take advantage of the current perception regarding the appropriateness of folktales for children in order to direct the text officially to them, while at the same time availing himself of the common conception of the child as a source of amusement in order to orient the text to the literary elite. However, in order to ensure that the upper classes would read his work, he felt obliged to "equip" it with signs that would indicate who the true audience was, while also making possible the duplicity of the text. While the folktale formulas designated the official audience, the breaking of such formulas—in addition to lending an ironic and satirical aspect to the text—marked the unofficial audience, the literary elite. Numerous accounts from the period testify to Perrault's success in attracting his unofficial audience to reading these texts—perhaps even more so than their officially intended audience—as Muir states:

> A feature of these salons, male and female alike, was the reading aloud of pasquinades, vaudevilles, sonnets à bouts-rimés, and similar short pieces: and the Comtesse d'Aulnoy seems to

have introduced the telling of fairy-stories in the female salons. The idea caught on and became the rage. The fashion
eventually extended to the male writers—The curious point
to be taken is that the stories were devised or adapted from
ancient originals, for the amusement not of children but of
adults. The consequence is that, although the characters and
the background belong superficially to fairy-tales, most of
them are too sophisticated for children.[14]

It is therefore evident that Perrault, like many of his contemporaries, did not write his famous tales for children alone,
but also, or perhaps mainly, for the pleasure of his friends. It
seems that the following quotation about his contemporary
Mlle l'Héritier also applies to Perrault himself: "Mademoiselle l'Héritier wrote for the amusement of her friends and
all of her writings bear the imprint of her 'salon wit.'"[15]

The Function of the Duality of the Intended Audience

Perrault had to emphasize the fact that children were the
official audience of his work because this was a condition for
its acceptance by high society. Even scholars who see the text
as meant primarily for children agree that at least part of it is
aimed at adults, as Soriano, for example, says: "It is always
addressed to an audience of children, no doubt, but at the
same time allowing a wink in the direction of the adult."[16]
Whether the text was intended entirely for adults or only
partially so, there is no disagreement that the ironic and satirical tone of the text, particularly as it is expressed in the
tragic ending of the tale, is meant for adults, and not for children. By means of the tragic ending, Perrault created a satire
about the city gentleman who does not hesitate to take advantage of the poor village girl. The text's satirical nature depends primarily on the moral, which comes at the end. From
this ending it is made clear that the wolf is not a real wolf,
but rather represents all sorts of people whom an innocent
village girl must beware of:

Who does not know that these gentle wolves
Are of all such creatures the most dangerous.[17]

The depiction of the gentleman abusing the innocent village girl is further strengthened in the text by the erotic elements that accompany her description: her beauty, the color red which is her symbol, and of course the erotic bed scene, in which she is surprised to discover what "grandmother" looks like in bed, after the latter asks her to undress and to come lie with her: "Little Red Riding Hood took off her cloak, but when she climbed up on the bed she was astonished to see how her grandmother looked in her nightgown."[18] It is clear that the erotic aspect encourages the reading of the text as the story of a gentleman exploiting the innocence of a village girl and enjoying her charms, rather than simply as the story of a little girl who is devoured by a wolf.

The child concept of Perrault's day provided the background for *Les Contes* and the mask necessary for their acceptance by the literary elite. However, in addition to the changes that later took place in the conception of the child, the nature of the texts meant for him also changed, as well as in the way the child himself was depicted in different texts. These changes were among the factors causing the transformation of "Little Red Riding Hood" from Perrault's version to the later one that the Brothers Grimm collected and committed to writing—along with their own revisions and alterations—a century later.

Differences between Versions of "Little Red Riding Hood": Perrault vs. the Brothers Grimm

Folktale research has dealt at length with the differences between the tales of Perrault and different versions of tales similar to his published by the Brothers Grimm. Scholars are divided regarding the origins of the texts and their degree of "originality," accounting for the similarities and differences in them by various methods. Some explain them using the historic-geographic method, while others prefer to look at cross-cultural relationships[19] or the crossover from one national culture to another.[20] Other researchers deny the possibility of a direct connection between Perrault's tales and those of the Brothers Grimm, attributing the similarities and differences to the intermediary influences of Tieck, whom the Brothers Grimm refer to in their commentary on "Little Red Riding Hood": "Perrault's 'Little Red Riding Hood' which Tieck elegantly reworked in his romantic drama . . ."[21]

Rather than getting involved in this complex argument, or refuting the conclusions of this or that researcher, I would like to propose an alternative way of accounting for the differences between Perrault's version and that of the Brothers Grimm: One could also regard the differences between the two as the result of the different perceptions of the concept of childhood which prevailed in each of the two periods in question, thereby yielding differing assumptions concerning the intended audience and the manner in which the child is presented in the texts.

In the hundred years that had passed since Perrault's days, a revolutionary change had taken place in the child concept. The "amusement" perception of the child was replaced in the Grimm Brothers' day by an "educational" perception which gave primary importance to a new and heretofore unheard of concept: that of educating the child. Consequently, an educational system evolved, the needs of which largely dictated both the nature of works written for children, and above all the literary models then dominating the literary scene.

The Brothers Grimm, like other writers of the mid-nineteenth century, adopted the new image of the child, stressing his straightforwardness and the ability, uniquely his, to look at the world in a special way. They expressed this view in the introduction to *Kinder- und Hausmärchen*, claiming to transmit the text from the child's point of view: "There runs throughout these narratives that quality of purity which makes children appear to us so wonderful and happy. The tales have, so to speak, the selfsame shining eyes open as far as they can possibly be while the rest of the body is still fragile, weak and unskilled for earthly labor."[22]

However, in contradistinction to Perrault, whose official audience was the child, the Brothers Grimm did not intend their text for children at first, although the book's title indicates the origin of the texts: they were collected from household members—maidservants—and children. The tales were first intended for adult members of the literary elite, for the accepted literary tastes—a return to the primary sources and to nature were in vogue—enabled them to enjoy such texts. The Brothers Grimm did not have the option of directing their works to adults and children at one and the same time, for according to the current child concept, the child was seen as an entity distinct from the adult, with different needs and capabilities of understanding. In order nevertheless to enable children to read their tales, the Brothers Grimm thought it necessary to revise them, gearing them to a child's level of understanding, particularly from a stylistic point of view. This they did starting with the second edition, in the introduction to which they outlined the principles that guided them in their endeavor to render the texts suitable for children.

In spite of this, the Brothers Grimm still recognized the possibility that there would be parents who would deem the book inappropriate for their children, forbidding them to read it: "Therefore we have taken care to leave out of this new edition expressions which were not suitable for children. Yet there may be objections. One or another parent may find material embarrassing or offensive, so that they would not be comfortable putting the book into the hands of children. In such well-founded individual cases, the parents have an easy choice to make."[23] In this introduction, two new ideas are evident which apparently were a major part of the changes that occurred in the text since Perrault's time. As stated above, one idea expressed the supposition that the child is an entity distinct from the adult. The other expressed the belief that the adult is responsible for satisfying the child's needs, and that the latter must be under his direct and constant supervision.

The differences between the versions of Perrault and the Brothers Grimm thus consist of more than just different assumptions about the audience and the fact that in the Grimm text there is no trace of the protracted game which Perrault played with his audience. Another striking difference between the texts is the distinctive way the child and everything connected with him is presented in each. In the Grimm version of "Little Red Riding Hood" the two beliefs that were combined in the child concept of the time are evident, particularly in the portrayal of intrafamilial relations, the simple honesty of the child, and the need to guide and instruct him. These viewpoints will be treated here through an examination of the differing tones of the two texts, and their divergent endings, as well as less salient differences.

Differences in Tone and Ending

As many scholars have asserted, the most salient differences between Perrault and the Brothers Grimm lie in the tone of the texts, ironic versus naive, and in the ending, happy versus tragic.

It seems that the difference in tone is due to the differing intentions of the authors. Whereas Perrault used satire and irony to address the literary elite, the Brothers Grimm made a noticeable effort to preserve the illusion of the naive narrator, considered crucial to the "authenticity" of the text. Although they freely admitted reworking the oral text—the written version is probably very different from it and closer to Tieck's,[24]—they still took pains to keep intact the naive character of the narrator, mainly by preserving the naive tone.

The other striking difference is, as noted earlier, the ending. In Perrault's version, the story ends when the wolf devours the girl, followed by a moral in rhyming verse. The Grimm version, on the other hand, offers two alternative endings, the common denominator between them being that the girl is not harmed in the end. In the first alternative, she is punished—the grandmother and the girl are at first devoured by the wolf, but are later rescued by the hunter, who also kills the wolf; however in the second alternative the wolf is drowned before it has a chance to harm the girl or her grandmother.

The drastic change in the nature of the tale's ending, completely changing its significance, raises the question why there was the need to insert such an ending at all, apart from the question of whether or not it was organic to the text.[25] In other words, what function did the addition of this ending to the text serve?

It is clear that turning the tragic ending into a happy one was first and foremost the result of the need to fit the story into the pattern of the folktale. The happy ending is considered an indispensable component of the folktale; it can be said to be a distinctive feature which differentiates folktales from literary tales. Hence the Brothers Grimm, or the anonymous narrator who added the happy ending (from the point of view of the function of the ending it is immaterial who was responsible for the addition, rather it is important to understand why it was necessary) could not deviate from the pattern, unlike Perrault, who intentionally departed from it at decisive points in the story. However, the selection of this specific ending has implications above and beyond the folktale pattern, reflecting also the educational views of the day. According to these views, the child must derive a moral lesson from every event, experience, or story to which he is exposed. Punishment was itself perceived as an integral part of the educational process—and in this respect the "Red Riding Hood" of the Brothers Grimm was no different. It is interesting to note that the Brothers Grimm themselves were pleased with the "educational" nature of the tales, seeing it as further proof that the text was suitable for children.[26]

Bolte and Polívka[27] suggest that this specific ending was chosen because it already existed in the folktale inventory in the tale "The Wolf and the Seven Young Kids." Because the wolf's role as protagonist is common to both tales, its choice presented a "natural" and ready-made solution. Even if we accept this explanation, it does not contradict the one offered above. Moreover, we must not ignore the fact that in the tale "The Wolf and the Seven Young Kids" the element of learning a lesson is absent. This is a feature which exists only in the text of "Red Riding Hood," which strengthens the assumptions made about the text regarding the education of the child and the process of reward and punishment.

This difference between the versions of Perrault and the Brothers Grimm changed not only the ending of the text, but also its meaning and moral. Unlike Perrault's Little Red Riding Hood, the Grimms' Little Red Riding Hood has the opportunity to learn a lesson, and indeed avails herself of the opportunity. Whereas Perrault's moral emphasizes the wolf, thereby pointing to the gentleman from the city, the moral of the Brothers Grimm's version stresses Little Red Riding Hood's learning a lesson. Thus the tale was transformed from a satire to a tale about reward and punishment and learning a lesson.

The difference in emphasis in the two versions and in their general significance explains the total omission of the erotic scene and the erotic elements from the Grimm version, and was probably also the reason for some less obvious changes. In Perrault's version there are only slight hints as to the relationship between family members, while in the Grimm version they are quite explicit. Examples include the grandmother's love for the girl, the mother's feeling of respnsibility for the grandmother, and the girl's love for her grandmother.

While in Perrault's version the grandmother's love for the girl is not mentioned at all, in the Grimm version her love for Little Red Riding Hood is boundless, and she makes her the red hood as a symbol of her love. Hence the hood serves a different function in each of the two versions: for Perrault it symbolizes the girl's eroticism, whereas for the Brothers Grimm it is an expression of the grandmother's deep love.

Perrault	*The Brothers Grimm*
The good woman made her a little red hood, which became her so well that everywhere she went by the name of Little Red Riding Hood.[28]	But it was her grandmother who loved her most. She could never give the child enough. One time she made her a present, a small, red velvet cap, and since it was so becoming and the maiden insisted on always wearing it, she was called Little Red Cap.[29]

In the Grimm version, the mother's feeling of responsibility for the grandmother is far greater than in Perrault's version. Whereas in Perrault's, the girl is sent to the grandmother's house because the mother has baked flat cakes and because she has heard that the grandmother is sick, in the Grimm version the mother has precise knowledge of the grandmother's condition, and consequently sends the girl to help her. In the Grimm version family ties are much stronger than in Perrault's:

Perrault	*The Brothers Grimm*
One day her mother, who had just made and baked some cakes, said to her: "Go and see how your grandmother is, for I have been told that she is ill. Take her a cake and this little pot of butter."[30]	One day her mother said to her, "Come, Little Red Cap, take this piece of cake and bottle of wine and bring them to your grandmother. She's sick and weak, and this will strengthen her."[31]

The bond between the girl and her grandmother is also less haphazard in the Grimm version. In Perrault's version, the girl picks flowers for her own enjoyment alone, while in the Grimm version she picks them to bring as a gift to her grandmother:

Perrault	*The Brothers Grimm*
. . . and the little girl continued on her way by the	Little Red Cap looked around and saw how the rays of the

longer road. As she went she amused herself by gathering nuts, running after the butterflies, and making nosegays of the wild flowers which she found.[32]

sun were dancing through the trees back and forth and how the woods were full of beautiful flowers. So she thought to herself, If I bring Grandmother a bunch of fresh flowers, she'd certainly like that.[33]

Family ties and the great amount of attention paid to children—a phenomenon which was nonexistent in Perrault's time[34]—took on a central importance in the century following Perrault, and were apparently also among the reasons for the discrepancy between the texts in the presentation of family ties. Similarly, different assumptions regarding the rearing of children are discernible in the two versions.

In Perrault's day there was no educational system in the modern sense of the term, nor was the need for the systematic education of the child recognized. In the time of the Brothers Grimm, on the other hand, not only was an educational system already established, but it was seen as an essential condition for the normal development of the child, and as part of the adult's responsibility toward him. Views about children's education are expressed in the Grimm version first and foremost in the directions which the mother gives the little girl about how she should conduct herself at her grandmother's house, directions which are totally absent from the Perrault version. The mother instructs the girl to behave nicely: "And when you enter her room, don't forget to say good morning, and don't go peeping in all the corners."[35] She admonishes her not to turn off the path: "Get an early start, before it becomes hot, and when you're out in the woods, be nice and good and don't stray from the path, otherwise you'll fall and break the glass, and your grandmother will get nothing."[36]

The girl does not obey, and is therefore punished. However, she ultimately learns her lesson. What is even more important from an educational standpoint is the alternative ending of the text, which furnishes proof that the lesson has indeed been learned: "Meanwhile, Little Red Cap thought to herself, Never again will you stray from the path by yourself and go into the forest when your mother has forbidden it."[37]

Although the notion that adults are duty-bound to guide their children and that they are responsible for the behavior of the latter did not yet exist in Perrault's time, it became the basis for the mother-daughter relationship in the Grimm version. Moreover, the school, an institution lacking in Perrault's day, became not just a recognized institution, but a hated one. In the version of the Grimm Brothers, when the wolf encounters Little Red Riding Hood in the woods, he says something that could not have appeared in Perrault's version: she looks as sad as if she were going to school: "You march along as if you were going straight to school."[38]

In the century following Perrault's lifetime, the concept of children's education took definite shape. This new concept, which struck deep roots in the educational system developed during the same period, lent a great deal of importance to children's reading material, thus creating an intellectual climate suitable for the composition of an official children's literature. Henceforth the prevalent educational concept has been largely responsible for the norms governing writing for children, and to it are attributable the changes that have occurred in twentieth-century adaptations of "Little Red Riding Hood."

Modern Adaptations of "Little Red Riding Hood"

The perception of children's literature as an educational tool of the first order, stressing that reading materials for children must serve educational goals, has remained basically unchanged from the nineteenth century until our own time. At the basis of official children's literature today is the assumption that reading materials for children must be suitable from an educational standpoint, and must contribute to their development. Nevertheless, a change has taken place since the nineteenth century in the educational views regarding the child's needs and his comprehension capabilities. Paralleling the change in these perceptions, a change has taken place in the nature of the norms of writing for children. So, for instance, folktales were kept from children at the beginning of the nineteenth century because it was feared that literature dealing with fantasy would corrupt the child. The educational establishment in those days preferred "realistic" texts, in which the featured images were death and disease.[39] Folktales were preserved in non-canonical literature, commonly in the form of chapbooks. However, with the changes that came about in the concept of education since the second half of the nineteenth century, fantastic literature also underwent a rehabilitation. Fantasy was no longer considered harmful, but was rather seen as an essential factor in the child's normal development. Consequently, there began to appear numerous editions of folktales which were adapted in various ways, mainly in an attempt to infuse them with instructive morals. Since that time folktales have become regularly featured on the children's Western literature shelf, and have been published in many editions. The number of different editions of the Grimm tales for children in English, French, German, and Hebrew is in the tens, if not hundreds, appearing in editions differing greatly from each other. However, all the versions of the children's folktales have a common denominator: behind them stand various views on the child and his educational needs. Even when a complete and precise edition of the original version of the Grimm tales for children comes out, its appearance is generally explained not only by the classical status of the text, but also using a psychological argument, as there are psychologists who attach importance to the child's full acquaintance with the text, even seeing it as a requisite part of his emotional development.[40]

In contrast to this, in a large number of children's editions it is assumed that the original text of the Brothers Grimm is beyond the comprehension level of the child, revealing too much of "reality" to him. There is a great deal of correspondence between these two views and the varied adaptations of children's folktales. The differences between them correspond to the different ways of treating these two matters.

In order to discuss the nature of the modern adaptations of "Little Red Riding Hood" for children, three versions have been selected as samples, enabling us to learn about the norms that guide the reworking of folktales for children, and about the procedures involved in such adaptations. The versions chosen are Modern Promotions (n.d.), Puppet Book, 1970; [41] and A Pop-Up Book (n.d.).

The Comprehension Capacity of the Child and Possibilities of "Exposure"

Assumptions regarding the child's comprehension capacity are expressed in the texts first and foremost in the tone of the story. Unlike the naive tone typical of the Grimms' style, adaptations for children are characterized by an authoritative, condescending tone. This is particularly obvious at the points in the story where the narrator fears that the child may not understand on his own. So, for example, the narrator of the Puppet edition explains the little girl's name: "That is exactly why she was called Little Red Riding Hood." In this adaptation, even the wolf's slyness is explained to the audience, because it is assumed that the child cannot figure this out for himself: "The crafty old wolf really knew where grandmother lived. He also knew that the path across the meadow was the shortest way to reach grandmother's house."

The adaptor of the Pop-Up edition, on the other hand, is afraid that the child will not be able to understand by himself that the wolf disguised himself as the grandmother, and therefore explains, "She was surprised to see her granny in bed (you see, she thought the wolf was her granny)."

However, the connection between the principles of adaptation and the adaptors' assumptions are most obvious in the various solutions which they propose for any bit of information which is considered unpleasant, especially the "violent" scenes existing in the original. This is the reason that in the Modern Promotion version the grandmother is not sick, it being merely implied that she is "not well," and in the Pop-Up edition, the grandmother's condition is not mentioned at all, the mother simply suggesting to the girl that she go visit her: "Why don't you go and visit Granny—I'm sure she would be pleased to see you."

The most interesting thing in the adaptations of "Little Red Riding Hood" for children is the manner in which the issue of "violence" is treated, as this is considered the least appropriate information for children. The adaptor of the Puppet edition is the most extreme, completely doing away with the potentially violent scene, making sure that even the wolf escapes unscathed: "When the wolf saw the hunter's long rifle, he had a change of mind. Now it was his turn to be frightened. He had time for just one yelp before running out of the house as quickly as he could." Other adaptors, however, elect to punish the wolf, apparently so as to see poetic justice done. Nevertheless, they omit the violent scenes between the wolf, the grandmother, and the girl. In the Puppet edition, the grandmother hides in the closet, escaping harm, and the girl is rescued before the wolf has a chance to devour her. "But grandmother saw the wolf too! She dashed into her clothes closet and locked the door behind her, doing it so quickly that the wolf hardly knew what was happening. At that moment a hunter passed the house. He heard Little Red Riding Hood's frightened scream and burst open the door." The adaptor of the Pop-Up edition provides a similar solution: "Fortunately, at that moment, the forester arrived. He ran inside and was just in time to rescue the little girl. Red Riding Hood breathed a sigh of relief when she realized what a narrow escape she had had."

The assumption that a text for children must not be injurious to the child's development, but on the contrary must justify its existence by contributing to that development, is expressed not only in global additions or omissions, but also in minor details, such as what items Little Red Riding Hood brings to her grandmother. Whereas in the original text she brings her cake and wine, every adaptation has her bringing something else, depending on the adaptor's views about what is best for the child. So, for instance, the adaptor of the Puppet edition disapproves of alcohol, and therefore has

Little Red Riding Hood bring fruit, rather than wine: "One day her mother packed a basket with cake and fruit." In the eyes of the adaptor of the Modern Promotion edition, cake is also undesirable for the child (as representing sweets), and hence it is replaced with nutritious foods, bread and honey: "One day her mother told her to take a basket of bread and honey to her grandmother who was sick." In the Puppet edition the baked goods disappear altogether, and the victory party is celebrated with milk alone: "They were all so happy that they decided to have a party then and there. Grandmother served glasses of milk to her visitors . . ."

This brief survey of three adaptations of "Little Red Riding Hood" from among hundreds testifies to the deep relationship between the cultural concept of the child and the way in which that culture produces texts for children, a connection which on certain occasions has provided material for parodies of folktales. If we were to reconstruct a hypothetical history of children's literature, it is safe to assume that if the literary establishment at the beginning of the nineteenth century had accepted folktales, it would have seen to it that death, violence, and cruelty—common themes in the literature of the time—were stressed in children's folktales, unlike adaptations from the second half of the nineteenth and the twentieth centuries.

Children's literature in the nineteenth and twentieth centuries is therefore grouped under the same entry. But when the texts under that entry are examined, it becomes clear that there are great differences between them. What determines their nature is not their official entry, but rather the way in which the concept of the child is perceived in a given society, a concept which is in large part responsible for the specific application of this entry in every period.

Notes

1. J. R. Townsend, *Written for Children* (London: Penguin, 1977), 17.

2. P. Ariès, *Centuries of Childhood* (New York: Vintage, 1962).

3. I. Weber-Kellermann, *Die Kindheit: Eine Kulturgeschichte* (Frankfurt a/M.: Insel Verlag, 1979); M.-L. Plessen and P. von Zahn, *Zwei Jahrtausende Kindheit* (Köln: VSG, 1979).

4. For an exhaustive discussion about this aspect, see Ariès, *Centuries of Childhood*, 50–61; Plessen and von Zahn, *Zwei Jahrtausende Kindheit*.

5. Quoted in Ariès, *Centuries of Childhood*, 131.

6. Ibid., 95–98.

7. M. Soriano, *Les Contes de Perrault* (Paris: Gallimard, 1968), 38.

8. Ibid., 69.

9. Ibid., 25.

10. Ibid., 66–67.

11. Ibid., 31.

12. Gilbert Rouger, ed., *Contes de Perrault* (Paris: Garnier, 1967–1972), 115. Italics are mine.

13. Soriano, 154–155.

14. P. Muir, *English Children's Books* (New York: Fredrick A. Praeger, 1969), 36.

15. Soriano, 65.

16. Ibid., 155.

17. Rouger, *Contes de Perrault*, 115.

18. Ibid., 114–115.

19. J. Bolte and G. Polívka, *Anmerkungen zu den Kinder- und Hausmärchen der Brüder Grimm*, vol. 4 (Hildesheim: Georg Olms, 1963 reprint of 1913 edition), 261–277.

20. H. V. Velten, "The Influence of Charles Perrault's Contes de ma Mère l'Oie on German Folklore," *Germanic Review* 5 (1930), 4–18.

21. Brüder Grimm, *Kinder- und Hausmärchen*, vol. 3 (Stuttgart: Reclam, 1890), 59.

22. Ibid., 16.

23. Ibid., 17.

24. R. Hagen, "Perraults Märchen und die Brüder Grimm," *Zeitschrift für Deutsche Philologie* 74 (1955), 392–410.

25. On this question see Velten, "The Influence of Charles Perrault's Contes de ma Mère l'Oie."

26. See their introduction to the *Kinder- und Hausmärchen*, 17.

27. Bolte and Polívka, *Anmerkungen*, vol. 1, 234–237.

28. Rouger, *Contes de Perrault*, 113.

29. Brüder Grimm, *Kinder- und Hausmärchen*, 156–157.

30. Rouger, *Contes de Perrault,* 113.

31. Brüder Grimm, *Kinder- und Hausmärchen,* 157.

32. Rouger, *Contes de Perrault,* 114.

33. Brüder Grimm, *Kinder- und Hausmärchen,* 158.

34. For a discussion of the development of the nuclear family, see Ariès, *Centuries of Childhood,* 339–407.

35. Brüder Grimm, *Kinder- und Hausmärchen,* 157.

36. Ibid.

37. Ibid., 159.

38. Ibid., 157–158.

39. For a detailed discussion on this matter, see Ariès, *Centuries of Childhood,* chs. 2–4.

40. B. Bettelheim, *The Uses of Enchantment* (New York: Knopf, 1976).

41. No pagination for the Puppet Book or A Pop-Up Book versions.

Fairy Tale and Dream:
"Little Red Riding Hood"

Another way of looking at "Little Red Riding Hood" from the perspective of childhood is provided by psychoanalytic theory. According to this theory, infantile experience and conditioning in a given culture are likely to be reflected in that culture's projective systems, which include dreams and folktales. If one accepts this premise, then it becomes possible to read back from projective material, such as fairy tales, to critical infantile thought and behavior.

Among the many psychoanalysts who have sought to explicate the purported unconscious content of fairy tales, none was more prolific and insightful than Géza Róheim (1891–1953). Born in Hungary, Róheim was first trained in folklore and ethnography. After discovering Freud's work in psychoanalysis, Róheim became an enthusiastic member of Freud's group of disciples, and he was perhaps one of the first to seek to apply psychoanalytic theory to nonwestern cultures. Thanks to financial support from Princess Marie Bonaparte, another Freudian follower, Róheim carried out fieldwork in Somaliland, Central Australia, and Normanby Island in Melanesia. Despite his fieldwork overseas, Róheim never lost interest in European folklore, especially folktales. In his numerous analyses of European tales, Róheim, unlike most psychoanalysts, utilized versions other than the Grimm text, a reflection of his initial training in folklore.

Róheim's sometimes brilliant analyses of specific folktales have received almost no attention from folklorists or

Reprinted from *The Psychoanalytic Study of the Child* 8 (1953), 394–403; only 394–398 have been reprinted here.

psychoanalysts. One reason is that Róheim's style of data presentation is often undisciplined. It is a combination of apparent free association and leaps in thought. Typically, he makes authoritative pronouncements without adequate supporting data. Róheim also had pet theories, one of which was the dream origin of myth and folktale. In his 1953 book *The Gates of the Dream* and in a series of posthumously published analyses of individual tales, Róheim tried to demonstrate the validity of his dream origin theory. One obvious difficulty with Róheim's dream origin theory is that it is by no means clear why dreams produce folktales. It is just as likely that folktales produce dreams. Dreams are culture-bound, and one could certainly argue that an individual's dreams are partly determined by the folktales to which that individual has been exposed. All one can state with any certainty is that there may be parallels in structure and content between the dreams and folktales of a given culture, but that says nothing about either dreams or folktales being logically or psychologically prior to one another.

In the following brief essay, Róheim summarizes his dream origin theory, then applies his theory to "Little Red Riding Hood," making some astute observations about the unconscious content of the tale.

The following fairy tale is analyzed in terms of a new view of mythology and the folk tale. The main stream of the argument is discussed extensively in my book, *The Gates of the Dream* (1953), and in many of my other papers.[1] To put this theory briefly: It seems that dreams and myths are not merely similar but that a large part of mythology is actually derived from dreams. In other words, we can not only apply the standard technique of dream interpretation in analyzing a fairy tale but actually can think of tales and myths as having arisen from a dream, which a person dreamed and then told to others, who retold it again, perhaps elaborated in accord with their own dreams.

"Little Red Riding Hood"

In Grimm's version (no. 26) Rotkäppchen is told by her mother to take a slice of cake and a bottle of wine to her sick grandmother. She is warned against dallying on the way; she is to go straight to grandmother and say "Good morning" like a good little girl. She meets the wolf and, not knowing what an evil character she is talking to, they start a conversation. The wolf finds out all about her and her grandmother. While she is gathering flowers, the wolf runs to the grandmother's house, swallows the grandmother and dresses up in her clothes.

The wolf lies down on the bed and, when the little girl arrives, he pretends that he is the grandmother. The child approaches the bed and is surprised when nobody answers her "Good morning." "Grandmother, why do you have such big ears?" she asks.

"So I can hear what you are saying."

"Why do you have such big eyes?"

"Because I want to see you."

"Why do you have such a big mouth?"

"Because I want to eat you."

And the wolf jumped out of bed and swallowed Rotkäppchen.

The wolf fell asleep after this meal and started to snore. A hunter heard his snore; fearing the wolf may have eaten the grandmother, he did not shoot the wolf, but instead took a pair of scissors to open the stomach of the sleeping wolf. After a few cuts he saw the shining red cap and out came the little girl. A few more cuts and the grandmother came out, too. Rotkäppchen filled the inside of the wolf with stones and *when he awoke* he wanted to run away but the heavy stones pulled him down and he collapsed and was dead. Rotkäppchen, however, had learned her lesson and will henceforth obey her mother.

To go on sleeping after its stomach has been cut open several times is quite an achievement, even for a folktale wolf. We can only understand this if we assume that the wolf, the grandmother, and the little girl are essentially the same person.

In the second version recorded by Grimm the wolf does not swallow either the child or the grandmother but pretends to be Rotkäppchen and asks the grandmother to let it come in. The grandmother keeps the door closed and the wolf sits on the roof, waiting for the moment *when it gets dark* and it can swallow Rotkäppchen. The grandmother puts water in which she had boiled sausages in a trough. The smell of the sausages tempts the wolf, he keeps sniffing, moving closer and closer, till he falls from the roof straight into the boiling water and is drowned.

In another German version the wolf calls himself a doctor and tells Rotkäppchen to pick various healing herbs for her grandmother. All of these are named after the wolf (*Wolfswurz, Wolfsmilch,* etc.) and all are poisonous.[2]

To accuse such an innocent person as Little Red Riding Hood of being no better than the wolf seems far-fetched. However, in a French story of Valencay[3] we find the Chaperon Rouge eating its grandmother's breasts, drinking its grandmother's blood. In the Haute Bretagne story the redbreast sings:

> Tu bois le sang de ta grandmère, ma petit fille
> Tu bois le sang de ta grandmère.[4]

If we assume that all three protagonists of the story are one and the same person, the emphasis must be placed on the sleeping wolf. Red Riding Hood is swallowed into her own "sleep-womb," which is at the same time the inside of her mother. The hunter would then be correctly interpreted as the father figure, as a rival for the inside (or breast) of the mother.[5] In one of the German versions (Southern Tyrol) it is the father who chops the wolf's head off.[6]

The problem becomes more complicated if we consider Perrault's version and some other French parallels. Here the story has no happy ending, the wolf eats the Chaperon Rouge.[7] In the story as told in Haute Bretagne[8] and in Valencay[9] and as in Perrault, the wolf devours the little girl. In a Swedish ballad the girl is supposed to stay awake all night to keep vigil over a corpse. She cries: "Dear wolf do not bite me, I give you my silk shirt." But the wolf will have nothing less than her blood. She climbs a tree, the wolf is after her. The girl screams in agony, her lover hears it, but he arrives too late; what is left of her is only a bleeding arm.[10]

We notice that the emphasis is being gradually shifted, the wolf becomes a wolf in the popular American sense of the word. The *moralité* added to Perrault's story makes this quite clear. Little girls, especially pretty ones, should avoid talking to strangers, that is, to wolves who pretend to be nice and courteous. In the Valencay story we have the devil instead of the wolf. In the story as told at Nievre it is a werewolf (*loup-garou*), the typical symbol of male aggression and sexuality.[11] This double meaning of the wolf-symbol explains the stories that end in disaster; they are written from a pedagogical angle.

In one of the French versions the ambisexuality of the heroine is emphasized. In the story as told at Tourangelle, the heroine is called Fillon-Fillette, that is, half girl, half boy. Instead of the wolf we have an ugly man (or the devil) with a sow on a string.[12] Since there is nothing in the plot to explain the bisexual character of the heroine, we can only assume that this trait has been displaced from the ogre to the heroine. In the case of the ogre, we have an original "swallowing" or "sleep-womb" and superimposed on this the werewolf or the male as aggressor. Looking at the whole thing from the point of view of my dream theory, that is, the dreamer or sleeper as being in his own body, we can understand the underlying identity of the nice little girl and the terrible wolf.

In some of the French stories the girl escapes by telling the wolf that she has to go out for a minute to defecate.[13] In one story the devil falls into the water and, giving chase to Jeannette, he tells his sow to lap up the river, but the sow fails and they both drown.[14] In one of the Grimms' versions the wolf, attracted by the smell of sausages, falls off the roof into the boiling water. We assume that the dreamer awakes owing to some somatic pressure such as thirst, hunger, or the need to defecate. When the sleeping wolf's inside is filled with stones and it goes on sleeping, the only way we can understand this is if we assume that the sleeper really ought to have a bowel movement (stones in the intestines) but this is in conflict with the desire to go on sleeping. As for the motive of hunger or orality it is amply represented (1) by the food the child is supposed to bring to its grandmother, (2) by the child eating the grandmother, (3) the wolf eating both grandmother and grandchild.

The whole story is not unlike the initiation of witches at Normanby Island. The young witch or candidate is supposed to disappear in the mouth of the old witch (her mother, or grandmother) and to come out through the vagina. They add that it is really the door of a house, but she imagines it is a mouth. The only plausible explanation for this is a dream in which the door symbolizes body orifices.

If we apply Lewin's concept of the "oral triad" (1950) to this story everything seems to work out quite nicely. We have the "wish to eat" (the bottle of wine and the cake carried by the girl to the grandmother), sleep (grandmother inside wolf, Riding Hood inside wolf), and the wish to be devoured. However, this theory fails to account for several important traits of the story. It does not account for the dreamer's awakening, which is caused by hunger or thirst (orality) or excremental pressure. I assume that we have a dream that represents sleep (return to the inside, or womb). Ferenczi[15] has said that in the oral stage the tooth is the tool used by the infant for boring itself back into the womb. This means that aggression is combined with regression and it follows that the idea of being swallowed, being eaten, is the talio aspect of this aggression. The cannibal child creates a cannibal mother. This also explains a theme that occurs in most of these stories. In the Grimm story it is expressed in the dialogue:

"O Grandmother why do you have such big ears?"

"In order that I can hear you better."

"Grandmother, why do you have such big eyes?"

"In order to see you better."

"Why such big hands?"

"To grab you," etc.

"Why such a big mouth?"

"To eat you."

The big eyes mean the same thing as the big mouth—the rest of the details are just added in folk tales. The infant eats the breast, the infant eats and sees, and desires and is, therefore, the original aggressor.[16] In reverse form ogres are not only cannibals but frequently have big eyes.

The father imago is clearly recognizable as the rival for the inside of the mother.[17] In other words, the oedipus complex goes back to the oral and to the uterine regressive organization.

In a Transylvanian Gypsy story an old grandfather lives in a hut with his grandchildren. The wolf tells the children that the grandfather has sent him with a cake and they open the door for him. He jumps in, eats them all, and then he finds a big bottle of brandy which he drinks. Consequently he falls asleep and starts snoring. Grandfather comes home, opens the wolf's stomach with his knife (penis), and the children jump out. The grandfather then hides the children. He took dry lime, filled the wolf's stomach with it, and then he sewed it together so that it was closed. The wolf awoke, felt thirsty, ran to the brook, and drank a lot of water. The lime in its inside was now burning so that the wolf burst and died.[18] Here the whole story is displaced to the male. The grandfather cuts the children out of the "sleep-womb." The wolf is thirsty; that is, the sleeper is thirsty or hungry or wants to defecate. Somatic pressure and the fantasy of the father imago compel the sleeper to leave the womb. Some people awaken at a certain time without an alarm clock; duty, the superego, the father imago, will not let them continue to sleep. The old-style mythological commonplace of the red hood symbolizing the sun or the dawn[19] should not be discarded as long as we know that the light enters the picture, not as a cosmic phenomenon, but as the moment of awakening.

Notes

1. G. Róheim, "The Story of the Light that Disappeared," *Samiksa* 1 (1948); "The Panic of the Gods," *Psychoanalytic Quarterly* 21 (1952); "The Evil Eye," *American Imago* 9 (1952), also in *The Yearbook of Psychoanalysis* 9 (New York: International Universities Press, 1953); "The Wolf and the Seven Kids," *Psychoanalytic Quarterly* 22 (1953); "Dame Holle or Dream and Folk Tale," in Robert Lindner, ed., *Explorations in Psychoanalysis: Essays in Honor of Theodor Reik* (New York: Julian Press, 1953); "The Language of the Birds," *American Imago* 10 (1953); *Hungarian and Vogul Mythology* (New York: American Ethnological Society, 1954).

2. L. Bechstein, *Märchenbuch* (Leipzig: Hesse und Becker Verlag, n.d.). Cf. also *Archiv für Geschichte und Altertumskunde von Oberfranken* 22 (1859), 229–232.

3. *Melusine* 6 (1892–1893), 237–238.

4. *Melusine* 3 (1886–1887), 397.

5. B. D. Lewin, "Phobic Symptoms and Dream Interpretation," *Psychoanalytic Quarterly* 21.

6. J. Bolte and G. Polivka, *Anmerkungen zu den Kinder- und Hausmärchen* (Leipzig, 1913).

7. A. Lang, *Perrault's Popular Tales* (Oxford, 1888).

8. *Melusine* 3 (1886–1887), 397.

9. *Melusine* 6 (1892–1893), 237–238.

10. The Grimms' notes to the story. Quoted from E. G. Geijer and A. A. Afzelius, *Svenska folk-visor från forntiden*, vol. 3 (Stockholm, 1818), 68–69.

11. *Melusine* 3 (1886–1887), 428–429.

12. *Melusine* 9 (1898–1899), 90–91.

13. *Melusine* 3 (1886–1887), 428–429; *Melusine* 6 (1892–1893), 237–238.

14. *Melusine* 9 (1898–1899), 90.

15. Sandor Ferenczi, *Thalassa: A Theory of Genitality* (New York: The Psychoanalytic Quarterly, Inc., 1938; first published in German as *Versuch einer Genitaltheorie*, Leipzig: Internationaler Psychoanalytischer Verlag, 1924). .

16. E. Bergler, *The Basic Neurosis* (New York: Grune & Stratton, 1949).

17. B. D. Lewin, "Phobic Symptoms."

18. H. Wlislocki, *Märchen und Sagen Transsilvanischer Zigeuner* (Berlin: Nicolai, 1886).

19. L. Frobenius, *Zeitalter des Sonnengottes* (Berlin: Reimer, 1904).

Little Red Cap and the Pubertal Girl

One reason folklorists and others are suspicious of psychoanalytic interpretations of fairy tales is that different psychoanalysts propose entirely different interpretations of the
same fairy tales. In theory, if a method of analysis were truly
valid, so it is argued, then the results of such a method ought
to be replicable. The fact that there may be as many different
psychoanalytic readings of a particular fairy tale as there are
psychoanalysts attempting such readings does not tend to
inspire confidence in the approach.

Bruno Bettelheim, a leading psychoanalyst, devoted an
entire book, *The Uses of Enchantment* (1976), to explicat-
ing European fairy tales from a psychoanalytic viewpoint.
His interesting discussion of "Little Red Riding Hood" differs markedly from the analysis offered by Róheim. Whereas
Róheim tended to emphasize infantile *oral* characteristics
of the tale, Bettelheim draws attention to pubertal *genital*
features of the same tale. The two interpretations are not
necessarily mutually exclusive. A tale might reflect both a
baby's picture of parents and an adolescent's struggle with
the same parents at a later period in life. Or perhaps both
interpretations are incorrect, being little more than psychoanalysts' own subjective associations to "Little Red Riding
Hood." Readers must decide for themselves as to the plau-
sibility of Róheim's and Bettelheim's psychoanalytic interpretations of the tale.

Other psychoanalytic readings of "Little Red Riding Hood"
include Erich Fromm, *The Forgotten Language* (New York:

Grove Press, 1951), 235–241; Lilla Veszy-Wagner, "Little Red Riding Hoods on the Couch," *Psychoanalytic Forum* 1 (1966), 400–415; and Carl-Heinz Mallet, *Fairy Tales and Children* (New York: Schocken Books, 1984), 100–127.

A charming, "innocent" young girl swallowed by a wolf is an image which impresses itself indelibly on the mind. In "Hansel and Gretel" the witch only planned to devour the children; in "Little Red Riding Hood" both grandmother and child are actually swallowed up by the wolf. Like most fairy tales, "Little Red Riding Hood" exists in many different versions. The most popular is the Brothers Grimm's story, in which Little Red Cap and the grandmother are reborn and the wolf is meted out a well-deserved punishment.

But the literary history of this story begins with Perrault.[1] It is by his title, "Little Red Riding Hood," that the tale is best known in English, though the title it was given by the Brothers Grimm, "Little Red Cap," is more appropriate. However, Andrew Lang, one of the most erudite and astute students of fairy tales, remarks that if all variants of "Little Red Riding Hood" ended the way Perrault concluded his, we might as well dismiss it.[2] This would probably have been its fate if the Brothers Grimm's version had not made it into one of the most popular fairy tales. But since this story's known history starts with Perrault, we shall consider—and dismiss—his rendering first.

Perrault's story begins like all other well-known versions, telling how the grandmother had made her granddaughter a little red riding hood (or cap), which led to the girl's being known by that name. One day her mother sent Little Red Riding Hood to take goodies to her grandmother, who was sick. The girl's way led her through a forest, where she met up with the wolf. The wolf did not dare to eat her up then because there were woodcutters in the forest, so he asked Little Red Riding Hood where she was going, and she told him. The wolf asked exactly where Grandmother lived, and the girl gave the information. Then the wolf said that he would go visit Grandmother too, and he took off at great speed, while the girl dallied along the way.

The wolf gained entrance at the grandmother's home by pretending to be Little Red Riding Hood, and immediately swallowed up the old woman. In Perrault's story the wolf does not dress up as Grandmother, but simply lies down in her bed. When Little Red Riding Hood arrived, the wolf asked her to join him in bed. Little Red Riding Hood undressed and got into bed, at which moment, astonished at how Grandmother looked naked, she exclaimed, "Grandmother, what big arms you have!" to which the wolf answered: "To better embrace you!" Then Little Red Riding Hood said: "Grandmother, what big legs you have!" and received the reply: "To be better able to run." These two exchanges, which do not occur in the Brothers Grimm's version, are then followed by the well-known questions about Grandmother's big ears, eyes, and teeth. To the last question the wolf answers, "To better eat you." "And, in saying these words, the bad wolf threw himself on Little Red Riding Hood and ate her up."

There Lang's translation ends, as do many others. But Perrault's original rendering continues with a little poem setting forth the moral to be drawn from the story: that nice girls ought not to listen to all sorts of people. If they do, it is not surprising that the wolf will get them and eat them up. As for wolves, these come in all variations; and among them the gentle wolves are the most dangerous of all, particularly those who follow young girls into the streets, even into their homes. Perrault wanted not only to entertain his audience, but to teach a specific moral lesson with each of his tales. So it is understandable that he changed them accordingly.[3] Unfortunately, in doing so, he robbed his fairy stories of much of their meaning. As he tells the story, nobody warned Little Red Riding Hood not to dally on the way to Grandmother's house, or not to stray off the proper road. Also, in Perrault's version it does not make sense that the grandmother, who has done nothing wrong at all, should end up destroyed.

Perrault's "Little Red Riding Hood" loses much of its appeal because it is so obvious that his wolf is not a rapacious beast but a metaphor, which leaves little to the imagination of the hearer. Such simplifications and a directly stated moral turn this potential fairy tale into a cautionary tale which spells everything out completely. Thus the hearer's imagination cannot become active in giving the story a personal meaning. Captive to a rationalistic interpretation of the story's purpose, Perrault makes everything as explicit as possible. For example, when the girl undresses and joins the wolf in bed and the wolf tells her that his strong arms are for embracing her better, nothing is left to the imagination. Since in response to such direct and obvious seduction Little Red Riding Hood makes no move to escape or fight back, either she is stupid or she wants to be seduced. In neither case is she a suitable figure to identify with. With these details Little Red Riding Hood is changed from a naïve, attractive young girl, who is induced to neglect Mother's warnings and enjoy herself in what she consciously believes to be innocent ways, into nothing but a fallen woman.

It destroys the value of a fairy tale for the child if someone details its meaning for him; Perrault does worse—he belabors it. All good fairy tales have meaning on many levels; only the child can know which meanings are of significance to him at the moment. As he grows up, the child discovers new aspects of these well-known tales, and this gives him the conviction that he has indeed matured in understanding, since the same story now reveals so much more to him. This can happen only if the child has not been told didactically what the story is supposed to be about. Only when discovery of the previously hidden meanings of a fairy tale is the child's spontaneous and intuitive achievement does it attain full significance for him. This discovery changes a story from something the child is being given into something he partially creates for himself.

The Brothers Grimm recount two versions of this story, which is very unusual for them.[4] In both, the story and the heroine are called "Little Red Cap" because of the "little cap of red velvet which suited her so well that she would not wear anything else."

The threat of being devoured is the central theme of "Little Red Riding Hood," as it is of "Hansel and Gretel." The same basic psychological constellations which recur in every person's development can lead to the most diverse human fates and personalities, depending on what the individual's other experiences are and how he interprets them to himself. Similarly, a limited number of basic themes depict in fairy stories quite different aspects of the human experience; all depends on how such a motif is elaborated and in what context events happen. "Hansel and Gretel" deals with the difficulties and anxieties of the child who is forced to give up his dependent attachment to the mother and free himself of his oral fixation. "Little Red Cap" takes up some crucial problems the school-age girl has to solve if oedipal attachments linger on in the unconscious, which may drive her to expose herself dangerously to the possibility of seduction.

In both these fairy tales the house in the woods and the parental home are the same place, experienced quite differently because of a change in the psychological situation. In her own home Little Red Cap, protected by her parents, is the untroubled pubertal child who is quite competent to cope. At the home of her grandmother, who is herself infirm, the same girl is helplessly incapacitated by the consequences of her encounter with the wolf.

Hansel and Gretel, subjects of their oral fixation, think nothing of eating the house that symbolically stands for the bad mother who has deserted them (forced them to leave home), and they do not hesitate to burn the witch to death in an oven as if she were food to be cooked for eating. Little Red Cap, who has outgrown her oral fixation, no longer has any destructive oral desires. Psychologically, the distance is enormous between oral fixation symbolically turned into cannibalism, which is the central theme of "Hansel and Gretel," and how Little Red Cap punishes the wolf. The wolf in "Little Red Cap" is the seducer, but as far as the overt content of the story goes, the wolf doesn't do anything that does not come naturally—namely, it devours to feed itself. And it is common for man to kill a wolf, although the method used in this story is unusual.

Little Red Cap's home is one of abundance, which, since she is way beyond oral anxiety, she gladly shares with her grandmother by bringing her food. To Little Red Cap the world beyond the parental home is not a threatening wilderness through which the child cannot find a path. Outside Red Cap's home there is a well-known road, from which, her mother warns, one must not stray.

While Hansel and Gretel have to be pushed out into the world, Little Red Cap leaves her home willingly. She is not afraid of the outside world, but recognizes its beauty, and therein lies a danger. If this world beyond home and duty becomes too attractive, it may induce a return to proceeding according to the pleasure principle—which, we assume, Little Red Cap had relinquished due to her parents' teachings in favor of the reality principle—and then destructive encounters may occur.

This quandary of standing between reality principle and pleasure principle is explicitly stated when the wolf says to Little Red Cap: "See how pretty the flowers are which are all around you. Why don't you look about? I believe you don't even hear how beautifully the little birds are singing. You walk along with singlemindedness and concentration as if you were going to school, while everything out here in the woods is merry." This is the same conflict between doing what one likes to do and what one ought to do which Red Cap's mother had warned her about at the outset, as she admonished her daughter to "walk properly and don't run off the road. . . . And when you come to Grandmother's place, do not forget to wish her a 'Good morning,' and don't look into all the corners as soon as you arrive." So her mother is aware of Little Red Cap's proclivity for straying off the beaten path, and for spying into corners to discover the secrets of adults.

The idea that "Little Red Cap" deals with the child's ambivalence about whether to live by the pleasure principle or the reality principle is borne out by the fact that Red Cap stops gathering flowers only "when she had collected so many that she could not carry any more." At that moment Little Red Cap "once more remembered Grandmother and set out on the way to her." That is, only when picking flowers is no longer enjoyable does the pleasure-seeking id recede and Red Cap become aware of her obligations.[5]

Little Red Cap is very much a child already struggling with pubertal problems for which she is not yet ready emotionally because she has not mastered her oedipal conflicts. That Little Red Cap is more mature than Hansel and Gretel is shown by her questioning attitude toward what she encounters in the world. Hansel and Gretel do not wonder about the gingerbread house, or explore what the witch is all about. Little Red Cap wishes to find out things, as her mother's cautioning her not to peek indicates. She observes that something is wrong when she finds her grandmother "looking very strange," but is confused by the wolf's having disguised himself in the old woman's attire. Little Red Cap tries to understand, when she asks Grandmother about her big ears, observes the big eyes, wonders about the large hands, the horrible mouth. Here is an enumeration of the four senses: hearing, seeing, touching, and tasting; the pubertal child uses them all to comprehend the world.

"Little Red Cap" in symbolic form projects the girl into the dangers of her Oedipal conflicts during puberty, and then saves her from them, so that she will be able to mature conflict-free. The maternal figures of mother and witch which were all-important in "Hansel and Gretel" have shrunk to insignificance in "Little Red Cap," where neither mother nor grandmother can do anything—neither threaten nor protect. The male, by contrast, is all-important, split into two opposite forms: the dangerous seducer who, if given in to, turns into the destroyer of the good grandmother and the girl; and the hunter, the responsible, strong, and rescuing father figure.

It is as if Little Red Cap is trying to understand the contradictory nature of the male by experiencing all aspects of his personality: the selfish, asocial, violent, potentially destructive tendencies of the id (the wolf); the unselfish, social, thoughtful, and protective propensities of the ego (the hunter).

Little Red Cap is universally loved because, although she is virtuous, she is tempted; and because her fate tells us that trusting everybody's good intentions, which seems so nice, is really leaving oneself open to pitfalls. If there were not something in us that likes the big bad wolf, he would have no power over us. Therefore, it is important to understand his nature, but even more important to learn what makes him attractive to us. Appealing as naïveté is, it is dangerous to remain naïve all one's life.

But the wolf is not just the male seducer, he also represents all the asocial, animalistic tendencies within ourselves. By giving up the school-age child's virtues of "walking singlemindedly," as her task demands, Little Red Cap reverts to the pleasure-seeking Oedipal child. By falling in with the wolf's suggestions, she has also given the wolf the opportunity to devour her grandmother. Here the story speaks to some of the Oedipal difficulties which remained unresolved in the girl, and the wolf's swallowing Little Red Cap is the merited punishment for her arranging things so that the wolf can do away with a mother figure. Even a four-year-old cannot help wondering what Little Red Cap is up to when, answering the wolf's question, she gives the wolf specific directions on how to get to her grandmother's house. What is the purpose of such detailed information, the child wonders to himself, if not to make sure that the wolf will find the way? Only adults who are convinced that fairy tales do not make sense can fail to see that Little Red Cap's unconscious is working overtime to give Grandmother away.

Grandmother, too, is not free of blame. A young girl needs a strong mother figure for her own protection, and as a model to imitate. But Red Cap's grandmother is carried away by her own needs beyond what is good for the child, as we are told: "There was nothing she would not have given the child."

It would not have been the first or last time that a child so spoiled by a grandmother runs into trouble in real life. Whether it is Mother or Grandmother—this mother once removed—it is fatal for the young girl if this older woman abdicates her own attractiveness to males and transfers it to the daughter by giving her a too attractive red cloak.

All through "Little Red Cap," in the title as in the girl's name, the emphasis is on the color red, which she openly wears. Red is the color symbolizing violent emotions, very much including sexual ones. The red velvet cap given by Grandmother to Little Red Cap thus can be viewed as a symbol of a premature transfer of sexual attractiveness, which is further accentuated by the grandmother's being old and sick, too weak even to open a door. The name "Little Red Cap" indicates the key importance of this feature of the heroine in the story. It suggests that not only is the red cap little, but also the girl. She is too little, not for wearing the cap, but for managing what this red cap symbolizes, and what her wearing it invites.

Little Red Cap's danger is her budding sexuality, for which she is not yet emotionally mature enough. The person who is psychologically ready to have sexual experiences can master them, and grow because of it. But a premature sexuality is a regressive experience, arousing all that is still primitive within us and that threatens to swallow us up. The immature person who is not yet ready for sex but is exposed to an experience which arouses strong sexual feelings falls back on Oedipal ways for dealing with it. The only way such a person believes she can win out in sex is by getting rid of the more experienced competitors—hence Little Red Cap's giving specific instructions to the wolf on how to get to Grandmother's house. In doing this, however, she also shows her ambivalence. In directing the wolf to Grandmother, she acts as if she were telling the wolf, "Leave me alone; go to Grandmother, who is a mature woman; she should be able to cope with what you represent; I am not."

This struggle between her conscious desire to do the right thing and the unconscious wish to win out over her (grand)mother is what endears the girl and the story to us and makes her so supremely human. Like many of us when we were children and caught in inner ambivalences that, despite our best efforts, we could not master, she tries to push the problem onto somebody else: an older person, a parent or parent substitute. But by thus trying to evade a threatening situation, she nearly gets destroyed by it.

As mentioned before, the Brothers Grimm also present an important variation of "Little Red Riding Hood," which essentially consists of only an addition to the basic story. In the variation, we are told that at a later time, when Little Red Cap is again taking cakes to her grandmother, another wolf tries to entice her to stray from the direct path (of virtue). This time the girl hurries to Grandmother and tells her all about it. Together they secure the door so that the wolf cannot enter. In the end, the wolf slips from the roof into a trough filled with water and drowns. The story ends, "But Little Red Cap went gaily home, and nobody did any harm to her."

This variation elaborates on what the hearer of the story feels convinced of—that after her bad experience the girl realizes that she is by no means mature enough to deal with the wolf (the seducer), and she is ready to settle down to a good working alliance with her mother. This is symbolically expressed by her rushing to Grandmother as soon as danger threatens, rather than her thinking nothing of it, as she did in her first encounter with the wolf. Little Red Cap works with her (grand)mother and follows her advice—in the continuation, Grandmother tells Red Cap to fill the trough with water that smells of sausages which had been cooked in it, and the smell attracts the wolf so that he falls into the water—and together the two easily overcome the wolf. The child thus needs to form a strong working alliance with the parent of the same sex, so that through identification with the parent and conscious learning from her, the child will grow successfully into an adult.

Fairy stories speak to our conscious and our unconscious, and therefore do not need to avoid contradictions, since these easily coexist in our unconscious. On a quite different level of meaning, what happens with and to Grandmother may be seen in a very different light. The hearer of the story rightly wonders why the wolf does not devour Little Red Cap as soon as he meets her—that is, at the first opportunity. Typically for Perrault, he offers a seemingly rational explanation: the wolf would have done so were it not afraid of some woodcutters who were close by. Since in Perrault's story the wolf is all along a male seducer, it makes sense that an older man might be afraid to seduce a little girl in the sight and hearing of other men.

Things are quite different in the Brothers Grimm's tale, where we are given to understand that the wolf's excessive greed accounts for the delay: "The wolf thought to itself, 'That young tender thing, what a fat mouthful, it'll taste much better than the old one: you have to proceed craftily so that you catch both.'" But this explanation does not make sense, because the wolf could have gotten hold of Little Red Cap right then and there, and later tricked the grandmother just as it happens in the story.

The wolf's behavior begins to make sense in the Brothers Grimm's version if we assume that to get Little Red Cap, the wolf first has to do away with Grandmother. As long as the (grand)mother is around, Little Red Cap will not become his.[6] But once the (grand)mother is out of the way, the road seems open for acting on one's desires, which had to remain repressed as long as Mother was around. The story on this level deals with the daughter's unconscious wish to be seduced by her father (the wolf).

With the reactivation in puberty of early Oedipal longings, the girl's wish for her father, her inclination to seduce him, and her desire to be seduced by him, also become reactivated. Then the girl feels she deserves to be punished terribly by the mother, if not the father also, for her desire to take him away from Mother. Adolescent reawakening of early emotions which were relatively dormant is not restricted to Oedipal feelings, but includes even earlier anxieties and desires which reappear during this period.

On a different level of interpretation, one could say that

the wolf does not devour Little Red Cap immediately upon meeting her because he wants to get her into bed with him first: a sexual meeting of the two has to precede her being "eaten up." While most children do not know about those animals of which one dies during the sex act, these destructive connotations are quite vivid in the child's conscious and unconscious mind—so much so that most children view the sexual act primarily as an act of violence which one partner commits on the other. I believe it is the child's unconscious equation of sexual excitement, violence, and anxiety which Djuna Barnes alludes to when she writes: "Children know something they can't tell; they like Red Riding Hood and the wolf in bed!"[7] Because this strange coincidence of opposite emotions characterizing the child's sexual knowledge is given body in "Little Red Riding Hood," the story holds a great unconscious attraction to children, and to adults who are vaguely reminded by it of their own childish fascination with sex.

Another artist has given expression to these same underlying feelings. Gustave Doré, in one of his famous illustrations to fairy tales, shows Little Red Riding Hood and the wolf in bed together.[8] The wolf is depicted as rather placid. But the girl appears to be beset by powerful ambivalent feelings as she looks at the wolf resting beside her. She makes no move to leave. She seems most intrigued by the situation, attracted and repelled at the same time. The combination of feelings her face and body suggest can best be described as fascination. It is the same fascination which sex, and everything surrounding it, exercises over the child's mind. This, to return to Djuna Barnes's statement, is what children feel about Red Riding Hood and the wolf and their relation, but can't tell—and is what makes the story so captivating.

It is this "deathly" fascination with sex—which is experienced as simultaneously the greatest excitement and the greatest anxiety—that is bound up with the little girl's Oedipal longings for her father, and with the reactivation of these same feelings in different form during puberty. Whenever these emotions reappear, they evoke memories of the little girl's propensity for seducing her father, and with it other memories of her desire to be seduced by him also.

While in Perrault's rendering the emphasis is on sexual seduction, the opposite is true for the Brothers Grimm's story. In it, no sexuality is directly or indirectly mentioned; it may be subtly implied, but, essentially, the hearer has to supply the idea to help his understanding of the story. To the child's mind, the sexual implications remain preconscious, as they should. Consciously a child knows that there is nothing wrong with picking flowers; what is wrong is disobeying Mother when one has to carry out an important mission serving the legitimate interest of the (grand)parent. The main conflict is between what seem justified interests to the child and what she knows her parent wants her to do. The story implies that the child doesn't know how dangerous it may be to give in to what she considers her innocuous desires, so she must learn of this danger. Or rather, as the story warns, life will teach it to her, at her expense.

"Little Red Cap" externalizes the inner processes of the pubertal child: the wolf is the externalization of the badness the child feels when she goes contrary to the admonitions of her parents and permits herself to tempt, or to be tempted, sexually. When she strays from the path the parent has outlined for her, she encounters "badness," and she fears that it will swallow up her and the parent whose confidence she betrayed. But there can be resurrection from "badness," as the story proceeds to tell.

Very different from Little Red Cap, who gives in to the temptations of her id and in doing so betrays mother and grandmother, the hunter does not permit his emotions to run away with him. His first reaction on finding the wolf sleeping in the grandmother's bed is, "Do I find you here, you old sinner? I have been looking for you for a long time"—and his immediate inclination is to shoot the wolf. But his ego (or reason) asserts itself despite the proddings of the id (anger at the wolf), and the hunter realizes that it is more important to try to rescue Grandmother than to give in to anger by shooting the wolf outright. The hunter restrains himself, and instead of shooting the animal dead, he carefully cuts open the wolf's belly with scissors, rescuing Little Red Cap and her grandmother.

The hunter is a most attractive figure, to boys as well as girls, because he rescues the good and punishes the bad. All children encounter difficulties in obeying the reality principle, and they easily recognize in the opposite figures of wolf and hunter the conflict between the id and the ego-superego aspects of their personality. In the hunter's action, violence (cutting open the belly) is made to serve the highest social purpose (rescuing the two females). The child feels that nobody appreciates that his violent tendencies seem constructive to him, but the story shows that they can be.

Little Red Cap has to be cut out of the wolf's stomach as if through a Caesarean operation; thus the idea of pregnancy and birth is intimated. With it, associations of a sexual relation are evoked in the child's unconscious. How does a fetus get into the mother's womb? wonders the child, and decides that it can happen only through the mother having swallowed something, as the wolf did.

Why does the hunter speak of the wolf as an "old sinner" and say that he has been trying to find him for a long time? As the seducer is called a wolf in the story, so the person who seduces, particularly when his target is a young girl, is popularly referred to as an "old sinner" today as in olden times. On a different level, the wolf also represents the unacceptable tendencies within the hunter; we all refer on occasion to the animal within us, as a simile for our propensity for acting violently or irresponsibly to gain our goals.

While the hunter is all-important for the denouement, we do not know where he comes from, nor does he interact with Little Red Cap—he rescues her, that's all. All through "Little Red Cap" no father is mentioned, which is most unusual for a fairy story of this kind. This suggests that the father is present, but in hidden form. The girl certainly expects her father to rescue her from all difficulties, and particularly those emotional ones which are the consequence of her wish to seduce him and to be seduced by him. What is meant here by "seduction" is the girl's desire and efforts to induce her father to love her more than anybody else, and her wish that he should make all efforts to induce her to love him more than anybody else. Then we may see that the father is indeed present in "Little Red Cap" in two opposite forms: as the wolf, which is an externalization of the dangers of overwhelming Oedipal feelings, and as the hunter in his protective and rescuing function.

Despite the hunter's immediate inclination to shoot the wolf dead, he does not do so. After her rescue, it is Little Red Cap's own idea to fill the wolf's belly with stones, "and as it woke up, it tried to jump away, but the stones were so heavy that it collapsed and fell to its death." It has to be Little Red Cap who spontaneously plans what to do about the wolf and goes about doing it. If she is to be safe in the future, she must be able to do away with the seducer, be rid of him. If the father-hunter did this for her, Red Cap could never feel that she had really overcome her weakness, because she had not rid herself of it.

It is fairy-tale justice that the wolf should die of what he tried to do: his oral greediness is his own undoing. Since he tried to put something into his stomach nefariously, the same is done to him.[9]

There is another excellent reason why the wolf should not die from having his belly cut open to free those he swallowed up. The fairy tale protects the child from unnecessary anxiety. If the wolf should die when his belly is opened up as in a Caesarean operation, those hearing the story might come to fear that a child coming out of the mother's body kills her. But if the wolf survives the opening up of his belly and dies only because heavy stones were sewn into it, then there is no reason for anxiety about childbirth.

Little Red Cap and her grandmother do not really die, but they are certainly reborn. If there is a central theme to the wide variety of fairy tales, it is that of a rebirth to a higher plane. Children (and adults, too) must be able to believe that reaching a higher form of existence is possible if they master the developmental steps this requires. Stories which tell that this is not only possible but likely have a tremendous appeal to children, because such tales combat the ever-present fear that they won't be able to make this transition, or that they'll lose too much in the process. That is why, for example, in "Brother and Sister" the two do not lose each other after their transformation but have a better life together; why Little Red Cap is a happier girl after her rescue; why Hansel and Gretel are so much better off after their return home.

Many adults today tend to take literally the things said in fairy tales, whereas they should be viewed as symbolic renderings of crucial life experiences. The child understands this intuitively, though he does not "know" it explicitly. An adult's reassurance to a child that Little Red Cap did not "really" die when the wolf swallowed her is experienced by the child as a condescending talking down. This is just the same as if a person is told that in the Bible story Jonah's being swallowed by the big fish was not "really" his end. Everybody who hears this story knows intuitively that Jonah's stay in the fish's belly was for a purpose—namely, so that he would return to life a better man.

The child knows intuitively that Little Red Cap's being swallowed by the wolf—much like the various deaths other fairy-tale heroes experience for a time—is by no means the end of the story, but a necessary part of it. The child also understands that Little Red Cap really "died" as the girl who permitted herself to be tempted by the wolf; and that when the story says "the little girl sprang out" of the wolf's belly, she came to life a different person. This device is necessary because, while the child can readily understand one thing being replaced by another (the good mother by the evil stepmother), he cannot yet comprehend inner transformations. So among the great merits of fairy tales is that through hearing them, the child comes to believe that such transformations are possible.

The child whose conscious and unconscious mind has become deeply involved in the story understands that what is meant by the wolf's swallowing grandmother and girl is that

183

because of what happened, the two were temporarily lost to the world—they lost the ability to be in contact and to influence what goes on. Therefore somebody from the outside must come to their rescue; and where a mother and child are concerned, who could that be but a father?

Little Red Cap, when she fell in with the wolf's seduction to act on the basis of the pleasure principle instead of the reality principle, implicitly returned to a more primitive, earlier form of existence. In typical fairy-story fashion, her return to a more primitive level of life is impressively exaggerated as going all the way to the prebirth existence in the womb, as the child thinks in extremes.

But why must the grandmother experience the same fate as the girl? Why is she both "dead" and reduced to a lower state of existence? This detail is in line with the way the child conceives of what death means—that this person is no longer available, is no longer of any use. Grandparents must be of use to the child—they must be able to protect him, teach him, feed him; if they are not, then they are reduced to a lower form of existence. As unable to cope with the wolf as Little Red Cap is, the grandmother is reduced to the same fate as the girl.[10]

The story makes it quite clear that the two have not died by being swallowed. This is made obvious by Little Red Cap's behavior when liberated. "The little girl sprang out crying: 'Ah, how frightened I have been; how dark it was inside the wolf's body!'" To have been frightened means that one has been very much alive, and signifies a state opposite to death, when one no longer thinks or feels. Little Red Cap's fear was of the darkness, because through her behavior she had lost her higher consciousness, which had shed light on her world. Or as the child who knows he has done wrong, or who no longer feels well protected by his parents, feels the darkness of night with its terrors settle on him.

Not just in "Little Red Cap" but throughout the fairy-tale literature, death of the hero—different from death of old age, after life's fulfillment—symbolizes his failure. Death of the unsuccessful—such as those who tried to get to Sleeping

Beauty before the time was ripe, and perished in the thorns—symbolizes that this person was not mature enough to master the demanding task which he foolishly (prematurely) undertook. Such persons must undergo further growth experiences, which will enable them to succeed. Those predecessors of the hero who die in fairy stories are nothing but the hero's earlier immature incarnations.

Little Red Cap, having been projected into inner darkness (the darkness inside the wolf), becomes ready and appreciative of a new light, a better understanding of the emotional experiences she has to master, and those others which she has to avoid because as yet they overwhelm her. Through stories such as "Little Red Cap" the child begins to understand—at least on a preconscious level—that only those experiences which overwhelm us arouse in us corresponding inner feelings with which we cannot deal. Once we have mastered those, we need not fear any longer the encounter with the wolf.

This is reinforced by the story's concluding sentence, which does not have Little Red Cap say that she will never again risk encountering the wolf, or go alone in the woods. On the contrary, the ending implicitly warns the child that withdrawal from all problematic situations would be the wrong solution. The story ends: "But Little Red Cap thought 'as long as you live, you won't run off the path into the woods all by yourself when mother has forbidden you to do so.'" With such inner dialogue, backed up by a most upsetting experience, Little Red Cap's encounter with her own sexuality will have a very different outcome, when she is ready—at which time her mother will approve of it.

Deviating from the straight path in defiance of mother and superego was temporarily necessary for the young girl, to gain a higher state of personality organization. Her experience convinced her of the dangers of giving in to her Oedipal desires. It is much better, she learns, not to rebel against the mother, nor try to seduce or permit herself to be seduced by the as yet dangerous aspects of the male. Much better, despite one's ambivalent desires, to settle for a while longer for the protection the father provides when he is not seen in his seductive aspects. She has learned that it is better to build Father and Mother, and their values, deeper and in more adult ways into one's superego, to become able to deal with life's dangers.

There are many modern counterparts to "Little Red Cap." The profundity of fairy tales when compared to much of today's children's literature becomes apparent when one parallels them. David Riesman, for example, has compared "Little Red Riding Hood" with a modern children's story, *Tootle the Engine,* a Little Golden Book which some twenty years ago sold in the millions.[11] In it, an anthropomorphically depicted little engine goes to engine school to learn to become a big streamliner. Like Little Red Riding Hood, Tootle has been told to move only on the tracks. It, too, is tempted to stray off them, since the little engine delights in playing among the pretty flowers in the fields. To stop Tootle from going astray, the townspeople get together and conceive of a clever plan, in which they all participate. Next time Tootle leaves the tracks to wander in its beloved meadows, it is stopped by a red flag wherever it turns, until it promises never to leave the tracks again.

Today we could view this as a story which exemplifies behavior modification through adverse stimuli: the red flags. Tootle reforms, and the story ends with Tootle having mended its ways and indeed going to grow up to be a big streamliner. *Tootle* seems to be essentially a cautionary tale, warning the child to stay on the narrow road of virtue. But how shallow it is when compared with the fairy tale.

"Little Red Cap" speaks of human passions, oral greediness, aggression, and pubertal sexual desires. It opposes the cultured orality of the maturing child (the nice food taken to Grandmother) to its earlier cannibalistic form (the wolf swallowing up Grandmother and the girl). With its violence, including that which saves the two females and destroys the wolf by cutting open its belly and then putting stones into it, the fairy tale does not show the world in a rosy light. The story ends as all figures—girl, mother, grandmother, hunter, and wolf—"do their own thing": the wolf tries to run away and falls to its death, after which the hunter skins the wolf and takes its pelt home; Grandmother eats what Little Red Cap has brought her; and the girl has learned her lesson. There is no conspiracy of adults which forces the story's hero to mend her way as society demands—a process which denies the value of inner-directedness. Far from others doing it for her, Little Red Cap's experience moves her to change herself, as she promises herself that "as long as you live, you won't run off the path into the woods."

How much truer both to the reality of life and to our inner experiences is the fairy tale when compared with *Tootle*, which uses realistic elements as stage props: trains running on tracks, red flags stopping them. The trappings are real enough, but everything essential is unreal, since the entire population of a town does not stop what it is doing, to help a child mend his ways. Also, there was never any real danger to Tootle's existence. Yes, Tootle is helped to mend its ways; but all that is involved in the growth experience is to become a bigger and faster train—that is, an externally more successful and useful adult. There is no recognition of inner anxieties, nor of the dangers of temptation to our very existence. To quote Riesman, "there is none of the grimness of Little Red Riding Hood," which has been replaced by "a fake [ordeal] which the citizens put on for Tootle's benefit." Nowhere in *Tootle* is there an externalization onto story characters of inner processes and emotional problems pertaining to growing up, so that the child may be able to face the first and thus solve the latter.

We can fully believe it when at the end of *Tootle* we are told that Tootle has forgotten it ever did like flowers. Nobody with the widest stretch of imagination can believe that Little Red Riding Hood could ever forget her encounter with the wolf, or will stop liking flowers or the beauty of the world. Tootle's story, not creating any inner conviction in the hearer's mind, needs to rub in its lesson and predict the outcome: the engine will stay on the tracks and become a streamliner. No initiative, no freedom there.

The fairy tale carries within itself the conviction of its message; therefore it has no need to peg the hero to a specific way of life. There is no need to tell what Little Red Riding Hood will do, or what her future will be. Due to her experience, she will be well able to decide this herself. The wisdom about life, and about the dangers which her desires may bring about, is gained by every listener.

Little Red Riding Hood lost her childish innocence as she encountered the dangers residing in herself and the world, and exchanged it for wisdom that only the "twice born" can possess: those who not only master an existential crisis, but also become conscious that it was their own nature which projected them into it. Little Red Riding Hood's childish innocence dies as the wolf reveals itself as such and swallows her. When she is cut out of the wolf's belly, she is reborn on a higher plane of existence; relating positively to both her parents, no longer a child, she returns to life a young maiden.

Notes

1. Charles Perrault, *Histoires ou Contes du temps passé, avec des Moralitez* (Paris, 1697). The first English translation which appeared in print was by Robert Samber, *Histories or Tales of Past Times* (London, 1729). The best known of these tales have been reprinted in Iona and Peter Opie, *The Classic Fairy Tales* (London: Oxford University Press, 1974). They can also be found in Andrew Lang's fairy books—"Little Red Riding Hood" is included among the tales of *The Blue Fairy Book* (London: Longmans, Green, ca. 1889).

2. Andrew Lang, *Perrault's Popular Tales* (Oxford: At the Clarendon Press, 1888). There he writes: "If 'Little Red Riding Hood' ended, in all variants, where it ends in Perrault, we might dismiss it, with the remark that the *machinery* of the story is derived from 'the time when beasts spoke,' or were believed to be capable of speaking. But it is well known that in the German form, 'Little Red Cap' (Brothers Grimm 26), the tale by no means ends with the triumph of the wolf. Little Red Cap and her grandmother are resuscitated, 'the wolf it was that died.' This may either have been the

original ending, omitted by Perrault because it was too wildly impossible for the nurseries of the time of Louis XIV, or children may have insisted on having the story "turn out well." In either case the German *Märchen* preserves one of the most widely spread mythical incidents in the world—the reappearance of living people out of the monster that has devoured them."

Interestingly enough, it is the Perrault version Andrew Lang chose to include in his *Blue Fairy Book*. Perrault's story ends with the wolf victorious; thus it is devoid of escape, recovery, and consolation; it is not—and was not intended by Perrault to be—a fairy tale, but a cautionary story which deliberately threatens the child with its anxiety-producing ending. It is curious that even Lang, despite his severe criticisms of it, preferred to reproduce Perrault's version. It seems that many adults think it better to scare children into good behavior than to relieve their anxieties as a true fairy tale does.

There is a considerable literature dealing with Perrault and his fairy tales. The most useful work—comparable to what Bolte and Polívka did for the Brothers Grimm's tales—is Marc Soriano, *Les Contes de Perrault* (Paris: Gallimard, 1968).

3. When Perrault published his collection of fairy tales in 1697, "Little Red Riding Hood" already had an ancient history, with some elements going very far back in time. There is the myth of Cronos swallowing his children, who nevertheless return miraculously from his belly; and a heavy stone was used to replace the child to be swallowed. There is a Latin story of 1023 (by Egbert of Lièges, called *Fecunda ratis*) in which a little girl is found in the company of wolves; the girl wears a red cover of great importance to her, and scholars tell that this cover was a red cap. Here, then, six centuries or more before Perrault's story, we find some basic elements of "Little Red Riding Hood": a little girl with a red cap, the company of wolves, a child being swallowed alive who returns unharmed, and a stone put in place of the child.

There are other French versions of "Little Red Riding Hood," but we do not know which of them influenced Perrault in his retelling of the story. In some of them the wolf makes Little Red Riding Hood eat of Grandmother's flesh and drink of her blood, despite warning voices which tell her not to. Two of these French versions of "Little Red Riding Hood" are published in *Melusine* 3 (1886–1887) and *Melusine* 6 (1892–1893). If one of these stories was Perrault's source, one can well understand that he eliminated such vulgarity as unseemly, since his book was designed for perusal at the court of Versailles. Perrault not only prettified his stories, he also used affectation, such as the pretense that his stories were written by his ten-year-old son, who dedicated the book to a princess. In Perrault's asides and the morals appended to the stories, he speaks as if he were winking at the adults over the heads of the children.

4. Their collection of fairy stories, which contained "Little Red Cap," appeared first in 1812—more than one hundred years after Perrault published his version.

5. Two French versions quite different from Perrault's make it even more obvious that Little Red Riding Hood chose to follow the path of pleasure, or at least of greater ease, although the path of duty was also brought to her attention. In these renderings of the story Little Red Riding Hood encounters the wolf at a fork in the road—that is, a place where an important decision has to be made: which road to follow. The wolf asks: Which road will you take, that of the needles or that of the pins? Little Red Riding Hood chooses the road of the pins because, as one version explains, is is easier to fasten things together with pins, while it is much harder labor to sew them together with needles. At a time when sewing was very much a work task expected of young girls, taking the easy way of using pins instead of needles was readily understood as behaving in accordance with the pleasure principle, where the situation would require acting according to the reality principle.

6. It is not all that long since, in certain peasant cultures, when the mother died, the oldest daughter took her place in all respects.

7. Djuna Barnes, *Nightwood* (New York: New Directions, 1937). T. S. Eliot, Introduction to *Nightwood.*

8. *Fairy Tales Told Again*, illustrated by Gustave Doré (London: Cassel, Petter and Galpin, 1872). The illustration is reprinted in Opie and Opie, *The Classic Fairy Tales.*

9. In some other renderings Little Red Cap's father happens to come on the scene, cuts the wolf's head off, and thus rescues the two females. (For alternative versions of "Little Red Cap," see Johannes Bolte and Georg Polívka, *Anmerkungen zu den Kinder- und Hausmärchen der Brüder Grimm*, 5 vols. [Hildesheim: Olms, 1963].) Maybe the shift from cutting open the stomach to cutting off the head was made because it was Little Red Cap's father who did it. A father's manipulating a stomach in which his daughter temporarily dwells comes too close for comfort in suggesting a father in sexual activity connected with his daughter.

10. That this interpretation is justified is borne out by the second version of the story presented by the Brothers Grimm. It tells how the second time around Grandmother protects Little Red Cap against the wolf, and successfully plans his demise. This is how a (grand)parent is supposed to act; if she does, neither (grand)parent nor child needs to fear the wolf, however clever it may be.

11. Gertrude Crampton, *Tootle the Engine* (New York: Simon and Schuster, 1946), a Little Golden Book.

Interpreting "Little Red Riding Hood" Psychoanalytically

All knowledge is partial, and the scholarship devoted to "Little Red Riding Hood" demonstrates this again and again. Few of those who have written extensively on the tale are aware of the possible Asian cognates widely reported in China, Japan, and Korea. Few are aware of the several psychoanalytic interpretations of the tale. Róheim's 1953 essay, for example, is mentioned in none of the other discussions of the tale presented here, not even in Bettelheim's extensive 1976 consideration of "Little Red Riding Hood." One cannot help but wonder what Róheim or Bettelheim would make of some of the details reported in the Asian cognates.

No doubt there are additional scholarly references to "Little Red Riding Hood" which have escaped my notice. Nevertheless, in the following concluding essay I shall try to review the various attempts I have found to elicit possible underlying meanings of "Little Red Riding Hood" before seeking to evaluate the previous psychoanalytic interpretations of the tale. If Róheim and Bettelheim had considered the Asian cognates of the tale in conjunction with the probable French oral versions, I believe they might have observed an anal component in addition to the possible oral and genital elements of the tale. In any event, it is surely a valid academic credo that anyone carrying out research on a topic should avail himself of all previous scholarship on the same topic. One should begin one's research where earlier schol-

Reprinted from James M. McGlathery, ed., *The Brothers Grimm and Folktale* (Urbana: University of Illinois Press, 1988), 16–51, by permission of the University of Illinois Press. Copyright © 1988 by the Board of Trustees of the University of Illinois.

ars left off. One of the principal goals of the present casebook is to make it easier for future interpreters of "Little Red Riding Hood" to see what earlier critics had to say and perhaps how and why they went astray.

Variation is a key concept in folkloristics. It is variation that in part distinguishes folklore from so-called "high culture" and "mass culture." High culture and mass culture are fixed in print or on videotape or film. A novel, short story, or poem does not change over time, although readers' perceptions and understandings of such literary products may well do so.

In marked contrast, folklore, with its characteristics of multiple existence and variation, is ever in a state of flux. There is no one single text in folklore; there are only texts. Folklore once recorded from oral tradition does not cease to be, but rather continues on its often merry way from raconteur to raconteur, from generation to generation. It is precisely this continuous process of oral transmission (or learning by example in the case of gestural or material folklore) that makes it possible for folklore to adapt to each individual or group among which it circulates.

Literature and mass or popular culture seem hopelessly rigid and inflexible in comparison with folklore. In studying them one must either seek to reconstruct the intellectual Zeitgeist or governing world-view paradigm present when the literary effort or popular/mass cultural product was created, or else abandon such a historical approach in favor of "new criticism" or its successors in an attempt to investigate how an old literary favorite is understood by yet one more set of readers.

The lack of flexibility in the texts of literary and popular culture is compensated for by the flexibility in interpretive approaches. Egyptologist Van Baaren has sagely observed that because biblical myths (e.g., in Genesis) are fixed and are part of a written tradition of organized religions, they cannot vary with each generation as an oral myth might. In-

stead the variation can occur only in the critical interpretation of biblical myths.[1] New generations are not really free
to tamper with the sacred text, but they can occasionally
offer new critical perspectives on the fixed texts as the history of biblical criticism over many centuries attests.

In folkloristics, the scientific study of folklore, the overwhelming amount of variation in texts—we have more than
one thousand versions of many of the standard Indo-European
märchen—may have discouraged those interested in interpretation. The comparative method, or Finnish method as it
is sometimes termed, rarely leads to interpretation, that is,
the interpretation of a folktale's content. It is a tedious and
tiring task merely to assemble all one thousand versions of
the Kind and Unkind Girls (AT 480) or Cinderella (AT 510A)
and further to arrange to have all these texts translated into
the native language of the researcher carrying out the comparative study.[2] At best or at most, the exhausted comparative folklorist may reluctantly guess at the possible historical relationships existing between subtypes of a given tale
type, or at the possible direction of diffusion—did a particular European tale type move from the Near East to continental Europe or from continental Europe to the Near East?

The failure of the folklorists to interpret the data they so
assiduously gather from informants in the field and which
they afterwards so painstakingly classify has left the field of
interpretation by default to non-folklorists. These scholars,
including literary critics, anthropologists, historians, and
psychoanalysts, among others, have been more than willing
to venture interpretations of folklore. As a result, we usually
find in terms of the two methodological steps essential for
the study of folklore in literature and culture—*identification*
and *interpretation*—one of two extremes.[3] The folklorists,
who delight in flaunting their expertise in identification, are
quick to point out that a specific text is a version of a particular tale type, but they utterly fail to interpret that text.
Non-folklorists are unable or unwilling to identify a text in
terms of tale type, but they feel perfectly free to interpret a
given text. Identification without interpretation, as prac-

ticed by too many folklorists, is sterile—publishing collections of tales with the notes limited to enumerating the relevant tale type numbers. Interpretation without proper identification may be equally unfortunate. One might, for instance, wrongly assume that a tale had been invented by a particular author or was peculiar to one culture or historical period, where in fact the existence of earlier versions of the same tale type in other cultures could easily disprove such an unwarranted initial assumption.

Germanicists and psychoanalysts, for example, have had a long tradition of interpreting the Grimm tales. Since the founder and early practitioners of psychoanalysis were native speakers of German, it made sense for them to choose samples from the celebrated Grimm canon on those occasions when they sought to consider folklore as grist for the psychoanalytic mill. The problem from the folkloristic perspective of limiting one's data base to a Grimm tale is twofold. For one thing, it is never appropriate to analyze a folktale (or any other exemplar of a folklore genre) on the basis of a single text. Literary scholars, accustomed as they are to working with "the" text rather than with "a" text, have simply taken the Grimm (or, if of the French persuasion, the Perrault) text as "the" text for analysis. Psychoanalysts have done much the same.

The second problem from the folklorist's perspective is that the Grimms' versions of tales are at least one full step removed from pure oral tradition. Although the Grimms claimed that they were recording authentic, unadulterated tales as they fell from their informants' untutored lips, source criticism over the years, thanks in part to the Grimms' own notes, has disproved conclusively this idyllic claim. When the Grimms, especially Wilhelm, who was more concerned than Jacob with the later editions of the *Kinder- und Hausmärchen*, began to combine different versions of the same tale type, to "present many versions as one" as they put it, they committed a cardinal sin in folklore, though to be sure it was one often committed by nineteenth-century collectors. The resultant composite text, made up as it was of dif-

195

ferent portions of different versions of the same tale type, constitutes what folklorists call fakelore, not folklore.[4] This means that many of the tales altered in the Grimm canon never were actually told orally in precisely that form by anyone before the publication of the Grimms' doctored texts.

It is well to keep in mind that fairy tales are first and foremost an *oral* form. So from that point of view, any written version is suspect. I am speaking here of "volksmärchen," not "kunstmärchen." Kunstmärchen constitutes yet another area of inquiry, namely, artistic or literary tales composed by known authors, perhaps inspired by a folk model. But there are varying degrees of accuracy in the written texts of oral tales collected in the nineteenth century. Nineteenth-century collector E. T. Kristensen (1843–1929) of Jutland, one of the greatest folklore collectors who ever lived, made a serious attempt to record oral fairy tales verbatim.[5] The Grimm brothers, regrettably, did not report their tales verbatim from their informants. Comparisons of the "same" tale in different editions of the *Kinder- und Hausmärchen* show just how much rewriting was done.[6]

The error of studying an international oral fairy tale on the basis of a single text is thus compounded by the fact that the Grimm version is not even an authentic oral version of that tale type. The folklorist would accordingly ask Germanicists and psychoanalysts who have written on fairy tales the following questions: Why, if there are one thousand versions of a tale type in print or readily available in folklore archives, would one want to limit one's analysis to a single version of the tale under investigation? And if one did want to limit analysis to a single version, why would one choose the Grimm text when we have indisputable evidence establishing that the Grimm version is *not* an authentic oral version of that tale?

It can certainly be argued that the Grimm fairy tale canon has its own existence as a kind of literary creation based in part on oral sources, and as a separate and unquestionably important and influential literary creation, it deserves study by literary critics. The essential point is that while one may legitimately analyze a Grimm tale, it should not be treated as the most common or most authentic form of that particular tale. Some ambitious scholars have sought to extrapolate general German values and worldview from the tales in the Grimm corpus. They would have been far better off examining the substantial body of bona fide German oral fairy tales in print. This is the fundamental distinction between analyzing literature and analyzing folklore. A student of Irish culture would be better advised to read Irish folktales and legends than the literary oeuvre of James Joyce. Joyce was a literary genius, an exception within his own or any culture, and much of his idiosyncratic and esoteric musings reflect the mind of James Joyce, not Ireland at large.

But all this is wishful thinking. By far the majority of published interpretations of fairy tales depend almost exclusively upon the Grimm canon. Certainly this is true in the case of psychoanalytic studies of folktales. There are dozens and dozens of psychoanalytic readings of fairy tales, most of which are totally ignored by literal-minded folklorists frightened and evidently greatly threatened by any thought that fairy tales might have symbolic import. Nearly every psychoanalytic reading of fairy tales uses the Grimm version as the sole point of interpretive departure. A few folklorists have bothered to read Bruno Bettelheim's *The Uses of Enchantment* (1976), but not many have read earlier psychoanalytic treatments of fairy tales by Géza Róheim and others. Róheim was actually trained as a folklorist and was much more conversant with comparative folkloristics than Bettelheim.

I should like to illustrate the pitfalls of relying too heavily upon literary, derivative, and bowdlerized renderings of what are wrongly believed to be authentic folktales by considering the case of "Little Red Riding Hood" (AT 333). In this particular instance, we are victimized by not one, but at least two distinct reworkings of the original oral tale.

The first was that of Perrault. His literary versions of 1695 and 1697 omitted many of the details of the oral tale. French folklorist Paul Delarue, among others, has established that

197

the oral tradition which preceded Perrault told of a girl (who wore no red hood) carrying a hot loaf of bread and a bottle of milk to her grandmother. On the way, she meets a wolf who asks her what path she is taking to her grandmother's house: the path of needles or the path of pins? The girl indicates that she will take the path of pins. Meanwhile the wolf enters the grandmother's house, kills the grandmother, and puts some of her flesh in the cupboard and a bottle of her blood on the shelf. The girl finally arrives, gives the bread and milk to the wolf disguised as grandmother, who invites her to eat some of the meat and wine. After she does so, a little cat remarks "A slut is she who eats the flesh and drinks the blood of her granny." The wolf then instructs the little girl to undress herself. When she asks where to put her apron, bodice, dress, petticoat, and long stockings, the wolf replies each time with "Throw them into the fire, my child, you won't be needing them any more." Then comes the celebrated dialogue which begins "Oh, Granny, how hairy you are!" "The better to keep myself warm, my child." Hereafter come nails to scratch oneself, shoulders to carry firewood, ears to hear you with, nostrils to sniff tobacco with, and ending with a mouth to eat you with. At that point, the little girl, in danger, says, "Oh, Granny, I've got to go badly. Let me go outside." The wolf replies, "Do it in the bed, my child!" "Oh no, Granny, I want to go outside." "All right, but make it quick." The wolf attaches a woolen rope to her foot and lets her go outside. When the little girl is outside, she ties the end of the rope to a plum tree in the courtyard. The wolf becomes impatient and says, "Are you making a load out there? Are you making a load?" When he realizes that nobody answers him, he jumps out of bed and sees that the little girl has escaped. He follows her, but arrives too late at her house, just at the very moment she enters.[7]

Perrault left out such "crude" elements as the cannibalistic eating of grandmother's flesh, the ritualistic strip-tease, and the ploy of going outside to defecate to escape the wolf's clutches.[8] Perrault also changed the ending of the story by having the little girl devoured by the wolf.

The overtly cannibalistic component of AT 333 is dramatically affirmed in a north Italian version of the tale collected in 1974. In this version a dialogue between Little Red Riding Hood and the wolf takes place which parallels and to some extent prefigures the traditional dialogue known to all devotees of the tale. Arriving at the grandmother's house, Little Red Riding Hood tells the wolf, whom she does not recognize under the grandmother's clothing, that the long trip has made her very hungry. "If you are hungry," says the wolf, "open the kneading trough and eat two or three tortellini which remain on a plate." While she eats, the wolf murmurs, "Eat the ears of your grandmother!" "Are you still hungry? In a pan are two or three lasagne," and he murmurs, "Eat the intestines of your grandmother!" "Are you still hungry? In a pan are remaining two or three manfettini," and he murmurs, "Eat the teeth of your grandmother." "Are you thirsty? In the corner is a bottle of red wine. . . . Drink the blood of your grandmother."[9]

Despite the existence of numerous oral versions of this tale type—Delarue examined more than thirty-five French texts—scholars continue to insist upon the priority of the Perrault telling of the tale. Folklorist Alexander Haggerty Krappe maintained in *The Science of Folklore* (1930) that "The story of Little Red Riding-Hood seems to be an invention of Perrault—at least no earlier variants are known, and the other French and Central European variants, not very many, to be sure, in all, show the unmistakable influence of the classical French text."[10] This statement articulates a typical literary bias, contending that oral traditions derive from an original written source, but it is demonstrably false. Perrault's source was oral tradition.

The alleged literary origin of "Little Red Riding Hood" was even espoused by Stith Thompson, who in *The Folktale* (1945) said, "This tale of Little Red Ridinghood has never had wide circulation where folktales are learned by word of mouth. Even in France and Germany, where the largest number is reported, practically all are based upon Perrault or Grimm. It does not extend east beyond the Russian border."[11]

This too is in error. Even a most cursory examination of Chinese, Japanese, and Korean versions of tale type 333 will establish that the oral tale *does* exist "beyond the Russian border." What is even more fascinating, this examination will document that some of the salient features of the pre-Perrault French oral tales are to be found in the Chinese, Japanese, and Korean traditions. Delarue, among European folklorists, appears to be one of the very few scholars to have been at all aware of the Asian versions of the tale type.[12]

The Chinese tale type 333C, The Tiger Grandma, as summarized in Nai-Tung Ting's *A Type Index of Chinese Folktales* (1978), presents a curious combination of The Wolf and the Kids (AT 123, Grimm no. 5) and the Glutton (Red Riding Hood) (AT 333, Grimm no. 26). In this tale, an ogress claims to be a relative of the children, usually a grandmother. The mother leaving home warns her children to watch the house and not open the door to strangers. The ogress, usually a wolf or tiger, comes to the house and asks the children to open the door. In some versions, the children meet the ogress on the way to see their grandmother and are invited to the house of the ogress, who claims to be their grandmother. Inside the house, the ogress's strange physical features are noticed by one or two of the older children. The surviving child hears the sound of biting and crunching in the dark and, asking to have some of the supposed grandmother's snack, is given a part of her sibling's body, usually a finger. She obtains permission to leave, typically with a rope tied to her body, which she later unties and puts around another object. When the ogress finds out she has been deceived, she searches and locates the fugitive, but the child talks her into letting a rope be tied to her body, after which the helpless ogress may be killed by having sharp or heavy objects thrown at her or having lime, salt water, or hot liquid poured on her body or into her mouth.[13]

Folklorist Wolfram Eberhard has written a monographic account of this popular Chinese tale type based upon some 241 Taiwanese texts of "Grandaunt Tiger." Some of the details he reports cannot help but remind us of the oral French versions. For example, in several Taiwanese texts, after the heroine asks to be allowed to leave to go to defecate, "the tiger tells the girl to relieve herself in the bed or in the room, but the girl objects saying that it would smell." Eberhard is able to illuminate the tiger's technique of tying a rope to the girl when she leaves to defecate. According to Eberhard, "The idea of the rope is nothing unusual to a Chinese. Toddlers are often prevented from getting into mischief or danger by having a rope tied to their legs, so that they can walk or crawl around but cannot get too far away."[14]

It is worth remarking that the elements common to the French and Chinese oral traditions, namely, the cannibalistic eating of a relative's flesh, the wolf or tiger's suggestion that the girl defecate in bed, and the device of escaping by tying a rope around a substitute object could not possibly have been transmitted by the Perrault literary version since these elements are *not* found in that version.

A summary of some seventy-three versions of AT 333A, The Gluttonous Ogress and Children, from Japan, as reported in Hiroko Ikeda's *A Type and Motif Index of Japanese Folk-Literature* (1971), reveals some of the same distinctive features. An ogress comes upon a woman, eats all the food she has, and then eats the woman, too. The ogress proceeds to the woman's house to eat the children; she is disguised as their mother. The ogress is asked by the suspicious children to put her hand through a hole and is told that the mother's hand is not so rough. The ogress leaves and returns after rubbing her hand with a taro leaf. This time the children claim that the ogress's voice is too hoarse to be that of their mother. She goes and returns after drinking oil (or sugar or honey) and is finally admitted. After going to bed, the ogress eats the baby. Hearing the munching sound, one of the children asks for the food and is given the baby's finger. The children insist that they need to go to the outhouse and are let out after ropes have been tied to them. They untie the ropes and climb up a tall tree. The ogress asks them how to climb the tree and, following their false instructions, falls from the tree to her death. In some versions, the children come down from the tree, cut the ogress open, and rescue their mother inside.[15]

The tale is equally popular in Korea. Eighteen versions are cited in In-Hak Choi, *A Type Index of Korean Folktales* (1979). They, too, include the detail that the children escape from the tiger by saying they have to go to the toilet.[16]

Even from these abbreviated summaries of the Chinese, Japanese, and Korean traditions, it should be obvious that the Perrault literary reworking of AT 333 is far from being the most typical version of the tale type. Once one admits that the Perrault version does not contain many of the most distinctive and essential traits of the oral tale, one may then turn to the Grimm version. A series of scholars have documented that the Grimm version came from Marie Hassenpflug, a woman with a French Huguenot background. Textual comparisons tend to substantiate the claim that the Grimms essentially reworked the Perrault version. Jack Zipes reminds us, "As is generally known, the major change made by the Grimms in their version of Little Red Cap was the happy ending. Here the Grimms borrowed a motif from the folk tale "The Wolf and the Seven Kids." A hunter saves Little Red Cap and her granny and they proceed to fill the wolf's belly with stones. When the wolf tries to jump up and escape, the stones cause his death."[17] If the Grimms have simply altered the Perrault version, then we would appear to have a case of a literary reworking of a literary reworking of an oral tale. The Grimm version of "Little Red Riding Hood" would thus be "twice removed" from genuine oral tradition.

The "twice-removed" status of the Grimm version of AT 333 should serve to illustrate the distinction made earlier between analyzing pure oral tradition and literary reworkings of that tradition. On the other hand, it should also be pointed out that the Grimms' restoration of the happy ending is entirely in accord with fairy tale morphology. Nearly all *oral* fairy tales end happily. Moreover, if we assume that AT 123 and AT 333 are probably cognates, possibly subtypes of the same general tale type (with the critical difference depending upon whether the wolf comes to the house of the children or the children come to the house of the wolf), then the possibility that the Grimms borrowed the ending of AT 123 to affix to the Perrault version of AT 333 may not be such a heinous literary crime. We have seen that in the Japanese versions of AT 333, the children in some instances cut the ogress open and rescue their mother inside.

The possible cognate relationship between AT 123 and AT 333 is actually hinted at by Stith Thompson insofar as he cross-references the two types in his revision of the tale type index. One of the weaknesses of the Aarne-Thompson tale type index system stems from Aarne's decision to classify folktales on the basis of dramatis personae rather than plot structure. Because of this arbitrary decision, AT 9B, In the Division of the Crop the Fox Takes the Corn, the Bear the More Bulky Chaff, is classified as an animal tale while the very same tale, if told of man and ogre rather than fox and bear, becomes AT 1030, The Crop Division. It is obvious that AT 9B and AT 1030 should be considered under the rubric of a single unifying tale type. In the same way, one can see that AT 43, The Bear Builds a House of Wood, the Fox of Ice, is equivalent to AT 1097, The Ice Mill. As a matter of fact, Thompson's synoptic summary of the latter tale type reads: "Like Type 43 with man and ogre in place of animals." In the same fashion, one may compare AT 34, The Wolf Dives into the Water for Reflected Cheese, with AT 1336, Diving for Cheese. Again, Thompson's summary of the latter includes "This is Type 34 with human actors."

The point in the present context is that it may not be at all unreasonable to consider AT 123 and AT 333 as part of one and the same tale type. Eberhard, an expert in Chinese folklore, comments, "The use of the Aarne-Thompson types involves . . . some difficulties when non-European tales are studied. In our case, the Grandaunt Tiger story is classified as AT 123, but one form of our tale is very similar to AT 333. . . . Yet for the Chinese, both variants are the same story, not different stories."[18]

If tale types AT 123 and AT 333 should prove to be cognate, then one must reexamine Jack Zipes' claim that "research has proven rather conclusively that Little Red Riding Hood is of fairly modern vintage. By modern, I mean that the basic elements of the tale were developed in an oral tradition during the late Middle Ages, largely in France, Tyrol, and northern Italy."[19] AT 123 goes back in time to classical antiquity as Haim Schwarzbaum reminds us in *The Mishle Shu' Alim (Fox Fables) of Rabbi Berechiah Ha-Nakdan* (1979).[20] For instance, the tale is an Aesopic fable. In Perry's *Aesopica*, we find a version of AT 123 with a curious phrase strangely reminiscent of the cannibalistic content of some of the oral versions of AT 333. When the wolf comes to the goat's door, he tries to imitate the mother goat's voice. The smart kid's response is, "Vocem matris audio; sed tu fallax et inimicus es, et sub matris voce nostrum quaeris sanguinem bibere et carnes edere."[21] Specifically, the kid's taunt that the wolf's disguise is just so he can "drink blood and eat flesh" is strikingly similar to the inversion in AT 333 where it is the wolf who dupes Little Red Riding Hood into drinking the blood and eating the flesh of her grandmother. French folklorist Marie Louise Tenèze, in an essay devoted to AT 123 as represented by some sixty French versions, considers it one of the most popular animal tales in France.[22] I cannot forbear remarking that the first word in Perry's Latin text in *Aesopica* is *Capella*, which means she-goat, and wonder if there could possibly be any phonetic connection between this word and the set of names for the heroine of AT 333 in the Romance language tradition (e.g., in Italian she is Cappuccetto). Stranger things have happened than to have original Latin words transformed into puzzling neologisms—for example, "hoc est corpus" becoming through parody of the Eucharist "hocus pocus," although this may be only a folk etymology.

In any event, I trust that this discussion of versions of AT 333 and AT 123 shows conclusively that interpreters of "Little Red Riding Hood" who have based their analyses on just the Grimm version or even just the two Grimm and Perrault versions have unnecessarily handicapped themselves. What are these various interpretations?

Perhaps the earliest were solar in nature. In 1865, Edward B. Tylor, regarded by some as the founding father of modern cultural anthropology, mentioned "Little Red Riding Hood" in his *Researches into the Early History of Mankind*, comparing the story to other accounts of swallowed protagonists and suggesting that it might have solar significance. The protagonist representing the sun was swallowed by night; the release from the monster's stomach signified the sun being set free at dawn. Tylor took up the subject again in his discussion of "sunset and sunrise myths" in *Primitive Culture* (1871).

> Stories belonging to the same group are not unknown in European folk-lore. One is the story of Little Red Riding-hood, mutilated in the English nursery version, but known more perfectly by old wives in Germany, who can tell that the lovely little maid in her shining red satin cloak was swallowed with her grandmother by the Wolf, but they both came out safe and sound when the hunter cut open the sleeping beast. Anyone who can fancy with prince Hal, "the blessed sun himself a fair hot wench in flame-coloured taffeta," and can then imagine her swallowed up by Skoll, the Sun-devouring Wolf of Scandinavian mythology, may be inclined to class the tale of Little Red Ridinghood as a myth of sunset and sunrise."[23]

George W. Cox, in *The Mythology of the Aryan Nations* (1870), offers a slight variant of this interpretation. "In Teutonic folk-lore the night of darkness is commonly the ravening wolf, the Fenris of the *Edda*. This is the evil beast who swallows up Little Red Cap or Red Riding Hood, the evening with the scarlet robe of twilight."[24] Here Little Red Riding Hood is the evening rather than the sun. It is somewhat ironic that Max Müller, the indefatigable champion of solar mythology, urged caution in interpreting the tale in this way. In a review of solar mythologist Hyacinthe Husson's *La chaîne traditionelle* (1874), in which Husson had suggested that Little Red Riding Hood was the dawn, Müller remarked that without proper supporting philological evidence, "It would be a bold assertion to say that the story of Red Riding

Hood was really a metamorphosis of an ancient story of the rosy-fingered Eos. . . ."[25] Note well the diversity of solar mythological opinion as to whether the tale's heroine is the sun, the evening, or the dawn. Then there was also the lunar school of interpretation, competing with its earlier solar counterpart, which insisted that Little Red Riding Hood, who disappeared and reappeared, was a moon figure.[26]

The pioneering Danish folklorist Axel Olrik published an essay in 1894 "Den lille Rødhaette" in which he took Tylor's comparative approach as a point of departure.[27] Assembling various examples of swallowing-monster narratives, Olrik sought to show that the monster represented death. Hence, he concluded that such stories constitute life-and-death struggles, and that is why the protagonist might be associated with "light" and the "sun" as rebirth images in contrast to "darkness" and "night." Olrik's interpretation drew fire from fellow Dane V. Holst, who contended that the monster in such tales represented spiritual and material oppression as manifested in unfair political and social conditions. This 1895 rejoinder would appear to be a precursor of Marxist readings of folklore materials. Olrik in his rebuttal of Holst strongly opposed such allegorical readings, at the same time refusing to admit that his own interpretation of "Little Red Riding Hood" was highly allegorical.[28]

Ritual or myth-ritual interpretations of "Little Red Riding Hood" are of two types. The first argues that the tale reflects a seasonal ritual in which typically spring conquers winter. This calendrical battle is the interpretation proposed by Saintyves.[29] Here Red Riding Hood is spring (or the month of May) escaping from the winter-wolf.[29] It is not unlike Olrik's life-and-death reading of the tale. The second type of ritual interpretation insists that fairy tales are remnants or reflections of puberty initiation rites. Vladimir Propp, for example, in his 1946 *Historical Roots of the Fairy Tale*, contended that fairy tales stemmed from an early matriarchal cultural stage of evolutionary development. The gist of this form of ritual interpretation might be summarized as follows: a girl leaves her childhood home, experiences the onset of menses, fulfills set tasks (especially those involved in cleansing a donor figure or a donor figure's dwelling), and finally marries, signifying maturation. One can readily see how Propp's 1928 *Morphology of the Folktale* led to this interpretation even though Alfred Winterstein had already proposed just such an interpretation of female fairy tales in his 1928 essay "Die Pubertätsriten der Mädchen und ihre Spuren im Märchen."[30]

Ritual interpretations of "Little Red Riding Hood" have continued unabated. Glauco Carloni's 1963 essay "La fiaba al lume della psicoanalisis" combines ritual and psychoanalytic approaches to the folktale, relying upon Saintyves and Propp for the ritual theory.[31] In similar fashion, Anselmo Calvetti, in his 1980 essay "Tracce di Riti di Iniziazione nelle Fiabe di Cappuccetto Rosso e delle tre ochine," relies not only on Propp and Lévi-Strauss, but also on Van Gennep's rites of passage insofar as he sees Little Red Riding Hood's departure from home as a rite of separation, her time in the woods as a marginal or liminal period, her being eaten by the wolf in the grandmother's house as an initiation test, and her being rescued from the wolf's stomach as her rebirth or readmission into adult society.[32] Yvonne Verdier's 1978 essay, "Le Petit Chaperon Rouge dans la tradition orale," which appeared in slightly abridged form in 1980, also adopts a ritual stance. "The sojourn in the little house of the grandmother presents all the characteristics of an initiation . . . her entrance is death, her leaving is birth . . . the little girl is instructed about her feminine future."[33]

There is simply no end to the interpretations offered of "Little Red Riding Hood." Marianne Rumpf's 1951 doctoral dissertation, "Rotkäppchen: Eine vergleichende Märchenuntersuchung," based on only forty versions of the tale, suggests after dismissing the interpretive efforts of Olrik and Saintyves that the tale is simply a warning or cautionary tale.[34] According to such a functional approach, the tale is told to keep young girls from straying from home into dangerous forests. The contrast between home and forest has also been a point of departure for structural and semiotic readings, of the tale with home representing "culture" and the outside world of the forest representing "nature."[35]

The nature-culture dichotomy reminds us of one of the most curious sets of folktale interpretations of all those proposed. These interpretations are inspired by anthroposophy, a school of spiritual science founded by Rudolf Steiner (1861–1925). Anthroposophical reasoning, similar to Jungian theory, argues that primeval man was in touch with nature and that this intuitive sense has been continually dulled by the inevitable encroachment of civilization. To get back in touch with archetypal reality—and Steiner does employ the term "archetype"[36]—one is advised to rediscover fairy tales and partake of the spiritual wisdom they contain. Wisdom is one of the key words in anthroposophy, and most of the numerous German books in this vein contain "Weisheit" somewhere in the title.[37]

In one typical reading of "Little Red Riding Hood" by Norbert Glas, first published in 1947, we are told: "The fairy stories collected by the brothers Grimm are an infinite source of . . . pictures of events taking place within the human soul. In modern times, as a result of childhood spent in towns and of the mechanisation of life, it becomes more and more difficult to apprehend the intimate stirrings of the soul and the spirit. . . ."[38] The essence of the interpretation is that grandmother is an old woman who is "weak and ill and in need of succour." Red Riding Hood comes to the rescue carrying "bread and wine." "In the Christian Church the Christ comes to the human being in the Bread and Wine; through the Bread and Wine sickness shall be healed." The huntsman signifies wisdom (not to be confused with "mere intellectual cleverness").[39] In another anthroposophical reading, the hunter is said to be reminiscent of the Holy Ghost.[40] In the end, the grandmother "eats the cake, the bread and drinks the wine; in other words, she receives the Holy Communion." Glas concludes, "The fairy tale 'Red Riding Hood' describes thus in a most wonderful way the victory of the human soul over the wild and tempting forces of the wolf which want to prevent it from treading the true path into the future."[41]

Steiner and his followers, it must be noted, have produced a large number of interpretive books on fairy tales in various languages going back at least to Steiner's own lecture *The Interpretation of Fairy Tales*, given in Berlin in December 1908. Anthroposophists are not much interested in criticisms of their approach. Indeed, Rudolf Steiner's own *The Mission of Folk-Souls in Connection with Germanic Scandinavian Mythology* (1929) bears a clear caveat on its title page: "Printed for Members of the School of Spiritual Science, Goetheanum, Class I. No person is held qualified to form a judgment on the contents of this work, who has not acquired—through the School itself or in an equivalent manner recognised by the School—the requisite preliminary knowledge. Other opinions will be disregarded; the authors decline to take them as a basis for discussion."[42]

The psychoanalytic study of "Little Red Riding Hood" began with Freud, not just because he was the founder of psychoanalysis but also because he specifically commented on the tale. In a paper "On the Sexual Theories of Children," published in 1908, Freud described the so-called cloacal theory of creation. Children ignorant of the birth process might logically assume that "babies" who grow in the body of the mother must exit the body in the same way that all objects located in the general area of the stomach leave the body, namely, via the anus. "The child must be expelled like excrement. . . . If in later childhood the same question is the subject of solitary reflection or of a discussion between two children, the explanations probably are that the baby comes out of the navel, which opens, or that the belly is slit and the child taken out, as happens to the wolf in the tale of Little Red Riding-Hood."[43] Freud continues, "If babies are born through the anus then a man can give birth just as well as a woman. A boy can therefore fancy that he too has children of his own without our needing to accuse him of feminine inclinations." Freud's remarkable insight about male pregnancy envy and how it might be manifested in anal terms has inspired analyses of creation myths, such as the creation of earth or man from mud or dust.[44] In the present context, we can only regret that Freud knew only the Grimm version of AT 333. What might he have thought in the light of versions of the same tale with explicit anality!

In his 1913 essay "The Occurrence in Dreams of Material from Fairy-Tales," Freud deals more extensively with "Little Red Riding Hood." A young male patient had a dream in which white wolves appeared in a tree. The patient remembered being "tremendously afraid of the picture of a wolf in a book of fairy tales. . . . He thought this picture might have been an illustration to the story of 'Little Red Riding Hood.'" Freud's knowledge of the Grimm canon stood him in good stead, for he suggested to the patient that the childhood image probably referred not to "Little Red Riding Hood" but to "The Wolf and the Seven Little Goats." "The white, too, comes into this story, for the wolf had his paw made white at the baker's after the little goats had recognized him on his first visit by his grey paw." Freud goes on to say, "Moreover, the two fairy-tales [that is, what folklorists now call AT 123 and AT 333] have much in common. In both there is the eating up, the cutting open of the belly, the taking out of the people who have been eaten and their replacement by heavy stones, and finally in both of them the wicked wolf perishes."[45]

Freud was not only interested in helping his patients, but also in the analysis of folklore. For Freud, folklore was an aid to understanding patients just as psychoanalysis was an aid to understanding folklore. Folklore and psychoanalysis were understood to be mutually or reciprocally beneficial. Freud concluded his essay: "If in my patient's case the wolf was merely a first father-surrogate, the question arises whether the hidden content in the fairy-tales of the wolf that ate up the little goats and of 'Little Red Riding Hood' may not simply be infantile fear of the father." Freud remarked that his patient's father had the habit of indulging in "affectionate abuse" and that he may have threatened in fun to "gobble him up." Another of Freud's patients told him that her two children could never get to be fond of their grandfather "because in the course of his affectionate romping with them he used to frighten them by saying he would cut open their tummies."[46] Freud reiterated his remarks about "Little Red Riding Hood" in the longer write-up of the same case in his 1918 paper "From the History of an Infantile Neurosis."[47]

The psychoanalytic treatment of "Little Red Riding Hood" continued with brief contributions by Otto Rank and Carl Jung. In 1912, Rank, no doubt influenced by Freud's 1908 paper "On the Sexual Theories of Children," attempted to survey what he termed "folk psychological parallels to infantile sexual theories." In his extensive consideration of myths and folktales, Rank judged "Little Red Riding Hood" to be the best-known illustration of the infantile notion of either opening or cutting the stomach to induce birth.[48] In 1913, the year that Jung began to reject psychoanalytic theory in favor of what was to become analytical psychology, he published "Versuch einer Darstellung der psychoanalytischen Theorie," in which he interpreted the wolf as the father, with the fear of being swallowed as an expression of fear of intercourse. Jung at this point was still very much under the influence of Freud.[49]

Perhaps the first significant psychoanalytic interpretation of "Little Red Riding Hood" was that written by Erich Fromm in 1951 in his book *The Forgotten Language*. He claimed, as so many psychoanalysts arrogantly do, that "Most of the symbolism in this fairy tale can be understood without difficulty." According to Fromm, "The 'little cap of red velvet' is a symbol of menstruation. The little girl of whose adventures we hear has become a mature woman and is now confronted with the problem of sex. The warning 'not to run off the path' so as not 'to fall and break the bottle' is clearly a warning against the danger of sex and of losing her virginity. The wolf's sexual appetite is aroused by the sight of the girl and he tries to seduce her."[50]

Fromm argues that the fairy tale is more than simply a moralistic tale warning of the danger of sex. He claims that the "male is portrayed as a ruthless and cunning animal, and the sexual act is described as a cannibalistic act in which the male devours the female." According to Fromm, this view is not held by women who like men and enjoy sex. It is an expression of a deep antagonism against men and sex. Fromm continues, "But the hate and prejudice against men are even more clearly exhibited at the end of the story . . . we must remember that the woman's superiority consists in her ability to bear children. How, then, is the wolf made ridiculous? By showing that he attempted to play the role of a pregnant woman, having living things in his belly. Little Red-Cap puts stones, a symbol of sterility, into his belly, and the wolf collapses and dies. His deed, according to the primitive law of retaliation, is punished according to his crime: he is killed by the stones, the symbol of sterility, which mock his usurpation of the pregnant woman's role."[51]

Fromm concludes "This fairy tale, in which the main figures are three generations of women (the huntsman at the end is the conventional father figure without real weight), speaks of the male-female conflict; it is a story of triumph by man-hating women, ending with their victory. . . ."[52]

Historian Robert Darnton in his 1984 book *The Great Cat Massacre* writes a devastating critique of Fromm's interpretation, based in part upon source criticism. Darnton notes that the symbols Fromm "saw in his version of the text were based on details that did not exist in the versions known to peasants in the seventeenth and eighteenth centuries." Darnton explains, "Thus he makes a great deal of the (non-existent) red riding hood as a symbol of menstruation and of the (nonexistent) admonition not to stray from the path into wild terrain where she might break it. The wolf is the ravishing male. And the two (nonexistent) stones that are placed in the wolf's belly, after the (nonexistent) hunter extricates the girl and her grandmother, stand for sterility, the punishment for breaking a sexual taboo. So, with an uncanny sensitivity to detail that did not occur in the original folktale, the psychoanalyst takes us into a mental universe that never existed, at least not before the advent of psychoanalysis."[53]

Darnton argues like a folklorist when he points out the fallacy of Fromm's analyzing a single version, namely, the

Grimm version of a tale type, but he himself errs when he seeks to extrapolate social history from such tales. Fairy tales are by generic definition fiction, *not* fact. Although occasional ethnographic or social facts may certainly be extracted from fairy tales, it is a methodological mistake to assume a one-to-one relationship between fairy tales and reality. A purely literal or historical approach to fairy tales yields precious little hard data. For one thing, it is not possible to "date" fairy tales in one particular century. Assuming, for example, that the Chinese, Japanese, and Korean versions of AT 333 cited earlier in this essay are indeed cognate with the French and other European versions of the tale type, one must assume a far greater time depth for the tale than the seventeenth century. Eberhard refers to a seventeenth-century Chinese version of AT 333, for example.[54] It would therefore be the height of folly to assume that most of the incidental details of the tale represent seventeenth-century peasant France.

Quite a different psychoanalytic interpretation of "Little Red Riding Hood" comes from Géza Róheim. In a 1940 essay, "The Dragon and the Hero," he offers brief exegeses of both AT 123 and AT 333. His basic view is that the tales reflect oral aggression on the part of infants. He cites a Romanian version of AT 123 in which the she-goat reveals to her children before leaving them what she will later say as a pass-word so that they will let her in. "It is all about the good things she is going to give them to eat. She has milk in the breast and cheese on her lips." Evidently, Róheim contends, "the narrative has something to do with the oral trauma. An absent nipple is a wicked child eating mother, and whenever the she-goat is not at home 'the wolf is at the door.' The youngest kid is probably the oldest and instead of wishing to rescue all the other kids swallowed by the wicked wolf-mother it really wishes to cut them out of its mother's body. As the wolf has become a wolf by not nursing its children, it dies in the attempt to assuage its thirst."[55] Róheim's preliminary analysis of "Little Red Riding Hood" is a bit more cryptic, although it is along similar lines: "the point is

that Little Red Riding Hood (as Wolf) eats the grandmother
first and is then eaten by the grandmother-wolf in the phase
of talio-anxiety."[56] What is important about Róheim's first
attempt at analyzing AT 333 is that it draws attention to the
cannibalistic component of the oral tales.

In the oral tales, the female protagonist does eat the body
of her grandmother. One might object that she does so un-
wittingly. She doesn't know that she is eating her grandmother's flesh and blood. But that is a necessary device in
folktale projections of psychological traumas. Oedipus in
theory didn't know he was marrying his mother after having
killed his father. In folklore fantasy, characters typically do
what they would like to do but which everyday society forbids. The sad part about most analyses of folklore is that
they wrongly emphasize the moralistic interdictions. Yes,
the interdictions are surely present, but what is critical in
folklore is that they are always violated. It is a mistake to
see only that the norms of a society are reflected in that society's folklore. Folklore articulates social sanctions at the
very same time that it permits, through wishful thinking,
escape from those very same social sanctions.[57]

Infants who breast-feed eventually learn that when their
teeth are in place, they possess their first real weapon. Any
mother or wet-nurse can testify to the pain that such little
teeth can inflict when a nursing baby becomes satiated or
unhappy during nursing. Through the principle of *lex talionis,* a guilty act is punished by the same means as those
employed in the commission of the original crime. Hence
biting or eating the mother's breast would be punishable by
the mother (or father) biting or eating the naughty infant.[58]

In 1953, the year of his death, Róheim published short separate essays on AT 123 and AT 333. In his study of AT 123,
"The Wolf and the Seven Kids," Róheim, unlike most psychoanalysts, makes good use of comparative data. He cites
an interesting version from Lorraine in which the wolf jumps
down the chimney into a cauldron of boiling milk. Róheim
writes, "The objectively good mother does not, moreover,
satisfy the insatiable cravings of the child and to that extent

becomes *ipso facto* an ogress. The infant's fantasy of being devoured by the mother is a fear through retaliation of its wish to devour the mother."[59] This remark would certainly apply to the story of "Little Red Riding Hood." The girl's attempt to devour her grandmother is followed immediately by the wolf-grandmother's attempt to devour her. This is precisely the plot of the oral French versions. Róheim's essay "Fairy Tale and Dream" offers an interpretation of the tale. After commenting upon the forced moralité in Perrault's story, which makes the wolf into the typical symbol of male aggression and sexuality, Róheim acutely remarks that such tales end in disaster for the young girl because they "are written from a pedagogical angle." When he returns to the oral versions, Róheim reiterates the same theory he proposed for AT 123. "Aggression is combined with regression and it follows that the idea of being swallowed, being eaten, is the talio aspect of this aggression. The cannibal child creates a cannibal mother."[60]

In the above discussion of Róheim's psychoanalytic interpretation of "Little Red Riding Hood," I have intentionally omitted some of the more controversial aspects of his analysis. For example, Róheim believes that fairy tales come from dreams. Parts of his interpretation are extremely hard to substantiate. He remarks, "To go on sleeping after its stomach has been cut open several times is quite an achievement, even for a folk-tale wolf. We can only understand this if we assume that the wolf, the grandmother, and the little girl, are essentially the same person."[61] Róheim continues, "Red Riding Hood is swallowed into her own 'sleep-womb' which is at the same time the inside of her mother. The hunter would then be correctly interpreted as the father figure, as a rival for the inside (or breast) of the mother."[62]

A number of other psychoanalytic treatments of "Little Red Riding Hood" can be mentioned briefly. In 1955, Elizabeth Crawford, inspired by Róheim's analysis of AT 123, wrote "The Wolf as Condensation." She argued that the wolf in that tale "is father and mother simultaneously." In her analysis, she continues her efforts to see the wolf as a complex figure, representing "good and bad, giver and taker, sexual object desired and feared. . . ." The complexity is summarized by her statement, "The wolf seduces, but the children invite seduction and danger."[63] Much the same argument could be sustained about the parental seduction of children fantasy. Parents may act seductively towards their own children, but children also engage in seductive behavior towards their own parents of the opposite sex.

In 1963, Glauco Carloni's insightful psychoanalytic treatment of "Little Red Riding Hood" drew heavily from Róheim, combining his approach with a ritual-initiation analysis deriving from Saintyves and Propp.[64] Also in 1963 appeared Julius E. Heuscher's *A Psychiatric Study of Fairy Tales.* Heuscher's mixture of Jungian theory, anthroposophy, and psychoanalysis is not always clear. With respect to "Little Red Riding Hood," his interpretation is in part Oedipal. He disagrees with Fromm's opinion that the huntsman is a weak figure. Rather he sees the huntsman as a "*strong* Father-image." According to Heuscher, "The huntsman who carries off the wolf's skin, combines now the human and sexual aspects of the male without being threatening. He shows that he has control over his animal drives."[65]

In 1966, Lilla Veszy-Wagner published her "Little Red Riding Hoods on the Couch" in *Psychoanalytic Forum,* accompanied by comments by four discussants and a final response by the author. Here we find the usual parochial lack of knowledge of tale types. The author begins by saying, "There seems to be no particularly relevant folkloristic material available to this story outside Europe so we may infer that problems pertaining to this tale seem to be more connected with the unconscious of the European mind."[66] One of her discussants, Mark Kanzer, offers the following psychoanalytic "translation" of "Little Red Riding Hood":

The pubescent girl, at the time of menstruation, defies her mother's warnings and enters into conversation with a strange man who accosts her. Taken to his room (which fuses in her unconscious with the bedroom of her parents), she inspects his body and is consumed sexually (just as mother has been by father). There follows (foreshortened in time) a pregnancy and delivery. However, a denial element is registered at this point: not the girl but the "wolf" becomes pregnant while she is delivered from his body by a good man, the hunter. The wolf, justly enough, succumbs to the perils of the pregnancy he has engendered.[67]

Kanzer adds that he finds some support for Fromm's suggestion that there is an allusion to the inability of the male wolf to bear children. "With the aid of the well-known equation, stones = feces, we find that he cannot, after all, convert his feces into children."

Another discussant, Thomas Mintz, proposes that the tale be looked at as a dream, in which case "one might see all the characters in the story as representing the dreamer: the wolf would represent sexual temptation and cannibalistic desires (the id) which must be killed off by the punishing huntsman (the superego) in order that the small child (the ego) will not be consumed and overwhelmed."[68]

No doubt the best-known psychoanalytic interpretation of "Little Red Riding Hood" is that written by Bruno Bettelheim in his 1976 book *The Uses of Enchantment*. To his credit, Bettelheim is aware that there are versions other than those of Perrault and the Grimms, but he makes absolutely no reference to any of the previous psychoanalytic treatments of the tale, such as those cited in this essay. Bettelheim's interpretation differs radically from Róheim's. For example, he claims that in contrast to Hansel and Gretel, who suffer from an oral fixation, "Little Red Cap, who has outgrown her oral fixation, no longer has any destructive oral desires."[69] I suggest that the overt cannibalistic details of the oral versions of AT 333 would not support Bettelheim's contention. When the protagonist devours her grandmother's body, that would seem to be prima facie "destructive oral desires."

Bettelheim, aware of the French versions of the tale in which Red Riding Hood has to choose between taking the road of needles and the road of pins, remarks in a footnote that pins represent the pleasure principle while needles represent the reality principle. His reasoning is that it is easier to fasten things together with pins; it is much more work to fasten things by needles, that is, by sewing. From this viewpoint, the girl's decision to take the path of pins signals her intention to indulge in the pleasure principle.[70]

For Bettelheim, the wolf is "not just the male seducer, he also represents all the asocial, animalistic tendencies within ourselves . . . Little Red Cap's danger is her budding sexuality, for which she is not yet emotionally mature enough."[71] Bettelheim maintains that Little Red Riding Hood's giving explicit directions to the wolf as to how to find grandmother's house is an admission that she is not ready for sexuality, but that grandmother, a mature woman, is. Bettelheim feels that the tale is basically an Oedipal one. "With the reactivation in puberty of early oedipal longings, the girl's wish for her father, her inclination to seduce him, and her desire to be seduced by him, also become reactivated. Then the girl feels she deserves to be punished terribly by the mother, if not the father also, for her desire to take him away from Mother."[72] Thus as long as mother or grandmother is around, the girl is not free to seduce/be seduced by the wolf. According to Bettelheim, the story "on this level deals with the daughter's unconscious wish to be seduced by her father (the wolf)."[73] This is why so many of the illustrations of the tale concentrate on the scene with Little Red Riding Hood in bed with the wolf. For Bettelheim, the father is present in the story in two forms: the wolf, "which is an externalization of the dangers of overwhelming oedipal feelings, and as the hunter in his protective and rescuing function."[74]

There have been psychoanalytic interpretations of "Little Red Riding Hood" since Bettelheim. For example, there is one included by Carl-Heinz Mallet in his *Kennen Sie Kinder?* (1981), among others.[75] However, few new insights have emerged. Not mentioned in this survey are various Jungian-inspired readings which, true to analytical psychology (as opposed to psychoanalysis), disavow the sexual content of fairy tales, preferring instead to emphasize individuation and maturation.[76]

What has been the reaction to these various psychoanalytic readings of the tale? We may consider that of Jack Zipes to be representative. Zipes's response to Bettelheim's treatment of "Little Red Riding Hood" is colored somewhat by his primary concern with the Grimms (and also Perrault's) manipulation of an oral tale. Zipes insists that these males twisted what was originally a girl-centered fairy tale (in which she triumphs unaided over the villainous wolf figure) into a story in which female sexuality is squelched and either a naughty female is killed by a male punishing wolf (Perrault) or a victimized female must await rescue at the hands of a male huntsman. Zipes traces these "civilizing" and moralizing trends through a host of literary editions and moreover adduces convincing evidence for his thesis from the illustrations in these children's books, illustrations drawn mainly by males, of course. From Perrault's conversion of "Little Red Riding Hood" into a cautionary tale to the Grimms' revision of the Perrault tale at the beginning of the nineteenth century, Zipes sees a shift of emphasis reflecting the growing impact of bourgeois morality. As Zipes remarks near the end of his important introductory essay in *The Trials and Tribulations of Little Red Riding Hood*, "Little Red Riding Hood is a *male* creation and projection. Not women but men—Perrault and the Brothers Grimm—gave birth to our common image of Little Red Riding Hood."[77] Zipes says further, "Viewed in this light, *Little Red Riding Hood* reflects men's fear of women's sexuality—and of their own as well. The curbing and regulation of sexual drives is fully portrayed in this bourgeois literary fairy tale on the basis of deprived male needs. Red Riding Hood is to blame for her own rape. The wolf is not really a male but symbolizes natural urges and social nonconformity. The real hero of the tale, the hunter-gamekeeper, is male governance."[78]

In a reprise essay of 1983–1984 entitled "A Second Gaze at Little Red Riding Hood's Trials and Tribulations," Zipes reiterates his view that the Perrault and Grimm versions "have served as models for numerous writers of both sexes throughout the world who have either amplified, distorted, or disputed the facts about the little girl's rape." In Zipes's words, "Instead of being raped to death, both grandma and granddaughter are saved by a male hunter or gameskeeper, who polices the woods. Only a strong male figure can rescue a girl from herself and her lustful desires."[79]

From this perspective, we can more easily appreciate Zipes' reaction to Fromm's and Bettelheim's psychoanalytic readings of "Little Red Riding Hood." First of all, Fromm and Bettelheim do not realize that the tale they analyze is "*not an ancient and anonymous folk tale reflecting 'universal' psychic operations of men and women, but rather it is the product of gifted male European writers, who projected their needs and values onto the actions of fictitious characters within a socially conventionalized genre.*"[80] Secondly, Zipes contends that Fromm, Bettelheim, and others have exacerbated the problem because they—as males—have interpreted the Perrault and Grimm versions "to reaffirm conventional male attitudes towards women; the girl is guilty because of her natural inclinations and disobedience."[81] Fromm, it may be recalled, claimed the tale displayed hate and prejudice against men and that it constituted a story of triumph by man-hating women, while Bettelheim felt that Little Red Cap's danger is her budding sexuality, for which she is not yet emotionally mature enough. In other words, both the male-altered tale *and* the male interpretations of this tale constitute a kind of male conspiracy to stereotype and dominate women.

Support for Zipes's position may be found in Eric Berne's pop(ular) psychology manual, *What Do You Say After You Say Hello?* (1972). Berne gives what he pretends might be a Martian's reaction to the tale:

> What kind of a mother sends a little girl into a forest where there are wolves? Why didn't her mother do it herself, or go along with LRRH? If grandmother was so helpless, why did

mother leave her all by herself in a hut far away? But if LRRH had to go, how come her mother had never warned her not to stop and talk to wolves? The story makes it clear that LRRH had never been told that this was dangerous. No mother could really be that stupid, so it sounds as if her mother didn't care much what happened to LRRH, or maybe even wanted to get rid of her. No little girl is that stupid either. How could LRRH look at the wolf's eyes, ears, hands, and teeth, and still think it was her grandmother? Why didn't she get out of there as fast as she could? And a mean little thing she was, too, gathering up stones to put into the wolf's belly. At any rate, any straight-thinking girl, after talking to the wolf, would certainly not have stopped to pick flowers, but would have said to herself: "That son of a bitch is going to eat up my grandmother if I don't get some help fast!"[82]

In similar fashion, Berne makes the Martian ponder the motivations of all the dramatis personae in the tale. The mother is evidently trying to lose her daughter "accidentally"; the wolf, instead of eating rabbits and such, is obviously overreaching himself; grandmother lives alone and leaves her door unlatched, so she may be hoping for something interesting to happen; the hunter is obviously a rescuer who enjoys working over his vanquished opponents with sweet little maidens to help; and "LRRH" tells the wolf quite explicitly where he can meet her again, and even climbs into bed with him. She is obviously playing "Rapo"—Berne is famous for coining the "games people play" metaphor—and ends up quite happy about the whole affair.[83]

Berne's Martian concludes his musing as follows:

The truth of the matter is that everybody in the story is looking for action at almost any price. If the payoff at the end is taken at face value, then the whole thing was a plot to do in the poor wolf by making him think he was outsmarting everybody, using LRRH as bait. In that case, the moral of the story is not that innocent maidens should keep out of forests where there are wolves, but that wolves should keep away from innocent-looking maidens and their grandmothers; in short a wolf should not walk through the forest alone. This also raises the interesting question of what the mother did after she got rid of LRRH for the day.[84]

This would certainly seem to be a fine example of Zipes's point that males insist upon projecting their sexual fantasies upon women. Men do not rape women; instead women ask to be raped. In Berne's terms, LRRH is playing "Rapo."

The problem with all this for the folklorist is that Zipes is really interested only in the particular impact of the Perrault and Grimm versions upon European society from the seventeenth century to the present. There is nothing wrong with such a scholarly concern, but it is *not* the same thing as being interested in the underlying, original oral folktale as such. We return to a theme mentioned at the outset of this essay. The study of one or two literary versions of an oral tale, no matter how important those literary versions may be, is no substitute for a full-fledged folkloristic study of the oral *and* literary versions of a given tale.

What then is one to make of all the various interpretations of "Little Red Riding Hood"? While they are not all mutually exclusive, one might wish to argue that some are more persuasive than others. Certainly the solar interpretations and others that depend upon one particular trait—for example, the red cap or hood, which in fact does *not* occur in the vast majority of available versions—are suspect. Within the more limited category of psychoanalytic interpretations, we clearly find discrepancies. Fromm suggests the tale is about the battle of the sexes; Róheim sees the tale as basically pre-Oedipal, with an emphasis upon infantile oral aggression; Bettelheim specifically denies such a theme. Recall Bettelheim's claim that Little Red Cap had outgrown her oral fixation and that she "no longer has any destructive oral desires." He opts for a more Oedipal or Electral interpretation. One could, of course, argue that fairy tales, like dreams, are over-determined; that is, they stem from more than one cause. In that event, a particular tale could contain both pre-Oedipal (in this case oral) *and* Oedipal elements.

From the vantage point afforded by folkloristics, we can see that most of the interpretations cited fail to make use of the full panoply of oral texts of "Little Red Riding Hood" that are available. No psychoanalytic (nor any other) interpretation of the tale has utilized the numerous versions of the basic tale type found in China, Japan, and Korea. (There are also many African versions of the tale type.[85]) The indisputable evidence of the existence of the tale in Asia would seem to militate against the notion that the tale was somehow a reflection of personality features restricted to Europe. Such a narrow Euro-centric approach to folklore in general and to fairy tales in particular would benefit greatly from taking account of cognate tales found in other parts of the world.

My own view, admittedly influenced by the various psychoanalytic essays devoted to the tale, is that there is good reason to believe that wishful thinking and regression abound. Any fairy tale with a female protagonist has a female antagonist. Hence I tend to agree with Verdier's interpretation of the tale as essentially an inter-generational conflict between daughter and mother. (The grandmother is an extended form of the mother imago.) But whereas Verdier sees this conflict only in "Little Red Riding Hood," I would use the Proppian model to suggest that same-sex rivalry is a standard feature of all oral fairy tales. Thus young girls have to contend with wicked stepmothers and witches while young boys have to struggle with male dragons or giants. The sexual identity of the donor (when he or she is distinct from the villain) may vary, but even here there is commonly a split parent, with the donor figure in "female" fairy tales being a kind female (e.g., a cow) and the donor figure in "male" fairy tales being a helpful wise old man.

In "Little Red Riding Hood" we find tremendous antagonism between heroine and female foe. We begin with a mother sending a hapless girl away from the safety of the home. This enforced abandonment (cf. weaning) leads the girl to take her revenge by eating her grandmother's flesh. If one stops to think about it, one can see that breast-feeding

223

constitutes a kind of eating of maternal flesh in order to obtain the necessary nourishing mother's milk. In oral versions of the tale, the heroine eats the flesh and blood of her grandmother, an unquestionably oral, aggressive act on the part of the girl. Infantile regression is also signaled by the desire to defecate *immediately* after eating. Here we have the first of a whole series of projective inversions or reversals. It is not the infant who seeks to "do it" in bed, but the wolf-grandmother who urges the child to do so. In other words, it is the parent who is not toilet trained while the child is. This explicit anal component of "Little Red Riding Hood" has received virtually no attention from commentators, probably because it was one of the "ruder" elements presumably intentionally omitted by Perrault in his version.

Eberhard observes that in the Chinese context, "it is also common that a grandmother or a mother shares her bed with one or two children."[86] In some of the Taiwanese versions of the tale type, we find a curious competition motif. "The tiger wants to eat the children, but cannot possibly eat both children at once and thus must try to eat one without arousing the suspicion of the other. Therefore the tiger declares that only one child may sleep with 'her,' the one who wins in a competition. The competition is usually that the girls must wash themselves, or more specifically, wash their feet. The one who is cleaner may sleep with the visitor."[87] The older girl, suspicious, remains "dirty on purpose" so as to discourage the tiger from sleeping with her. From a psychoanalytic perspective, we can see here an instance of projective inversion. In the infantile experience, the infant associates defecating in bed with the withdrawal and absence of the parent who normally sleeps with it. In the fairy tale projection, it is not the parent, but the infant who withdraws from the bed through the threat of defecation. Indeed, in the fairy tale projection, the parent-surrogate actually urges the infant to "do it in bed." This explains why the feigned wish to defecate in the tale is a reasonable and appropriate means of escaping from the parental bed.

The reversal of the parent-child toilet training schema—in which it is the parent who recommends doing it in bed while the child goes outside to the outhouse—is paralleled by other reversals in which the parent and child exchange places. Once outside, the child-heroine frees herself from the toddler's safety-line (rope) and later induces the tigress to have a similar line tied around her. In this way, it is the parent-figure who assumes the role of toddler-infant. Finally, in many of the Chinese versions of AT 333, the tiger grandmother is killed by having hot liquid poured on her body "or into her mouth." Remember the French (Lorraine) version cited by Róheim in which the wolf jumps into a cauldron of boiling milk. The original oral aggressive tendencies of the infant are displaced or projected onto the parent figure. It is then not the child who is hungry, but the parent. Little Red Riding Hood begins her adventure carrying food to her grandmother. As Róheim correctly observed, it is not the child who wants to eat up the parent; it is, through projective inversion, the parent who wants to eat up the child. Through lex talionis, the hungry parent is killed by having boiling fluid poured into his or her mouth, or the wolf dies by drowning in hot milk! Even in the peculiar Grimm addendum to their version of the tale, which tells of a second encounter with a wolf, the wolf is duped by oral temptation. Following her grandmother's instructions, Little Red Riding Hood pours the water in which yesterday's sausages were boiled into a trough. The wolf smells the scent of the sausages and falls down from the roof where he was ensconced to drown in the sausage-water.

The sequence of oral, anal, and finally genital themes in oral versions of "Little Red Riding Hood" would indicate that the application of psychoanalytic theory is not inappropriate. Chinese, Japanese, and Korean versions of the tale, in which the hero or heroine's siblings are swallowed by the ogress, have the added component of sibling rivalry.

All this leads me to conclude that the tale of "Little Red Riding Hood" is full of infantile fantasy. I believe that the

225

evidence of the tale's infantile nature has been available for centuries, but folklorists and literary scholars have chosen not to consider it. The cannibalistic eating of the mother's body, the reference to defecating in bed, the toddler's rope (which is a direct allusion to Little Red Riding Hood being a very young child), and the insistence upon Red Riding Hood's being called "little" all support the infantile-fantasy interpretation. Illustrators may very well depict her as a girl approaching adolescence, but her name calls attention to her littleness, as in Le *petit* chaperon rouge and Rotkäppc*hen*. But such clues have gone unnoticed by commentators, perhaps in part because of their resistance to psychoanalytic interpretations of fairy tales.

Some may feel that the present psychoanalytic reading of the tale somehow spoils the story by reducing it to a series of infantile wishes. Such individuals should keep in mind that all of us begin life as infants and that there is nothing wrong or unusual in retaining or even celebrating infantile desires and fears in fairy tale form. Genuine fairy tales are *always* told from the child's point of view, never the parents'. Furthermore, adults no matter how old they are never cease to be the children of their own parents. Giants and giantesses are nothing more than the infant's eye view of adults. Fairy tale content is sufficiently disguised symbolically so that adults seeking to fathom the depths of meaning in fairy tales can ignore or forget their earliest infantile thoughts. Perrault simply chose to edit out what he considered to be overly rude or earthy elements from the oral tale, but the basic tale, like all genuine folklore, survived.

The unconscious content of "Little Red Riding Hood" was not entirely removed by the efforts of either Perrault or the Grimm brothers. The extensive number of updatings, parodies, short stories, poems, and even cartoons based upon the tale, as documented by Hans Ritz, *Die Geschichte vom Rotkäppchen: Ursprunge, Analysen, Parodien eines Märchens* (1981); Jack Zipes, *The Trials and Tribulations of Little Red Riding Hood* (1983), and Wolfgang Mieder's essay "Survival Forms of 'Little Red Riding Hood' in Modern Society" (1982) all reveal how much "Little Red Riding Hood" is a part of contemporary culture.[88] Even the scholarship dedicated to "Little Red Riding Hood" can provide a source of amusement, as we see in Heinrich E. Kühleborn's *Rotkäppchen und die Wölfe* (1982), in which the research efforts of a certain Professor Wainbrasch [= brainwash] are reported in detail.[89]

To the extent that some of the poetic and cartoon derivatives of the tale are sexually explicit, I would argue that the moralizing effect of Perrault's cautionary tale version and the Grimm brothers' recension have not been successful in stifling the underlying content of the oral tale. The projective nature of "Little Red Riding Hood" with respect to key familial conflicts has survived the literary reworkings of the tale. While the oral versions are ever so much more explicit than most of the tame children's book adaptations, the basic infantile content remains intact. Perrault and the Grimms may have truncated the tale, but they could not destroy it. Folklorists know well that folklore once recorded does not cease to be. "*Little* Red Riding Hood" is a delightful and psychologically meaningful piece of folklore fantasy. It will remain important to children and adults in decades to come— even if the more explicit and direct oral versions remain in the shadow of the better-known Perrault and Grimm texts.

Notes

1. Th. P. Van Baaren, "The Flexibility of Myth," *Studies in the History of Religions* 22 (1972), 199–206, reprinted in Alan Dundes, ed., *Sacred Narrative: Readings in the Theory of Myth* (Berkeley, 1984), 217–224.

2. For representative comparative studies of folktales made by folklorists, see Warren E. Roberts, *The Tale of the Kind and the Unkind Girls* (Berlin, 1958) and Anna Birgitta Rooth, *The Cinderella Cycle* (Lund, 1951).

3. For a discussion of this methodology, see Alan Dundes, "The Study of Folklore in Literature and Culture: Identification and Interpretation," *Journal of American Folklore* 78 (1965), 136–142.

4. The term "fakelore" was coined by Richard M. Dorson. See his "Folklore and Fake Lore," *American Mercury* 70 (1950), 335–343. See also his article "Fakelore," *Zeitschrift für Volkskunde* 65 (1969), 56–64. For a consideration of the Grimms' tales as fakelore, see Alan Dundes, "Nationalistic Inferiority Complexes and the Fabrication of Fakelore: A Reconsideration of Ossian, the *Kinder- und Hausmärchen*, the *Kalevala*, and Paul Bunyan," *Journal of Folklore Research* 22 (1985), 5–18.

5. For an introduction to this extraordinary collector, see Joan Rockwell, *Evald Tang Kristensen: A Lifelong Adventure in Folklore* (Aalborg, Denmark, 1982).

6. For considerations of the differences from edition to edition of the Grimms' tales, see Heinz Rölleke, *Die älteste Märchensammlung der Brüder Grimm* (Cologny-Geneve, 1975), and John M. Ellis, *One Fairy Story Too Many: The Brothers Grimm and Their Tales* (Chicago, 1983). For a small sample of the changes in "Little Red Riding Hood" in the different editions, see Marianne Rumpf, "Rotkäppchen: Eine vergleichende Märchenuntersuchung" (Ph.D. diss., Göttingen, 1951), 97–98.

7. The details of the French oral versions of AT 333 were first masterfully surveyed by Paul Delarue. See "Le Petit Chaperon Rouge," *Bulletin folklorique d'île-de-France* 13 (1951), 221–228, 251–260, 283–291, where he considers some thirty-five French versions. See also his essay, "Les contes merveilleux de Perrault et la tradition populaire," *Bulletin folklorique d'île-de-France* 15 (1953), 511–517. For a summary in English of some of Delarue's conclusions, see his note to "The Story of Grandmother (T. 333)" in his *The Borzoi Book of French Folk Tales* (New York, 1956), 380–383. It is this version of the tale, circa 1885, which I have summarized in this essay. Literary scholars unfamiliar with folkloristics are genuinely puzzled by Delarue's claim that this "1885" text is the "source" of Perrault's seventeenth-century tale. How can a tale collected in the nineteenth century be "older" than one recorded in the seventeenth century? The answer is that comparative studies of many, many versions of a given tale type can establish with reasonable certainty what some, if not all, of the most ancient traits or details of a tale are or were. Delarue explains this when he notes that an examination of French and Italy-Tyrolean versions share common traits which are absent from Perrault's version. He concludes that it is plausible to assume that Perrault eliminated some of those salient traits that would have shocked

the society of his period. For the sceptical view, see Carole and D. T. Hanks, Jr., "Perrault's 'Little Red Riding Hood': Victim of the Revisers," *Children's Literature* 7 (1978), 76–77, n. 2. For Delarue's remarks, see *The Borzoi Book of French Folk Tales*, 383.

8. The idea of "strip-tease" I have borrowed from Marc Soriano, "Le Petit Chaperon Rouge," *Nouvelle Revue Française* 16 (1968), 429–443.

9. The version was first reported in Anselmo Calvetti, "Una versione romagnola di Cappuccetto Rosso," *In Rumâgna* 2 (1975), 85–95. The dialogue cited in the present essay is also found in Calvetti, "Tracce di Riti di Iniziazione nelle Fiabe di Cappuccetto Rosso e delle Tre Ochine," *Lares* 46 (1980), 487–496. (The dialogue is on page 488.) For similar Italian versions of the tale, see Paul Delarue, "Le Petit Chaperon Rouge," *Bulletin folklorique d'île-de-France*, 13 (1951), 257–259. For statistics demonstrating the frequency of the cannibalistic eating of the grandmother's flesh and blood, see page 260, and Rumpf, "Rotkäppchen," 51–54.

10. Alexander Haggerty Krappe, *The Science of Folklore* (New York, 1930), 38.

11. Stith Thompson, *The Folktale* (New York, 1945), 39.

12. For Delarue's discussion of the Asian analogues, see "Le Petit Chaperon Rouge," *Bulletin folklorique d'île-de-France*, 13 (1951), 286–289. See also Rumpf, "Rotkäppchen," 68. Although both Delarue and Rumpf tend to see the Asian tales as related to AT 123 rather than AT 133, Delarue does state that the Chinese tales have traits analogous to "Little Red Riding Hood" so particularized that they cannot possibly be attributed to coincidence. In other words, they are cognate. See Delarue, page 289. To be fair, it should be noted that Thompson does comment on AT 123's distribution in China, Japan, and Africa. See Thompson, page 40.

13. Nai-Tung Ting, *A Type Index of Chinese Folktales*, Folklore Fellows Communications no. 223 (Helsinki, 1978), 61–64.

14. Wolfram Eberhard, *Studies in Taiwanese Folktales*, Asian Folklore and Social Life Monographs (Taipei, 1970), 152, 54.

15. Hiroko Ikeda, *A Type and Motif Index of Japanese Folk-Literature*, Folklore Fellows Communications no. 209 (Helsinki, 1971), 91–92.

16. See tale type 100 in In-Hak Choi, *A Type Index of Korean Folktales* (Seoul, 1979), 27–28.

17. Jack Zipes, *The Trials and Tribulations of Little Red Riding Hood* (South Hadley, Mass., 1983), 15. See also Rolf Hagen, "Per-

raults Märchen und die Brüder Grimm," *Zeitschrift für Deutsche Philologie* 74 (1955), 392–410. For "Little Red Riding Hood," see 402–406.

18. Eberhard, *Taiwanese Folktales*, 166.

19. Zipes, *Trials and Tribulations*, 2.

20. Haim Schwarzbaum, *The Mishle Shu' Alim (Fox Fables) of Rabbi Berechiah Ha-Nakdan: A Study in Comparative Folklore and Fable Lore* (Kiron, 1979), 119–122.

21. Ben Edwin Perry, *Aesopica*, vol. I (Urbana, 1952), 614, no. 572.

22. Marie Louise Tèneze, "Aperçu sur les contes d'animaux les plus fréquemment attestés dans le repertoire français," in Georgios A. Megas, ed., *IV International Congress for Folk-Narrative Research in Athens, Lectures and Reports, Laographia* 22 (1965), 569–575.

23. Edward B. Tylor, *Researches into the Early History of Mankind* (Chicago, 1964), 206; *The Origins of Culture*, Part I of *Primitive Culture* (New York, 1958), 340–341.

24. George W. Cox, *The Mythology of the Aryan Nations*, vol. II (London, 1870), 351, n. 1.

25. F. Max Müller, "Note B. L'Aurore et le Jour," in *Selected Essays on Language, Mythology and Religion*, vol. I (London, 1881), 564. For the interpretation criticized by Müller, see Hyacinthe Husson, *La chaîne traditionelle* (Paris, 1874), 7. For references to other solar interpretations of "Little Red Riding Hood," see Zipes, *Trials and Tribulations*, 59, n. 1.

26. Ernst Siecke, *Indogermanische Mythologie* (Berlin, 1921), 66. According to Siecke, the wolf as swallower is the dark of the moon while Little Red Riding Hood is the bright moon which comes back to life after being released from the wolf's stomach.

27. Axel Olrik, "'Den lille Rødhaette' og andre Aeventyr om Mennesker, der bliver slugt levende," *Naturen og Mennesket* 11 (1894), 24–39.

28. V. Holst, "Aeventyr om menneskeslugende Uhyrer," *Naturen og Mennesket* 11 (1895), 187–189. For Olrik's rebuttal, see "Om Betydningen af Aeventyr," *Naturen og Mennesket* 11 (1895), 189–204. For these Danish references, I am greatly indebted to Bengt Holbek's important doctoral dissertation, "*Interpretation of Fairy Tales: Danish Folklore in a European Perspective*" (Helsinki, 1987), 233, 217–218. Inasmuch as Holbek uses "Little Red Riding Hood" as a sample tale to illustrate diverse approaches to content analysis, his dissertation provided many of the sources utilized in

the present essay. The point about Olrik's inconsistency, however, is mine.

29. Pierre Saintyves, *Les contes de Perrault et les récits parallèles* (Paris, 1923), 215–229.

30. Propp's 1946 book as yet has not been translated into English. Two chapters, however, appear in Vladimir Propp, *Theory and History of Folklore* (Minneapolis, 1984), 100–123, where his myth-ritual bias may be observed. For a more extreme argument that "Little Red Riding Hood" is the product of matriarchy, see M. Pancritius, "Aus mutterrechtlicher Zeit, Rotkäppchen," *Anthropos* 27 (1932), 743–778. The validity of Propp's brilliant morphological analysis of fairy tales fortunately is independent of his myth-ritual theorizing. See *Morphology of the Folktale* (Austin, 1968). For Winterstein's essay, see *Imago* 14 (1928), 199–274.

31. Glauco Carloni, "La fiaba al lume della psicoanalisi," *Revista di psicoanalisi* 9 (1963), 169–186. The analysis of "Little Red Riding Hood" is on pages 177–186.

32. For the application of Van Gennep's classic scheme to "Little Red Riding Hood," see Calvetti, "Tracce di Riti di Iniziazione," 489.

33. Yvonne Verdier, "Le Petit Chaperon Rouge dans la tradition orale," *Le débat* 3 (July–August 1980), 31–61. The initiation interpretation appears on page 54. The original article appeared as "Grands-mères, si vous saviez: le Petit Chaperon dans la tradition orale," *Cahiers de Littérature Orale* 4 (1978), 17–55.

34. Rumpf, "Rotkäppchen," 113–118, 121. See also the same author's *Ursprung und Entstehung von Warn- und Schreckmärchen*, Folklore Fellows Communications 160 (Helsinki, 1955). Although this approach has its advocates (e.g., Gottfried Henssen, "Deutsche Schreckmärchen und ihre europäischen Anverwandten," *Zeitschrift für Volkskunde* 50 ([1953], 84–97), it says little or nothing about the possible symbolic meanings of the tale. According to Propp's *Morphology*, a great many fairy tales involve interdictions. The point, however, is *not* that fairy tales have interdictions (to teach morality), but that the interdictions are invariably *violated*. It is the violation of the interdiction that makes the plot of fairy tales possible. This suggests that it is a truism but a gross over-simplification of "Little Red Riding Hood" to say it is a warning-tale for little girls to stay out of the forest! For a further consideration of "Little Red Riding Hood" as a moral cautionary tale, see Friedrich Wolfzettel, "Märchenmoral und Leseerwartung am Beispiel des Rotkäppchenstoffes," in Herbert Grabes, ed., *Text-Leser-*

Bedeutung (Grossen-Linden: Hoffmann Verlag, 1977), 157–175.

35. For a structural study of "Little Red Riding Hood," see Carsten Høgh, "Dansk på seminariet: 'Rødhaette' som metodeeksempel," *Kursiv,* 20 (1982), 9–18. For a semiotic study, see Victor Laruccia, "Little Red Riding Hood's Metacommentary: Paradoxical Injunction, Semiotics & Behavior," *Modern Language Notes,* 90 (1975), 517–534. For an essentially linguistic exercise in analyzing "Little Red Riding Hood" into sentences, see Gerald Prince, *A Grammar of Stories* (The Hague, 1973), 84–100. See also Joanne M. Golden, "Interpreting a Tale: Three Perspectives on Text Construction," *Poetics* 14 (1985), 503–524.

36. See Rudolf Steiner, *The Interpretation of Fairy Tales* (New York, 1929), 20. According to this 1908 lecture, "in a proper explanation of fairy tales it should always be recognised that we must go back to the archetype and identify it."

37. Representative titles include: Rudolf Meyer, *Die Weisheit der Schweizer Märchen* (Schaffhausen, 1944); Marie Brie, *Das Märchen im Lichte der Geisteswissenschaft* (Breslau, 1922); F. Eymann, *Die Weisheit der Marchen im Spiegel der Geisteswissenschaft Rudolf Steiners* (Bern, 1952); Ursula Grahl, *The Wisdom in Fairy Tales* (East Grinstead, 1955); and Rudolf Meyer, *Die Weisheit der deutschen Volksmärchen* (Frankfurt, 1981), first published in 1935. The Christian bias in anthroposophy is explicit. Grahl remarks "Moreover, these stories contain a deeply Christian element, as indeed there lives in all genuine fairy tales. This is true even of the stories that date back to pre-Christian times; for Christ was always known to men on earth." (39) For those interested, a major collection of Steiner-inspired books and monographs is to be found in the Steinerbiblioteket, which is a part of the Donnerska Institutet för Religionshistorisk och Kulturhistorisk Forskning, located in Turku, Finland.

38. N. Glas, *Red Riding Hood (Little Red Cap)* (East Gannicox, 1947), 3.

39. Ibid., 10–11, 21.

40. See Mellie Uyldert, "Roodkapje," in *Verborgen Wijsheid van het Sprookje,* 2d ed. (Amsterdam, 1969), 19–27. The interpretation of the hunter is on page 26. For the same author's interpretations of children's rhymes, see *Verborgen wijsheid van oude rijmen* (Amsterdam, 1972).

41. Glas, *Red Riding Hood,* 24. For additional anthroposophical readings of the tale, see the discussion in Holbek, "Interpreta-

tion of Fairy Tales," 226–228. For another such reading, see Roy Wilkinson, *The Interpretation of Fairy Tales* (East Grinstead, 1984), 18–19.

42. Rudolf Steiner, *The Mission of Folk-Souls in Connection with Germanic Scandinavian Mythology* (London, 1929). The preface was written in 1918 for the series of lectures which were given in Christiania (Oslo) in 1910.

43. Sigmund Freud, *Collected Papers*, vol. 2 (New York, 1959), 68–69.

44. See, for example, Alan Dundes, "Earth-Diver: Creation of the Mythopoeic Male," *American Anthropologist* 64 (1962), 1032–1050, reprinted in *Sacred Narrative: Readings in the Theory of Myth* (Berkeley, 1984), 270–294.

45. Freud, *Collected Papers*, vol. 4 (New York, 1959), 242.

46. Ibid., 243.

47. Freud, *Collected Papers*, vol. 3 (New York, 1959), 473–605. The clinical discussion of "Little Red Riding Hood" is on pages 498–515.

48. Otto Rank, "Völkerpsychologische Parallelen zu den infantilen Sexualtheorien: Zugleich ein Beitrag zur Sexualsymbolik," *Zentralblatt für Psychoanalyse* 2 (1912), 372–383, 425–437. The discussion of "Little Red Riding Hood" occurs on 426–427.

49. Carl G. Jung, "The Theory of Psychoanalysis," in *The Collected Works of C. G. Jung*, vol. 4, Bollingen Series XX (New York, 1961), 83–226. The consideration of "Little Red Riding Hood" is found on pages 210–211.

50. Erich Fromm, *The Forgotten Language: An Introduction to the Understanding of Dreams, Fairy Tales and Myths* (New York, 1951), 240.

51. Ibid., 241.

52. Ibid.

53. Robert Darnton, *The Great Cat Massacre and Other Episodes in French Cultural History* (New York, 1984), 11.

54. Eberhard, *Taiwanese Folktales*, 4.

55. Géza Róheim, "The Dragon and the Hero," *American Imago* 1, no. 2 (1940), 40–69. The discussions of AT 123 and AT 133 occur on pages 61–62 and 63, respectively.

56. Róheim, "The Dragon and the Hero," 63.

57. This is what William R. Bascom referred to as "the basic paradox of folklore." He concluded his classic statement on the functions of folklore by observing that while folklore "plays a vital role

in transmitting and maintaining the institutions of a culture and in forcing the individual to conform to them, at the same time it provides socially approved outlets for the repressions which these same institutions impose upon him." See "Four Functions of Folklore," *Journal of American Folklore* 67 (1954), 333–349, reprinted in Alan Dundes, ed., *The Study of Folklore* (Englewood Cliffs, 1965), 279–298.

58. It is my contention, incidentally, that the psychological origin of the widespread *vagina dentata* motif comes from a projection of the first weapon of the infant, that is, the teeth that bite the breast. As a male infant bites a female body protuberance, so later his fear of females finds expression in an imagined toothed vagina which threatens to bite his phallus.

59. Géza Róheim, "The Wolf and the Seven Kids," *Psychoanalytic Quarterly* 22 (1953), 253–256. The quotation is from p. 255.

60. Géza Róheim, "Fairy Tale and Dream," *The Psychoanalytic Study of the Child* 8 (1953), 397. "Little Red Riding Hood" is treated on pages 394–398.

61. Ibid., 395.

62. Ibid., 396.

63. Elizabeth Crawford, "The Wolf as Condensation," *American Imago* 12 (1955), 307–314.

64. Glauco Carloni, "La fiaba al lume della psicoanalisi," *Revista di psicoanalisi* 9 (1963), 169–186. Carloni is one of the very few interpreters of "Little Red Riding Hood" to acknowledge Róheim's brilliant analysis of the tale, although he unaccountably omits a formal reference in his footnotes.

65. Julius E. Heuscher, *A Psychiatric Study of Fairy Tales: Their Origin, Meaning and Usefulness* (Springfield, Ill., 1963), 73–79.

66. Lilla Veszy-Wagner, "Little Red Riding Hoods on the Couch," *Psychoanalytic Forum* 1 (1966), 400–415. The quotation is from p. 400.

67. Ibid., 410. Kanzer also refers to Róheim's essay, although his own summary of the content of "Little Red Riding Hood" owes little to Róheim's emphasis upon orality.

68. Ibid., 411.

69. Bruno Bettelheim, *The Uses of Enchantment: The Meaning and Importance of Fairy Tales* (New York, 1976), 170. The discussion of "Little Red Riding Hood" runs from pages 166–183.

70. Ibid., 171 n. For further discussion of the needles and pins alternatives, see Bernadette Bricout, "Les deux chemins du petit

chaperon rouge," in James Austin, et al., eds., *Fontieres du Conte* (Paris, 1982), 47–54.

71. Bettelheim, *The Uses of Enchantment*, 172, 173.

72. Ibid., 174, 175.

73. Ibid., 175.

74. Ibid., 178.

75. See Carl-Heinz Mallet, *Kennen Sie Kinder?* (Hamburg, 1981). The discussion of "Little Red Riding Hood" is on pages 81–112. The English edition is *Fairy Tales and Children* (New York, 1984). Not all psychoanalytic studies are truly psychoanalytic. See J. Geninasca, "Conte populaire et identité du cannibalisme," *Nouvelle Revue de Psychanalyse* 6 (1972), 215–230.

76. Jungian treatments include David L. Miller, "Red Riding Hood and Grand Mother Rhea: Images in a Psychology of Inflation," in James Hillman, ed., *Facing the Gods* (Irving, Tex., 1980), 87–99; Marzella Schäfer, *Märchen lösen Lebenskrisen*: Tiefenpsychologische Zugänge zur Märchenwelt für Eltern und Erzieher (Freiburg, 1983) ["Little Red Riding Hood" is the subject of the second chapter, pages 43–55]; and Verena Kast, *Märchen als Therapie* (Olten, 1986) ["Little Red Riding Hood" is the first tale analyzed, on pages 14–45].

77. Zipes, *Trials and Tribulations*, 56.

78. Ibid., 57.

79. "A Second Gaze at Little Red Riding Hood's Trials and Tribulations, *The Lion and the Unicorn*, 7–8 (1983–1984), 78–109. The quotation is from p. 81.

80. Ibid., 81–82.

81. Ibid., 83.

82. Eric Berne, *What Do You Say After You Say Hello? The Psychology of Human Destiny* (New York, 1972), 43.

83. Ibid., 44.

84. Ibid., 44–45.

85. For references to African versions, especially of AT 123, see May Augusta Klipple, "African Folk Tales with Foreign Analogues" (Ph.D., Indiana University, 1938), where more than a dozen versions of AT 123 are discussed on pages 86–92, 202–204. See also Erastus Ojo Arewa, *A Classification of the Folktales of the Northern East African Cattle Area by Types* (New York, 1980), 223–224, type 4024.

86. Eberhard, *Taiwanese Folktales*, 44.

87. Ibid., 46. See also p. 82.

88. Hans Ritz includes discussions of both scholarship and parodies in *Die Geschichte vom Rotkäppchen: Ursprünge, Analysen, Parodien eines Märchens* (Göttingen, 1981). The same is true of Jack Zipes, *The Trials and Tribulations of Little Red Riding Hood*. Zipes, however, has a special interest in political interpretations of the tale. Accordingly, he summarizes the argument of Hans-Wolf Jäger, who hypothesizes that the Grimms, having collected their tales during a period of French occupation, infused "Little Red Riding Hood" with anti-French sentiments. (See Jäger's essay earlier in this volume.) Wolfgang Mieder's extensive compilation of poems, parodies, and cartoons derived from "Little Red Riding Hood" documents the tale's continuity in the twentieth century. See "Survival Forms of 'Little Red Riding Hood' in Modern Society," *International Folklore Review* 2 (1982), 23–40. Also of interest are the eight poems referring to "Little Red Riding Hood" contained in Mieder, *Disenchantments: An Anthology of Modern Fairy Tale Poetry* (Hanover, N.H., 1985), 95–114. Folklorist Lutz Röhrich includes twelve parodies of the tale in *Gebärde–Metapher–Parodie: Studien zur Sprache und Volksdichtung* (Düsseldorf, 1967), 130–152. For a serious review of "Little Red Riding Hood" scholarship, see Hans T. Siepe, "Rotkäppchen einmal anders: Ein Märchen für den Französischunterricht," *Der Fremdsprachliche Unterricht* 65 (1983), 40–48.

89. Heinrich E. Kühleborn, *Rotkäppchen und die Wolfe: Von Märchen fälschem und Landschaftszerstörern* (Frankfurt am Main, 1982).

Selected Bibliography

Index

Suggestions for Further Reading
on "Little Red Riding Hood":
A Selected Bibliography

Bricourt, Bernadette. "Les Deux Chemins du Petit Chaperon Rouge." In *Frontieres du conte*, edited by James Austin, et al., 47–54. Paris: Centre National de la Recherche Scientifique, 1982. A discussion of the two alternative paths—of needles and of pins—in the French versions of "Little Red Riding Hood."

Bülow, Werner von. *Märchendeutungen durch Runen: Die Geheimsprache der deutschen Märchen. Ein Beitrag zur Entwickelungsgeschichte der deutschen Religion.* Hellerau bei Dresden: Hakenkreuz-Verlag, 1925. A brief discussion (pp. 28–32) of "Little Red Riding Hood" in excessively nationalistic and allegorical Teutonic terms, in which the sick grandmother represents the wisdom of ancient Aryan mother-right (law and order) which must be restored by the (grand)daughter so that the German soul can be reborn.

Burns, Lee. "Red Riding Hood." *Children's Literature* 1 (1972), 30–36. The author knows the French oral version but claims that its end "is farcical and anticlimactic in comparison with the Perrault and Grimm versions." He contrasts the "sly eroticism" in Perrault with the "repressed sexuality" in the Grimm version, and also discusses the modern versions of Walter de la Mare and Ann Sexton.

Calvetti, Anselmo. "Tracce di Riti di Iniziazione nelle Fiabe di Cappuccetto Rosso e delle tre Ochine," *Lares* 46 (1980), 487–496. Using a north Italian text collected in 1974 as a point of departure, the author applies Arnold van Gennep's classic rites of passage scheme to "Little Red Riding Hood." Her leaving home is a rite of separation; her encounter in the woods signifies a marginal state; her adventures at grandmother's house constitute an initiation; while the final rescue represents rebirth or admission into the adult world.

Calvetti, Anselmo. "Fungo Agarico Moscario e Cappuccio Rosso," *Lares* 52 (1986), 555–565. Apparently a serious addition to his earlier essay in which a hallucinogenic nonpoisonous *red-headed mushroom, Amanita muscaria,* is equated to Soma. Thus Little Red Riding Hood's red hood signifies this mushroom; she presumably picks the mushroom in the woods and ingests it, which accounts for her "temporary death" in the wolf's abdomen before being reborn at the end of the initiation ritual.

Carloni, Glauco. "La fiaba al lume della psicoanalisi," *Revista di psicoanalisi* 9 (1963), 169–186. After a general introduction the author analyzes "Cappuccetto Rosso," borrowing heavily from Fromm, Saintyves, and especially Róheim (pp. 177–186).

Crawford, Elizabeth. "The Wolf as Condensation," *American Imago* 12 (1955), 307–314. A psychoanalytic interpretation of the wolf in "Little Red Riding Hood" as "sexual object desired and feared" and as both mother and father figures.

Darnton, Robert. *The Great Cat Massacre.* New York: Vintage Books, 1985. The initial chapter, "Peasants Tell Tales: The Meaning of Mother Goose" (pp. 9–72), includes a brief but devastating critique of Fromm's and Bettelheim's interpretations of "Little Red Riding Hood" (pp. 9–13, 16–17) on the grounds that the text they analyzed never existed as a folktale but was largely a deviation by Perrault from oral tradition. He argues that genuine French fairy tales reflect eighteenth-century French peasant culture.

Delarue, Paul. "Les contes merveilleux de Perrault et la tradition populaire: I. Le petit chaperon rouge," *Bulletin folklorique d'Île-de-France* (1951), 221–228, 251–260, 283–291; (1953), 511–517. A leading scholar of the French folktale surveys thirty-five French versions (including oral ones) of "Little Red Riding Hood" and discusses Italian and Asian parallels. One of the first and most detailed comparative studies of the tale.

Deulin, Charles. *Les Contes de Ma Mere l'Oye avant Perrault.* Paris: E. Dentu, 1879. A short chapter (pp. 159–171) devoted to "Little Red Riding Hood" discusses mostly solar interpretations of the tale.

Dumézil, Georges. *Le Festin d'Immortalité: Etude de Mythologie Comparée Indo-Européenne,* 189–190. Paris: Librairie Orientaliste Paul Geuthner, 1924. The distinguished Indo-Europeanist mentions in passing (pp. 189–190) that "Little Red Riding Hood" is a folktale which has evolved considerably from its mythic beginnings but that the young girl's carrying a little pot of butter to her grandmother may be an echo or survival of earlier accounts in which ambrosia was the restorative or rejuvenating agent.

Fromm, Erich. *The Forgotten Language: An Introduction to the Understanding of Dreams, Fairy Tales and Myths.* New York: Grove Press, 1951. Includes his brief but often-cited interpretation of "Little Red Riding Hood" (pp. 235–241) as a sexual adventure involving the battle of the sexes. "It is a story of triumph by man-hating women."

Glas, Norbert. *Red Riding Hood: Meaning and Exact Rendering of Grimm's Fairy Tale.* East Gannicox: Education and Science Publications, 1947. This twenty-four-page pamphlet offers an anthroposophical interpretation of "Little Red Riding Hood," according to which the girl brings "the true Christian symbols of Bread and Wine" to heal her ailing grandmother. The wolf is the devil who is defeated.

Golden, Joanne M. "Interpreting a Tale: Three Perspectives on Text Construction," *Poetics* 14 (1985), 503–524. Utilizing reader-response theory, the author's pluralistic, formalistic rhetorical analysis of an English translation of Perrault's version of "Little Red Riding Hood" yields twenty-five speech acts, twelve major concepts, and a macro-structure of "a setting and six episodes."

Hagen, Rolf. "Perraults Märchen und die Brüder Grimm," *Zeitschrift für Deutsche Philologie* 74 (1955), 392–410. In this essay summarizing the results of his doctoral dissertation, the author discusses the relationship of Perrault's and Tieck's "Little Red Riding Hood" to that of the Grimms (pp. 402–406).

Haggart, Rev. James B. *Stories of Lost Israel in Folklore.* Thousand Oaks, Cal.: Artisan Sales, 1981. This unique Christian reading of "Little Red Riding Hood" (pp. 59–67) includes such reasoning as "Having decoded the character of Little Red Riding-Hood as Israel and the wolf as Imperial Rome, we can readily see that the central theme of our story revolves around the relationship of Israel with Rome" (p. 61).

Hanks, Carole, and D. T. Hanks, Jr. "Perrault's 'Little Red Riding Hood': Victim of the Revisers," *Children's Literature* 7 (1978), 68–77. The authors prefer the moralistic Perrault tale to both the Grimm version and the many American editions based on Grimm which eliminate the "sexuality and violent death which Perrault built into his tale." In a note (p. 76, n. 2) the authors express their doubt that an oral text collected as recently as the 1885 version cited by Delarue could possibly be considered the ancestor of Perrault's seventeenth-century tale.

Henssen, Gottfried. "Deutsche Schreckmärchen und ihre europäischen Anverwandten. Ein Beitrag zur vergleichenden Volks-kunde," *Zeitschrift für Volkskunde* 50 (1953), 84–97. The au-thor considers "Little Red Riding Hood" to be part of a Romance language oicotype (localized form) consisting of a warning or cau-tionary tale, in contrast to a Germanic and Slavic oicotype where the heroines escape from cannibalistic ogres.

Høgh, Carsten. "Dansk på seminariet: 'Rødhaette' som metodeek-sempel," *Kursiv* 2 (1982), 9–18. "Little Red Riding Hood" serves as a testing ground for structural and psychological interpreta-tions. A Lévi-Straussian opposition between culture (home) and nature (the woods) provides the basic matrix for the structural ar-gument with "contracts" broken and reestablished to regain ac-cess to home. A second set of models explains how the ego (Red Riding Hood) initially disregards superego (mother's warning) to fall victim to id (the wolf), with a final Jungian diagram showing how the heroine achieves individuation with the help of the col-lective unconscious.

Høgh, Carsten. "Oplevelse og metode—udelukker de to ting hi-nanden?—en replik til May Schack," *Kursiv* 2 (1983), 67–72. The author seeks to defend his original analysis against the cri-tique of May Schack.

Holbek, Bengt. *Interpretation of Fairy Tales: Danish Folklore in a European Perspective.* Folklore Fellows Communications no. 239. Helsinki: Academia Scientiarum Fennica. "Little Red Riding Hood" appears throughout this major contribution to the study of fairy tales as the standard exemplar text by which differ-ent folktale theories are demonstrated. See, for instance, pp. 221–228 as well as the numerous entries under AT 333 in the "Index of Tale Types" (p. 657).

Jones, Steven Swann. "On Analyzing Fairy Tales: 'Little Red Riding Hood' Revisited," *Western Folklore* 46 (1987), 97–106. Swann critiques Robert Darnton's critique of Fromm and Bettelheim on the grounds that Darnton's attempt to tie a fairy tale to a particu-lar historical time period (eighteenth-century France) is naïve. According to Swann, the tale reflects more psychology than history.

Jones, Steven Swann. "Response to Oring," *Western Folklore* 46 (1987), 112–114. Defends notion that "Little Red Riding Hood" "is more about a child's developing awareness of sexuality than it is about the savagery of eighteenth-century French life."

Kast, Verena. *Märchen als Therapie.* Olten: Walter-Verlag, 1986.

Kast, a Jungian therapist, devotes an early chapter (pp. 14–45) to "Little Red Riding Hood" and discusses the tale in terms of female adolescent individuation.

Kühleborn, Heinrich E. *Rotkäppchen und die Wölfe: Von Marchenfälschern und Landschaftszerstörern.* Frankfurt am Main: Fischer, 1982. An extended parody of "Little Red Riding Hood" research efforts.

Laruccia, Victor. "Little Red Riding Hood's Metacommentary: Paradoxical Injunction, Semiotics and Behavior," *Modern Language Notes* 90 (1975), 517–534. An ambitious attempt to apply Lévi-Straussian structural analysis to Perrault's version of the tale.

Legros, Élisée. "'L'Enfant dans le sac' et 'Le Petit Chaperon rouge,'" *Enquêtes du Musée de la Vie Wallonne* 7 (1954–1956), 305–328. A distinguished Belgian folklorist discusses versions of AT 327C, The Devil (Witch) Carries the Hero Home in a Sack, several of which are combined with AT 333. The sophisticated comparative analysis, which draws from Delarue and Henssen, suggests several traits which support the hypothesis that "Little Red Riding Hood" may have come to Europe from Asia.

Mallet, Carl-Heinz. *Fairy Tales and Children: The Psychology of Children Revealed through Four of Grimm's Fairy Tales.* New York: Schocken Books, 1984. One of the tales analyzed is "Little Red Riding Hood" (pp. 100–127). The author interprets the tale as a sexual adventure but with no explicit reference to any of the previous scholarship. The book was originally published in German under the title *Kennen Sie Kinder?* (Hamburg: Hoffmann und Campe, 1980). In the German edition, the discussion of "Little Red Riding Hood" occurs on pages 81–112. The author also published his analysis of the tale elsewhere. See "'Little Red Riding Hood': Rated R," *The Sciences* 24, no. 3 (May/June, 1984), 50–55.

Mieder, Wolfgang. "Survival Forms of 'Little Red Riding Hood' in Modern Society," *International Folklore Review* 2 (1982), 23–40. A marvelous and entertaining survey of thirty-eight adaptations of "Little Red Riding Hood" in modern dress including cartoons, advertisements, parodies, and poetry, with twenty-three illustrations, all of which attest to the continued popularity of the tale in the contemporary world.

Miller, David L. "Red Riding Hood and Grand Mother Rhea: Images in a Psychology of Inflation." In *Facing the Gods*, 87–99. Irving, Tex.: Spring Publications, 1980, pp. 87–99. A Jungian review of several Freudian readings of "Little Red Riding Hood" (pp. 89–91) which includes the comment that it was a "grand story before the analysts brought it into their consulting rooms."

Olrik, Axel. "'Den lille rødhaette' og andre Aeventyr om Mennesker, der bliver slugt levende," *Naturen og Mennesket* 11 (1894), 24–39. One of the pioneers of international folkloristics offers one of the first extensive interpretations of "Little Red Riding Hood." Surveying various swallowing-monster stories, Olrik argues that the monster in these narratives and in "Little Red Riding Hood" represents death. In the context of life-or-death struggles, it made sense to Olrik that the protagonist was frequently depicted in terms of light and the sun in opposition to death's association with darkness and night.

Oring, Elliott. "On the Meanings of Mother Goose," *Western Folklore* 46 (1987), 106–111. A response to Jones in which both psychoanalytic and ethnographic-historic approaches to "Little Red Riding Hood" (and folktales in general) are questioned on methodological grounds.

Pancritius, Marie. "Aus mutterrechtlicher Zeit, Rotkäppchen," *Anthropos* 27 (1932), 743–778. A far-ranging cross-cultural discussion of cannibalism and death rituals ending with a far-fetched analysis of "Little Red Riding Hood" as a journey to the land of the dead, with red connotating the color of the underworld.

Prince, Gerald. *A Grammar of Stories*. The Hague: Mouton, 1973. An appendix (pp. 84–100) in this technical linguistics treatise rewrites "Little Red Riding Hood" using a complex set of grammatical transformational rules.

Ritz, Hans. *Die Geschichte vom Rotkäppchen: Ursprünge, Analysen, Parodien eines Märchens*. Emstal: Muriverlag, 1981. 143 pp. A substantial discussion of "Little Red Riding Hood" texts from Perrault up to modern parodies. One of the best single sourcebooks for the study of the tale in its many manifestations.

Ritz, Hans. *Bilder vom Rotkäppchen. Das Märchen in 100 Illustrationen, Karikaturen und Cartoons*. Munich: Wilhelm Heyne Verlag, 1986. 127 pp. An excellent variety of contemporary advertising illustrations and cartoons based upon the story of "Little Red Riding Hood."

Röhrich, Lutz. "Zwölfmal Rotkäppchen." In *Gebarden-Metapher-Parodie*, Dusseldorf: Schwann, 1967. A selection of twelve parodies of "Little Red Riding Hood" (pp. 130–152).

Rumpf, Marianne. "Rotkäppchen: Eine vergleichende Märchenuntersuchung." Ph.D. diss., Göttingen, 1951. This 128-page historic-geographic comparative study is based upon only forty versions of the tale. The author is aware of the possible connection between AT 123, The Wolf and the Kids, and AT 333, as well as the possible Asian parallels. This study has been published (Berne: Peter Lang, 1989).

Schack, May. "Om metode og subjektivitet i forbindelse med tekstlaesning og undervisning," *Kursiv* 4 (1982), 70–75. Criticizes Høgh's analyses of "Little Red Riding Hood" on the grounds that they represent subjective interpretation masquerading as structural or psychological methodology.

Schäfer, Marzella. *Märchen lösen Lebenskrisen: Tiefenpsychologische Zugänge zur Märchenwelt für Eltern und Erzieher.* Freiburg im Breisgau: Herder, 1983. One chapter of this Jungian book (pp. 43–55) treats "Little Red Riding Hood" as a story of a young girl's growing self-consciousness of her own identity.

Siepe, Hans T. "Rotkäppchen einmal anders. Ein Märchen für den Französischunterricht," *Der Fremdsprachliche Unterricht* 65 (1983), 40–48. One of the most succinct summaries of "Little Red Riding Hood" scholarship to date.

Sixma van Heemstra, F. S. "Analyse van een sprookje," *Nehalennia* 3 (1958), 22–27. This Dutch author considers "Roodkapje" as a prehistoric tale to be understood in terms of gnostic-neoplatonic Christianity, a reading consonant with the tenets of anthroposophy.

Soriano, Marc. "Le petit chaperon rouge," *Nouvelle Revue Française* 16 (1968), 429–443. An authority on Perrault discusses the content and style of his version of "Little Red Riding Hood."

Taylor, Archer. "Little Red Riding Hood," *California Folklore Quarterly* 3 (1944), 318. A very brief note by the great comparative folklorist relates his own New England grandmother's oral version of "Little Red Riding Hood," in which the grandmother locks herself in a closet when the wolf arrives and later escapes to summon the woodchopper.

Uyldert, Mellie. *Verborgen Wijsheid van het Sprookje,* 2d ed. Amsterdam: De Driehoek, 1969. "Roodkapje" is the first tale analyzed (pp. 20–27) in this anthroposophical treatment of fairy tales. A struggle between day and night, light and dark, with Little Red Riding Hood representing day/light and the wolf being an archetype of darkness leads to an interpretation of the tale as a Christian allegorical drama, with the hunter who saves the heroine and her grandmother being compared to the Holy Ghost, the archangel Michael, and Jesus Christ.

245

Verdier, Yvonne. "Le Petit Chaperon Rouge dans la tradition orale," *Le debat* 3 (July–August) 1980, 31–61. A thorough discussion of the French oral versions of "Little Red Riding Hood" (comparing them with Perrault's text), ending with an interesting interpretation of the tale as a female initiation rite. The essay first appeared under the title "Grands-mères, si vous saviez, . . . le Petit Chaperon Rouge dans la tradition orale," *Cahiers de Littérature Orale* 4 (1978), 17–55.

Veszy-Wagner, Lilla. "Little Red Riding Hoods on the Couch," *Psychoanalytic Forum* 1 (1966), 400–415. Using clinical cases from her analytic practice, the author interprets "Little Red Riding Hood" as a partly pre-Oedipal story with the wolf being a "mother figure." The essay includes comments from four discussants plus a final rebuttal by the author.

Weiss, Harry B. *Little Red Riding Hood: A Terror Tale of the Nursery.* Trenton: privately printed, 1939. This nineteen-page pamphlet includes a valuable annotated list of some sixty English and American children's book editions of "Little Red Riding Hood."

Wichelhaus, Barbara. "Märchentext-Märchenbild: Eine Semiotische Untersuchung," *Semiosis* 3–4 (1985), 62–71. An analysis of the illustrations found in editions of "Little Red Riding Hood" in terms of "signs" of semantic import.

Wilkinson, Roy. *The Interpretation of Fairy Tales.* East Grinstead: Henry Goulden, 1984. Among the thirty-nine folktales analyzed anthroposophically is "Little Red Riding Hood" (pp. 18–19). The heroine is "the ego-conscious soul" who brings bread and wine (Holy Communion) to her grandmother. Swallowed by the wolf, the soul is engulfed by evil forces in a kind of initiation. Good triumphs over evil and the soul, having realized the dangers of the material world, knows in future which path to tread.

Wittgenstein, Ottokar. *Märchen, Traüme, Schicksale,* 2d ed. Munich: Kindler, 1981. An analysis of "Little Red Riding Hood" (pp. 211–227) consists in part of a clinician's recounting of his patients' interpretations of the tale plus his own admittedly idiosyncratic understanding of the story as a guide for children into the world of adulthood.

Wolfzettel, Friedrich. "Märchenmoral and Leseerwartung am Beispiel des Rotkäppchenstoffes." In *Text-Leser-Bedeutung: Untersuchungen zur Interaktion von Text und Leser,* edited by Herbert Grabes, 157–175. Grossen-Linden: Hoffmann, 1977. A survey of different literary readers' moral responses to "Little Red Riding Hood," including those of Anatole France and Alphonse Daudet.

Zipes, Jack. *The Trials and Tribulations of Little Red Riding Hood: Versions of the Tale in Sociocultural Context.* South Hadley, Mass.: Bergin & Garvey, 1983. 298 pp. The author presents thirty-one texts of "Little Red Riding Hood," nearly all literary, spanning the time period from 1697 until 1979. The book also includes more than seventy different types of illustrations of the tale. An excerpt from the author's masterful sixty-five page introduction has been included in this volume.

Zipes, Jack. "A Second Gaze at Little Red Riding Hood's Trials and Tribulations," *The Lion and the Unicorn* 7–8 (1983–1984), 78–109. A reprise of the author's argument that Perrault and the Grimms transformed an oral folktale where originally a young girl rescues herself into a narrative about rape in which the heroine, though victim, is blamed for the violation, concentrating especially upon evidence from sixteen illustrations of the young girl's encounter with the wolf from children's book editions.

Index

Index

historical approach, x, 89–120, 212–13

Holst, Dane V., 206

hunter, symbolism of, 99, 101, 109, 126, 174, 180–82, 208, 212, 216, 217, 219–20, 221

Hüsing, Georg: article by, 64–70

Husson, Hyacinth, 73–74, 79, 205

Jäger, Hans-Wolf, x, 125; article by, 89–120

Japanese versions, 13, 19, 57, 60, 61, 200, 201–2, 213, 223, 225

Jung, Carl G., 92, 211, 216, 218–19

Kanzer, Mark, 216–17

Kinder- and Hausmärchen, 7, 93, 145, 195, 196

Kleist, Heinrich von, 97, 98, 99

Köhler, Reinhold, 66

Korean versions, 13, 19, 57, 60, 61, 200, 202, 213, 223, 225

Krappe, Alexander Haggerty, 199

Kristensen, Evald Tang, 196

Kuhleborn, Heinrich E., 227

Kunstmärchen, 196

Lang, Andrew, 169, 170

Lefèvre, André, 74, 79

legend, definition of, 64

Lévi-Strauss, Claude, 207

Lewin, Bertram D., 164

lex talionis, 215

Linnig, Franz, 91

lunar mythology, 64, 65, 91, 206

Mallet, Carl-Heinz, 218

Marxist approach, 113, 124–25, 206

Mieder, Wolfgang, 226

Mintz, Thomas, 217

moral, attached to tale, 3, 6, 73, 124, 149, 163, 211, 215

Müller, Max, 205

myth, definition of, 64

myth-ritual theory, x, 71–88, 89, 206–7

Nordic mythology, 79, 80, 81, 82

Nourry, Emile. *See* Saintyves, P.

Oedipus complex, 174–75, 176, 178, 179, 182, 185, 218, 222

Olrik, Axel, 206, 207

oral aggression, 164, 165, 213–15, 222, 223, 224

Panzer, Friedrich, 94

peach-boy, tale of, 62

peach symbolism, 61–62

Perrault, Charles, ix, x, xi, 8, 14, 17, 18, 19, 20, 21, 66, 67, 72, 73, 83, 89, 95, 100, 101, 109, 111, 122, 124, 136, 138–52, 163, 169, 170, 171, 178, 195, 197, 198, 199, 201, 202, 217, 219, 220, 222, 227; article by, 3–6

Perry, Ben Edwin, 204

Ploix, Charles, 80

pregnancy envy, 209, 212

Propp, Vladimir, 206–7, 216, 223

psychoanalytic approach, xi, 59, 92, 159–67, 168–91, 209–27

Rank, Otto, 211

red hood: meaning of, 14, 18, 69, 74, 76, 80, 102–4, 109–11, 122, 165, 176, 205, 212

Riesman, David, 186, 187

Ritz, Hans, 226

roads of needles and pins, 15, 18–19, 20, 190, 198, 217–18

Róheim, Géza, xi, 168, 192, 197, 213–15, 216, 217, 222, 225; article by, 159–67

rope or string tied to heroine's body, 16, 19, 25, 44–46, 57, 82, 198, 201, 225, 226

Rumpf, Marianne, 91, 207